Possibilities and Impossibilities in a Contradictory Global Order

Stian Nordengen Christensen

2018
Torkel Opsahl Academic EPublisher
Brussels

ISBN: 978-82-8348-104-4 (print) and 978-82-8348-105-1 (e-book).

For my children

PREFACE

Understanding the basic principles that determine the shape and development of the international system has been a main academic interest of mine for the past two decades. In the existing literature on the international system, however, I have yet to find a theory that I see as satisfactory in explaining the international norms, regimes, institutions and policy formation. This book represents my own attempt to construct such a theory.

Furthermore, and based on this theory, the book aims to present possibilities for the future. In doing so, the main emphasis is on assessing the limits of the possible within the existing international system. As a student, I co-founded an academic journal for optimistic initiatives in international policy formation back in 2002. In many aspects, this book represents a continuation of that manner of thinking about the potential applicability of academic research.

While the experience I have gained through my chosen profession as a diplomat lies close to the present subject-matter, it is important to make it clear that my motivation for writing this book is entirely academic and based on the search for truth. If the reader should get the impression that there is any underlying political agenda in the text, personal or other, this is unintended. While it is difficult for any person to disregard his professional background, or the opinions this will inevitably shape, I have strived to ensure that the two worlds are kept separate, when writing this book. The text is based entirely on open sources, and has been written during my extended leave of absence from work in 2016–2017.

I am indebted to Andreas Løvold, Claire Hubert, Richard Scarborough, and Bjørn Klouman Bekken for their comments on parts of the text for this book, which caused major revisions that have doubtlessly improved the final product. While I am fortunate to have received their advice, I am responsible for the final product, including its conclusions, opinions and analyses. I would also like to thank the Torkel Opsahl Academic EPublisher for its detailed reviews of and work on the manuscript, in particular Morten Bergsmo, CHAN Ho Shing Icarus and SIN Ngok Shek.

Finally, I thank my wife, Kristine, for all of her love and support, which makes both my work and private life not only possible, but joyful.

TABLE OF CONTENTS

Preface.. *i*

Abbreviations.. *vii*

1. Paradigms of the International System 1
    1.1. The Key Concepts of the Paradigmatic Approach 1
    1.2. Theory of Paradigm Shifts 1
    1.3. International Relations Theory 2
    1.4. Previous Paradigms of the International System:
         The Westphalian System 4
    1.5. The Popular Sovereign Paradigm 11
         1.5.1. Elements of the Popular Sovereign Paradigm 11
         1.5.2. Treaty of Versailles: A Mix of Old and New 13
                1.5.2.1.   New Order: Self-determination with Constraints. 13
                1.5.2.2.   Balance of Power *v.* Community of Power 15
                1.5.2.3.   Sovereign Rights – Shifting from Old to New 16
                1.5.2.4.   Contradictions of the New System 17
    1.6. Significance of States' Differences 17
    1.7. Influence of States *v.* Non-State Actors and Supranational
         Entities 19
    1.8. Key Questions in Subsequent Chapters 21

2. Main Organs under the United Nations Charter 23
    2.1. Introduction 23
    2.2. The Trusteeship Council and Decolonisation 26
    2.3. The UN Security Council and Global Peace and Security 29
         2.3.1. Composition and Inequality in the Security Council 29
         2.3.2. The P5 and the Others 31
         2.3.3. The Veto 34
         2.3.4. The Security Council in Action 36
         2.3.5. System Integrity: The Security Council *vis-à-vis* Other
                UN Main Organs 40
         2.3.6. The Future of the Security Council: Reform, Paralysis or
                Disintegration? 42
                2.3.6.1.   Lack of Clarity of Rules 45

      2.3.6.2.   Institutional Checks and Balances on the
                Security Council 47
      2.3.6.3.   Clearer Rules on International Intervention 48
2.4. The United Nations General Assembly 50
    2.4.1. Significance 50
    2.4.2. Formal Equality between Sovereign States 51
    2.4.3. General Assembly in Action: Sovereign Perspective
         Inputs, Supranational Outputs... 53
    2.4.4. System Integrity: The General Assembly *vis-à-vis* Other
         UN Main Organs.. 55
    2.4.5. The Future of the General Assembly 56
2.5. The International Court of Justice.. 60
    2.5.1. Composition of the ICJ International Court of Justice: 61
    2.5.2. The Court in Action 63
    2.5.3. System Integrity: The Court *vis-à-vis* Other UN Main
         Organs 66
    2.5.4. Future of the Court: Possible and Impossible Reforms 66

3.   The World Trade Organization 71

3.1. Introduction and Historical Background 71
3.2. World Trade Organization Decision-Making and Negotiations 76
    3.2.1. Sovereign States' Dominance 76
    3.2.2. Special Issues of Cessation of Sovereign Rights in the
         Trade Area... 81
    3.2.3. The Disputes Settlement Mechanism: Supranational
         within Narrowly Defined Limits... 83
    3.2.4. System Integrity of the World Trade Organization 88
3.3. The Future of the World Trade Organization: Reform Proposals... 88
    3.3.1. Fundamental Obstacles to Reform 89
    3.3.2. Making Informal Procedures Formal................................. 90
    3.3.3. Increased NGO Participation 91
    3.3.4. Increased Secretariat Capacity and Independence 92
    3.3.5. Increased Accessibility of Dispute Settlement Mechanism . 93

4.   The Global Human Rights System 95

4.1. Introduction 95
4.2. Global Rules of Human Rights 98
    4.2.1. How Universal is the Universal Declaration of Human
         Rights? 103
    4.2.2. Human Rights and State Practice after the Adoption of
         the Universal Declaration of Human Rights....................... 107
         4.2.2.1.   Africa.. 108

4.2.2.2. Asia.. 110
4.2.3. Human Rights Treaty Law: The Covenants...................... 112
4.2.4. Degrees of Consensus Required for Universally Binding
Norms 114
4.2.5. Universally Binding Rules as International Customary
Law 118
4.3. Global Human Rights Bodies... 124
4.4. The UN Human Rights Council.. 126
4.4.1. Procedures and Instruments... 126
4.4.2. Instruments of the Human Rights Council....................... 128
4.4.3. Criticism of the Human Rights Council............................ 130
4.4.4. The Human Rights Council and the Boundaries of the
Possible.. 131
4.4.5. The Human Rights Council in Practice 134
4.5. System Integrity: The Human Rights Council *vis-à-vis* the UN
System in General 137
4.6. Future of the Global Human Rights System 140
4.6.1. Paradigmatic Limitations of the Human Rights Council... 140
4.6.2. Court-Like Entity for Human Rights? 141
4.6.3. Limiting Membership 142
4.6.4. Merging the Human Rights Council with the Third
Committee of the UNGA.. 143
4.6.5. Improving the Universal Periodic Review........................ 144
4.6.6. Enforcement against Human Rights Violators.................. 144
4.6.7. A Global Human Rights Court.. 145

5. International Humanitarian Law... 147

5.1. Introduction.. 147
5.2. Development of International Humanitarian Law Rules:
State Sovereignty *v.* Individual Rights 150
5.2.1. The 1949 Geneva Conventions....................................... 151
5.2.2. The 1977 Additional Protocols 155
5.2.3. How Universal are the Geneva Conventions and
Protocols? 159
5.2.4. The International Criminal Court 162
5.3. The Future of International Humanitarian Law and the
International Criminal Court 168

6. What the Future Holds.. 171

6.1. Benefits of the Paradigmatic Approach.................................. 171
6.2. Possibilities and Impossibilities in the Present International
System 173

6.3. Area-Specific Reforms 175
6.4. *Quo Vadis*? Risk of Rupture or Disintegration 179
6.5. Paradigm Shift: Rupture or Evolution 185
6.6. Future Paradigms of the International System 188

Index 193

TOAEP Team 197

Other Volumes in the Publication Series 199

ABBREVIATIONS

AP	Additional Protocol to the Geneva Conventions
ASEAN	Association of South-East Asian Nations
CCW	Convention on Certain Conventional Weapons
CEDAW	Convention on the Elimination of All Forms of Discrimination against Women
CRC	Convention on the Rights of the Child
DPRK	Democratic People's Republic of Korea (North Korea)
DSB	Dispute Settlement Body of the WTO
ECOSOC	UN Economic and Social Council
EU	European Union
GATT	General Agreement on Tariffs and Trade
HRC	UN Human Rights Council
ICC	International Criminal Court
ICCPR	International Covenant on Civil and Political Rights
ICESCR	International Covenant on Economic, Social and Cultural Rights
ICJ	International Court of Justice
ICRC	International Committee of the Red Cross
ICTR	International Criminal Tribunal for Rwanda
ICTY	International Criminal Tribunal for the former Yugoslavia
ITO	International Trade Organization
NATO	North Atlantic Treaty Organization
NGO	Non-governmental organisation
NHRI	National Human Rights Institute

OHCHR	UN Office of the High Commissioner on Human Rights
OIC	Organisation of Islamic Cooperation
P5	Permanent members of the UNSC
UDHR	Universal Declaration on Human Rights
UK	United Kingdom
UN	United Nations
UNDP	UN Development Programme
UNGA	UN General Assembly
UNSC	UN Security Council
UNSG	UN Secretary-General
UPR	Universal Periodic Review
US	United States
WTO	World Trade Organization

1

Paradigms of the International System

1.1. The Key Concepts of the Paradigmatic Approach

The fundamental concept of this book is that the international system should be understood as a framework that is based on a set of basic and enduring principles. These basic principles include such concepts as sovereign states being the decision makers, and the formal equality of sovereign states. This framework will be referred to as 'the paradigm'.

The paradigm should be understood both as the foundation and the outer boundaries of its content, which include the treaties, conventions, and international regimes of co-operation. Unlike the basic principles, these are not enduring fixtures. They can be changed as long as it does not conflict with the fundamental framework, that is, the paradigm. Thus, the international system can gradually accumulate norms and rules within the paradigm. However, such accumulation cannot go beyond the fundamental principles of the paradigm. This would require a paradigm shift.

1.2. Theory of Paradigm Shifts

Thomas Kuhn published his landmark theory on paradigm shifts in sciences in the *Structure of Scientific Revolutions* in 1962. The book argues that scientific progress should not be seen as an accumulative process, where theories develop over time by accumulation of ever increasing knowledge. Instead, science should be seen as developing in leaps.

An example is the change from the geocentric view of the universe (with Earth at the centre) to the heliocentric view (with the Sun at the centre). The former was the established scientific view from the Hellenistic age until the Modern era. Throughout the period, it progressed and developed in order to explain new observations. For example, a theory of 'epicycles' was suggested to explain why planets' distance from the Earth varied, despite the fundamental principle of planets moving in perfect circles around the Earth. However, if the planets moved in smaller circles *while* orbiting the Earth (an epicycle), this could explain perfectly well why the distance from the Earth varied. Only after the work of Nicolaus Copernicus and Johannes Kepler, did science shift to the heliocentric view, in which planets orbit the sun in elliptical movements. This paradigm completely replaced the geocentric paradigm with something new. Within the new paradigm, astronomical science then accumulated new knowledge and theories on the basis of new basic assumptions.

Another example is the shift from Newtonian physics to Relativity. While Newtonian physics at its time seemed to explain forces of the universe completely, the publication of the Special and General Theories of Relativity led to a radically new view of physics, where Newtonian laws could no longer be seen as fully precise.

This book argues that the international system should be seen as developing similarly. It argues that the present paradigm is made up of basic principles that are the enduring fixtures in the system. Within this paradigm, international relations play out, including formation of global rules and institutions. The book aims to show that the various rules and institutions of the international system since 1945 – such as the main UN organs, human rights, and the ICC – have all developed within this paradigm. It further attempts to show that this paradigm is characterised by internally conflicting principles, and is showing signs of disintegration, which will lead to a new paradigm sometime in the future. Finally, this book aims to explore which reforms can be possible within the present paradigm of the international system, and which reforms may well be desirable, but remain impossible, in the present framework.

1.3. International Relations Theory

Interpreting the international system as a paradigm is an alternative to the mainstream theories of international relations, which are realism, liberalism and constructivism. Realism considers, broadly speaking, international society to be anarchic and characterized by self-serving states seeking to gain advantage for themselves, where power is the ultimate broker.[1] This represents a more or less static view of the international system, with small or

---

[1] I describe realism here in line with, *inter alia*, Andrew Hurrell, see Andrew Hurrell, *On Global Order: Power, Values, and the Constitution of International Society*, Oxford University Press, Oxford, 2007, p. 296. For an example, see John J. Mearsheimer, *The Tragedy of Great Power Politics*, W.W. Norton and Company, New York, 2001, pp. 362–363. Realism, however, is defined as a spectrum of ideas – not capable of fair summary in one phrase – in William C. Wohlsworth, "Realism", Christian Reus-Smit and Duncan Snidal (eds.), *The Oxford Handbook of International Relations*, Oxford University Press, Oxford, 2008. All summaries are ultimately acts of simplification, and this is most definitely the case with how

even non-existent probabilities for systemic changes. Instead, changes are more often explained with reference to shifting power relations between states. Realism thus has limitations in regard to explaining, for example, why or how law can develop into a form that actually binds states to new patterns of behaviour. As will be discussed, there is strong evidence of changes in states' behaviour in the international system, which cannot easily be explained without references to changing international law.

Liberalism and Constructivism, on the other hand, face limitations in explaining why central features of the international system are so enduring. If, as 'commercial liberalism' proposes, globalization and global commercial interests lead to economic interdependence, free trade and general pacification in states' relations, why is it so difficult to set up a robust and predictable global system for regulating international trade? If, as 'neoliberal institutionalism' proposes, international institutions can both preserve peace and benefit states mutually, why is it impossible to reform the UN Security Council to make it a more effective, efficient and credible instrument world peace?[2]

Finally, Constructivism presumes that identities and interests of states can and do change, including through extension of international cooperation and collective identities. If so, however, why is it so difficult for states to set up global institutions with independence and power that can bind the states through rules and judgements, aiming at maximisation of the collective good? If sovereignty is "an ongoing accomplishment of practice", as Alexander Wendt argues, then it should also be possible to construct international organisations that do not rely on sovereign states as the final decision makers. However, as will be shown in subsequent chapters, no such institutions exist.[3]

I summarise the three main international relations traditions here. The alternative would be a lengthy discussion deviating from the purpose of this book, which is to outline a new theory based on the paradigmatic approach. For this reason, I keep the summaries short.

[2] The definitions of liberalism are taken from Jonathan Cristol, "Liberalism", in Patrick James (ed.), *Oxford Bibliographies*, Oxford University Press, Oxford (2017).

[3] Alexander Wendt, "Anarchy is what States Make of it: The Social Construction of Power Politics", in *International Organization*, 1992, vol. 46, no. 2, p. 413.

The realist approach is too static to fit with much of the real-world evidence, while the liberalist and constructivist approaches are too dynamic. A paradigmatic approach may be better suited to explain both the enduring and changing features of the international system.

1.4. Previous Paradigms of the International System: The Westphalian System

The Treaty of Westphalia, which ended the Thirty Years War in Europe in 1648, is commonly regarded as a starting point of the modern international system.[4] The framers of the treaty could not have imagined that this peace agreement would have such a profound and long-lasting influence.

The Thirty Years' War was fought over a range of issues, but the crux was the division between the Catholic and the Reformed Christian faiths. After thirty years of anarchy, famine and exhaustion, the Treaty of Westphalia represented a compromise, where states have the attained right to choose their religion.

This was a compromise, however, only in religious matters. In international relations, the treaty represented a complete shift. The power of the Catholic Church to define universal norms was shattered.[5] The treaty also effectively put an end to any reality of a unified Christian empire, under a Catholic emperor. Two of the basic principles underpinning the previous international system in Western Europe were thus removed, namely the universal obligation to follow Catholic Church rules, and the concept of an Emperor that (ideally) wielded universal temporal power in accordance with Church teachings.[6]

As in many other treaties, the treaty text itself only vaguely hinted at these tectonic shifts. Instead, it was framed as a continuation of sovereign princes' obligations toward the Emperor, although largely devoid of actual content. The treaty laid down a number of other provisions that safeguarded

---

[4] This is a basic theme in, for example, Henry Kissinger, *World Order*, Penguin Press, New York, 2014, particularly pp. 371–373. See also Hurrell, 2007, pp. 291–292, see *supra* note 1; or Antonio Cassese, *International Law*, Second Edition, Oxford University Press, Oxford, 2005, p. 36.

[5] Treaty of Westphalia: Peace Treaty between the Holy Roman Emperor and the King of France and their respective Allies, 24 October 1648, Article LXIV (http://www.legal-tools.org/doc/cbb7e7/).

[6] Cassese, 2005, p. 23, see *supra* note 4.

---

the princes' rights to form alliances, provided that they were not against the Emperor of the "public peace".[7] This ambiguous language allowed the Holy Roman emperors to persist in the pretence of being universal rulers of the Roman Empire until it was formally dissolved by Napoléon Bonaparte in 1806. However, the treaty *de facto* dissolved the Empire: the concept of universal political rule in Europe under a Roman Emperor had been eroding for centuries, but was, after the treaty, an empty shell. From 1648, the states of the Empire were free to choose their legal and belief systems, as well as to decide on their own foreign and military policies.

The era that followed, from 1648 to 1789, can be called the classic Westphalian era. The international system in Europe at that time – and increasingly in the world at large, through the conclusion of treaties between European states and states in Asia and Africa – was characterised by the following basic principles:

1. Sovereign states were the deciding authorities of the international system. They decided on all substantial matters, including their religion, internal laws, trade and tariffs, external alliances, use of force and declarations of war.

2. There were two tiers of states: sovereign states in Europe were formally equal, and different primarily in their capacity for use of force or economic pressure to coerce other states.[8] The equality of states applied only to European states and, later, to the US. States in Asia and Africa were not equal, and infringements on their sovereign rights – by Intra-European standards – were the norm, including coercion to cede special rights to Europeans in regard to practice of religion, immunity from domestic law, extension of trade privileges, and colonisation of territory.[9]

3. Sovereigns were primarily persons, such as monarchs, princes, popes, or emperors. Although there were variations of systems of governance – notably the Dutch Republic and the increasingly Parliamentarian rule in England – these were exceptions to the broadly accepted system of personal sovereignty.

---

[7]   Treaty of Westphalia, Article LXV, see *supra* note 5.

[8]   Cassese, 2005, p. 24, see *supra* note 4.

[9]   *Ibid.*, pp. 26–27.

4.   Authority was top-down, generally from the sovereign, through the nobility, to the other classes. There was no generally recognised right for all people to participate in state affairs, and certainly no equality between people regardless of ethnicity, class and gender.

The time of the classic Westphalian system is the era of which it is most correct to speak of an 'anarchic system' of state relations. There were very few international rules, and the ones that did exist, were weak. States tended to follow their perceived self-interests up to and including in use of force and declarations of war. Because of the lop-sided emphasis on sovereign states, international law was solely a matter between sovereigns, not between peoples. The threshold for war was very low and wars were frequent.

Throughout the era, however, competing ideas won more ground. Up until the seventeenth century, political philosophy tended to focus on the sovereign's rights, such as absolute rule by divine right, or a sovereign's duties, such as to maintain power and public order. Thomas Hobbes' theory, as laid out in *Leviathan* (1651), describes a theoretical social contract between a sovereign and its subjects, where the former gains power and the latter gains protection, but without any recognition of a right to revoke this agreement when breached. Even so, Hobbes' theory was a long way away from the theory of divine right to rule, which held sway in his own time.

Later in the era, there was a significant shift in the political philosophy. In John Locke's *Two Treatises on Government* in 1689, he justified the Glorious Revolution in England in 1688, when English parliamentarians and William of Orange overthrew the monarch James II. Jean-Jacques Rousseau published his influential *The Social Contract* in 1762, arguing that legitimate governance and laws must be founded on the common interest of the people, termed 'general will' by him. This represented a temporary culmination of this trajectory in the history of ideas, where the people of a state and not the head of state is seen as the legitimate source of authority.

It should be noted that 'general will' is not the same as the sum of opinions of the people, but an impersonal concept representing the common good. Thus, the general will can be realized by many different models of government, including communism, fascism, dictatorships or, of course, election-based democracies. The concept's core is that the will of the people – hereinafter referred to as the 'popular will' – is the source of legitimate governance. This view stood in stark contrast with both the view that sovereign authority was vested in a personal prince by God, and that legitimate sovereign authority should be based on personal inheritance.

The concept of popular will does not resolve specific questions of governance. For example, Napoléon Bonaparte may be (and was by many in his own time) seen as representing the popular will just as well as an elected National Assembly. Furthermore, it does not resolve the question of who 'the people' are, to which different ideologies, such as nationalism and communism, have different answers.

Already by the time of the French Revolution in 1789, there had been a change in the mind-set of many Europeans. The idea that sovereignty should be based on the will of the governed – contrary to the Westphalian system's basic assumptions of personal sovereignty and top-down rule – was the rallying call for a series of upheavals during a long period of revolutions in Europe, between 1789 and 1922. There were significant revolutions in England (1688) and the American colonies (1776) that were to a great extent justified on the same principle. The Revolution in 1789 in Europe's most powerful state, France, and the subsequent Wars of the French Revolution and Napoleonic Wars, increased the pace of the spreading of the revolutionary idea of popular will throughout all of Europe.

The international system, however, did not change as dramatically as could have been imagined. While the classic Westphalian system broke down during the Napoleonic wars, it was not replaced, but restored in a counterrevolutionary system, the Concert of the great powers 1815–1914. Since the traditional sovereigns won the Napoleonic wars and formed the power base on the European continent (primarily Russia, Austria, Prussia and France), the international system that followed sought to restore the traditional principles in the preceding era, with one exception. The ideal of a *balance of power* became the stated common objective of that international system. Thus, the international system after 1815 was a continuation of the Westphalian Paradigm, modified by the balance of power doctrine.

The concept of balance of power was not new. It was frequently and increasingly used by states to justify military actions in the seventeenth and eighteenth centuries.[10] It featured in the *Anti-Machiavel*, by Frederick the

---

[10] Walter Alison Philips, "Balance of Power", in *Encyclopaedia Britannica,* Encyclopaedia Britannica, Inc., London, 1911, vol. 3, p. 235.

Great of Prussia, who proclaimed it to be the main basis of peace in Europe.[11] It was also important in the various wars fought to curtail presumed French ambitions for a 'universal monarchy' in the eighteenth century, such as the War of Spanish Succession 1701–1714.[12] However, the great powers did not state the balance of power as their common objective clearly until the Final Act of the conference in Vienna in 1815.

The difference is significant. While the balance of power was previously argued to exist as a reality that was also desirable, the Concert of Vienna concluded that it was an objective to be pursued by the international community. Frederick the Great, for example, made it clear, in both his writing (The *Anti-Machiavel*) and his actions, that a monarch should pursue wars of interest.[13] When Frederick invaded and annexed Silesia from the Habsburg Empire in 1740, he did so almost entirely without any legal justification. This was in line with the practice of princes of the time.[14] In the Final Act of Vienna in 1815, however, the states of Europe agreed that their borders were finally settled and that any attempts to change them would require agreement of the eight signatory states.[15]

However, balance of power, as a policy objective, was the 'epicycle' of the classic Westphalian Paradigm. The victorious princes in continental Europe in 1815 wanted to return to the system they knew and which was definitively to their personal benefit. However, the Westphalian system rested on the idea of personal sovereignty. Within a century, it would be replaced almost completely by the notion that the popular will as the sole legitimate basis for sovereignty.

The framers of the Vienna system were unwilling or unable to recognise that the reality has shifted in such a way that the Westphalian system could not be fully restored. Therefore, the paradigm of the international

---

[11] Frederick II of Prussia, *Anti-Machiavel*, Chapter XXVI.

[12] Robert Tombs, *The English and their History: The First Thirteen Centuries (Kindle edition)*, Penguin, London, 2014, pp. 253 and 304, 335, and 340.

[13] *Ibid.*

[14] Christopher Clark, *Iron Kingdom: The Rise and Downfall of Prussia 1600–1947 (Kindle edition)*, Penguin, London, 2007, loc. 3757.

[15] Georges-Henri Soutou, "Was There a European Order in the Twentieth Century? From the Concert of Europe to the End of the Cold War", in *Contemporary European History*, 2000, vol. 9, no. 3, p. 330. The states were Austria, Russia, Prussia, Great Britain, France, Sweden-Norway, Portugal, and Spain (the latter ratified in 1817).

system did not change. Balance of power in the Vienna system was an 'epicycle' because it justified the continuation of the paradigm, yet conflicted with the evidence of observed reality. Sovereign princes' power was justified as necessary for keeping the peace, yet the institution of sovereign persons was increasingly an anachronism.

The Vienna system represented both the Westphalian Paradigm at the height of its importance, and the beginning of its decline. The former is evidenced by the fact that the balance of power did hold in Europe between 1815–1860, which is considerable, given the frequent wars in preceding centuries. Wars in Europe 1815–1860 occurred mostly in the fringes, not in the centre. Primarily, the armed conflicts occurred in the Balkans, where the Ottoman Empire was in retreat.[16]

The Westphalian Paradigm was declining, however, because two of the basic underlying principles were changing. The changes lead to increasing tensions and conflicts in the last decades of the period (1860–1918), resulting in paradigm change. Specifically, these principles were changing:

1. Sovereigns were no longer persons. Ideologically, absolutism was in full retreat, while the notion of popular will was rising rapidly. There were several revolutions in European countries between 1815 and 1914, and particularly in 1830 and 1848. Some countries had experienced fundamental shifts of power, others less so. Significantly, France became a Republic in 1871, and smaller states also established constitutional governments with powerful national assemblies, including Belgium (1830–31), Denmark (1849), and the Netherlands (1848). England had a national assembly with predominant influence over the government (increasing gradually after 1688). Similarly, the US had been ruled by elected representatives since independence, and its weight and influence in international affairs had been growing with its size, population, economy and military strength.

2. Authority was no longer solely a top-down process. Individuals and non-state groups in society increasingly gained rights that previously had been reserved for royalty, aristocracy or clergy, including to political participation. The new governments in unified Italy (1860) and Germany (1866–1870) preserved rule under strong monarchs, but were based on nationalistic ideology, in which the popular will is the

---

[16] Martti Koskenniemi, *The Gentle Civilizer of Nations: The Rise and Fall of International Law 1870 – 1960*, Cambridge University Press, Cambridge, 2001, p. 11.

theoretical basis of authority. All great powers of Europe and the US had national assemblies with increasing power and influence by the time of the outbreak of World War I.

The other factors underpinning the Westphalian Paradigm remained unchanged: sovereign states were still the determining agents of the system, deciding on all international matters, and being equal among themselves but unequal towards states in other parts of the world.

The decisive changes in the political realities in Europe meant that a change in the paradigm of the international system in some form was all but inevitable. However, it did not actually happen until after the calamity of the two world wars of the twentieth century. Until then, states' behaviour on the international scene conformed to the patterns of the past – rivalries between European powers for power and prestige gave impetus into the colonial race, particularly from 1885, and led to frequent war-scares in the lead-up to World War I.

One example is the Moroccan crisis in 1905, when the German Kaiser challenged French influence in Morocco by declaring his support for the sovereignty of the Sultan. The event escalated into a significant war-scare before being resolved through a conference of the great powers in 1906. Other examples include the Second Moroccan crisis in 1911, also between Germany and France; and the Bosnian crisis of 1908–1909, when Austria-Hungary annexed Bosnia from the Ottoman Empire, in spite of protests from Russia and other great powers.

Because the Westphalian Paradigm largely condoned self-interested acts by states up to and including war, it seems all but unavoidable that this would result in war sooner or later. Indeed, World War I was not particularly different from wars in the past, coming as a consequence of great power rivalries over influence, prestige and territory. The difference lies mainly in the severity of the costs in terms both of human lives and material values.

In regard to maintenance of peace, the Vienna system fared no better than the classic Westphalian system before it. On the contrary, the system paradoxically encouraged war. The relative legitimacy of wars of interests lead states to pursue such interests at the expense of other states. The balance of power objective then translated into a desirability of war to counteract wars of interests, because the latter upset the balance of power. Only after the two world wars would the international system enter into an era when the right to conduct wars would be restrained and the concept of international organisations with authority over states would be introduced.

1.5. The Popular Sovereign Paradigm

It can be debated whether World War I or II should be taken as the point of departure from the Westphalian system and the creation of the present-day system. Antonio Cassese argues that the Westphalian system survived World War I, considering that critical elements remained unchanged, but not World War II. He points to the lack of a general prohibition on war in the Charter of the League of Nations after World War I.[17] Another argument in favour of seeing World War II as the departing point is that most of the institutions set up after World War I dissolved (such as the League of Nations), while those set up after World War II have largely survived.

It seems clear that many elements of the post-World War I international order would not have been possible under the Vienna system. The League of Nations is one example, even though it eventually failed. Another was the complete breakthrough of popular will as the basis for legitimate governance in the international system. Prior to World War I, Russia, Germany, Austria-Hungary and the Ottoman Empire all had monarchical rules with considerable influence, but this had changed during and immediately after the war.

Seeing the paradigmatic change as occurring in relation to both world wars might make sense, as well: there was a clear break with the past after World War I, but the present international system was only shaped after World War II. Similar to the Treaty of Westphalia in 1648, the Versailles Treaty in 1919 represented a compromise between different principles. New ideas regarding self-determination of peoples and collective security – represented primarily by the Woodrow Wilson government of the US – and the legacy of the Westphalian Paradigm, represented primarily by the UK and France. The new paradigm only fully blossomed after 1945, leading to decolonisation and a virtual explosion of international laws and organisations.

1.5.1. Elements of the Popular Sovereign Paradigm

This new paradigm can be called the 'Popular Sovereign Paradigm'. The only continuity from the Westphalian Paradigm is that sovereign states still

---

[17] Cassese, 2005, pp. 36 and 39, see *supra* note 4.

form the basis of the system, as the primary actors, decision makers and – not least – the constituting powers. In all other respects, however, the system is different. The main change is in the concept of the 'sovereign', which is no longer assumed to be a person, nor has full powers of decision either in the international sphere or in domestic affairs. Instead, sovereignty is tempered by new factors, such as the concept of rule based on popular will, the growth of universal individual rights, universal laws and – to a lesser extent – supranational organisations, meaning organisations that can act independently of sovereign states and make decisions that are binding on them. The most significant feature of the paradigm is the continuation of sovereign states as decision makers combined with the dominance of the idea of popular will, hence the term 'popular sovereign paradigm'.

These are the fundamental principles of the Popular Sovereign Paradigm:

1. Sovereign states remain the decision makers of the international system. However, their powers are formally limited in two aspects:

    a. On matters deemed to be of paramount importance to the international system, such as international armed conflict, states exercise their authority legitimately only through permanent organisations of inter-state co-operation, such as the League of Nations and the United Nations.

    b. States' rights are constrained by universal and binding rules. These rules have increased to include, *inter alia*, prohibition of genocide, war of aggression, and forcible annexation of territory and, arguably, obligations to uphold a number of human rights, such as the prohibition on torture. While the rules are sometimes broken by some states, they are still binding, and serve to direct the behaviour of states in general.

2. Sovereign states are formally equal, but are different primarily in their capacity to influence other states through economic pressure, or the use of force.[18] There is no longer a two-tiered international society where some states can legitimately be at the mercy of others. Importantly, this led to a rapid decolonisation process after World War II.

---

[18]   Cassese, 2005, p. 24, see *supra* note 4.

3. Sovereigns base their legitimacy on the popular will, not personal or divine rights to rule. While there are exceptions, such as Morocco and Jordan, where hereditary monarchs wield actual power, the idea of rule by popular will is dominant on the global level. Popular will as basis for legitimacy extends to a number of states that are not democratic, such as the former Soviet Union and several of its successor states, Cuba and the DPRK. While ruling elites may not actually share power, their claim to power is, in almost all circumstances, justified as being for the public good.

4. Authority is no longer solely top-down. States differ widely in consultations with the public on their policies. Throughout the period, the right of political participation in the affairs of the state has become universally recognised, although not universally practiced.

1.5.2. Treaty of Versailles: A Mix of Old and New

The international system after World War I was set up by the victorious powers, primarily the US, the UK and France. As mentioned, the main features of the post-World War I international system were a mixture of the old system, defended by France and the UK, and the new, defended by the US. Toward the end of World War I, the principled statements of these powers show how different ideals were to play out.

1.5.2.1. New Order: Self-determination with Constraints

President Wilson, in his various speeches in 1917 and 1918, acted as a protagonist for a substantially new world order. Most well-known are the 14 points that he outlined as a basis for settlement of the war, in a speech to a joint session of the US Congress on 8 January 1918. Significantly, Wilson proposed, in his fifth point, "a free, open-minded, and absolutely impartial adjustment of all colonial claims, based upon a strict observance of the principle that in determining all such questions of sovereignty the interests of the populations concerned must have equal weight with the equitable claims of the government whose title is to be determined".[19] The notion of self-determination of colonial peoples represented a break with the previous international system, where European supremacy and colonial rights

---

[19] Woodrow Wilson, "Speech to Joint Session of Congress, 8 January 1918" (http://www.legal-tools.org/doc/12dcf6/).

were justified. For Wilson, the principle of self-determination applied to both Europe and the world at large, including the African and Asian colonies.[20] However, he also held the opinion that this should be realised gradually, and under the tutelage of established states.

This moderation made self-determination more palatable to the European allies, who saw the continued preservation of their empires through colonial administration as a core interest. Certainly, there was a real clash of principles between Wilson and the governments of the UK and France on this issue, which could not be resolved outright and ended up being deferred. Self-determination of colonial peoples is not clearly spelled out in the Versailles Treaty. Instead, Article 22 set out rules for the colonies of the defeated powers, which were organised as mandates under designated victorious powers.[21] While the article contains language regarding responsibility of the mandate-holders to develop the colonised peoples, it falls far short of a recognition of the right to self-determination. This left the issue of self-determination unresolved, extending the life of the European colonial empires for a few more decades. The Wilsonian policies, however, were a sign of changing times that led to decolonisation after World War II.

The Versailles Treaty did, however, represent a step toward self-determination for the peoples of Europe. Nine new states were set up in the treaty on the basis of nationality, including Poland, the Baltic states, Ukraine, and Hungary. In most cases, the principle of popular will required compromises, as peoples did not always fit into neat boxes in defined nations or territories. The nation-states of Czechoslovakia and Yugoslavia are examples of new states based on the principle of self-government, but the 'nations' were defined through diplomatic negotiations. Both states, of course, represented more than one nation, but were diplomatically defined as a unit.

In any case, the Versailles Treaty did represent a clearly different view of sovereigns in the international system than the Westphalian Paradigm. Peoples, or nations, were now the legitimate basis of sovereigns, not

---

[20] David Raic, *Statehood and the Law of Self-Determination*, Kluwer Law, The Hague, 2002, p. 182.

[21] Treaty of Versailles, "Part I, the Covenant of the League of Nations" (http://www.legal-tools.org/doc/a64206/).

---

persons. Immanuel Kant, in his essay *On Perpetual Peace*, from 1795, argued that one condition for a durable international peace would be to abolish the practice of one state acquiring another through inheritance, exchange, purchase or donation.[22] Europe's past has been the theatre of numerous wars resulting from the death of a sovereign and disagreements about the inheritance. After World War I, this particular challenge to international peace was no longer a reality. The concept of sovereignty as based on peoples and not persons was now the norm, rendering one of the basic principles of the classic Westphalian Paradigm obsolete.

1.5.2.2. Balance of Power *v.* Community of Power

A second central feature of the Versailles treaty is the discussion over the principle of balance of power as an objective of international relations. Wilson expressly opposed this concept. In his address to the Senate on 22 February 1917, he said that "There must be, not a balance of power, but a community of power; not organized rivalries, but an organized common peace". The subsequent year, Wilson referred to the balance of power as "the great game, forever discredited".[23] German Chancellor Count von Hertling expressed agreement, as did British Foreign Minister Arthur Balfour.[24]

The British acceptance of the Wilsonian view of international relations, however, was more convenient at the time when the US support to the war effort was critical, than during the negotiations over the Versailles Treaty. The Covenant of the League of Nations does not contain any but the vaguest language regarding common security obligations of the member states. Nor, on the other hand, does it contain any language that suggests that balance of power is the main objective. Again, the treaty represents the lack of a common vision, expressed in vague language. Thus, it exemplifies the transition between the Westphalian Paradigm and the Popular Sovereign Paradigm in regard to the balance of power *vis-à-vis* the abolition of wars of aggression.

---

[22] Immanuel Kant, *Perpetual Peace: A Philosophical Sketch,* 1795, Preliminary Article 2, p. 5 (http://www.legal-tools.org/doc/dc079a/).

[23] Woodrow Wilson, "Address to Congress 11 February 1918" (http://www.legal-tools.org/doc/17defb/).

[24] Georg von Hertling, "On President Wilson's Addendum to the Fourteen Points", 25 February 1918 (http://www.legal-tools.org/doc/aa13d4/); Arthur Balfour, "Speech to Parliament in Response to Woodrow Wilson's 11 February Speech to U.S. Congress", 27 February 1918 (http://www.legal-tools.org/doc/9afec3/).

The Covenant of the League of Nations does not render wars of aggression illegal. Instead, it sets up an obligation for its members to preserve against external aggression on territorial integrity or on the independence of League members, but without specification of subsequent collective action to be undertaken (Article 10). Matters of dispute or rupture were to be submitted either to arbitration or to the Council of the League (Article 12). War was justified only after a cooling off period of three months after the arbitration award. This can be contrasted with the stated principles in the UN Charter that "[a]ll Members shall refrain in their international relations from the threat or use of force against the territorial integrity or political independence of any state, or in any other manner inconsistent with the Purposes of the United Nations" (Article 1(4)).

The general prohibition of use of force except self-defence represents a clear difference between the Westphalian Paradigm and the Popular Sovereign Paradigm. While this principle is of course violated by some states, it forms a basic concept of international law to which most states in practice conform.

1.5.2.3. Sovereign Rights – Shifting from Old to New

Finally, it is significant that the Versailles treaty set up certain international organisations that were envisaged to have some influence over states on matters that previously had been clearly within the domain of sovereign rights. The League of Nations itself is the most important. Article 20 of the League's Covenant stated that no treaties inconsistent with the Covenant should be concluded. It was an expression, albeit weak, of the beginning of the concept of reining sovereign powers in through international organisations. Similarly, the Covenant set up the Permanent Court of International Justice, which was in most aspects a classic arbitral tribunal, but its ties with the League arguably also held a nascent idea of a supranational institution with powers over states that previous arbitral institutions did not have.

The League system, of course, broke down in the lead-up to World War II. For a number of reasons, it failed to include all the great powers in a meaningful way, including the US, Germany, Italy, Japan and the Soviet Union. It also failed to unite the great powers within the League to take decisive and concerted action when it was most needed, for example, in response the Spanish Civil war (1936–1939) or the Italian conquest of Abyssinia (Ethiopia) in 1935–36. It was only after World War II that the Popular Sovereign Paradigm found its lasting form.

1.5.2.4. Contradictions of the New System

The post-World War II international system also contains conflicting fundamental principles. On the one hand, it represents ideas that would have been unthinkable in the Westphalian Paradigm, such as the concept of popular will as the basis for sovereignty and the prohibition of the use of force other than in self-defence. On the other hand, it perpetuates the idea of sovereign states as the basis for the international system, which represents continuity from the Westphalian Paradigm. The Popular Sovereign Paradigm is therefore founded on contradictions, as will be discussed.

One main feature is the dilemma – which is not solvable either in principle or in practice – of the rights of sovereign states over internal matters as conflicting with an increasing body of universal law, which concerns particularly human rights and international humanitarian and criminal law. This dilemma is paradoxically produced by the states themselves through treaty law or customary law. Another internal conflict is the acceptance of a need for common commercial rules to facilitate trade, combined with the states' rights to preserve sovereignty, including creation and enforcement of its own commercial rules. Finally, there is the prohibition on use of force as contrasted with the lack of an effective common security mechanism, which remains elusive mainly due to states' concern for loss of sovereign rights.

These dilemmas form the conflict lines which shape the present international system, and will decide much of the system's future development. They are underlying causes for actual and potential conflicts between the present great powers, with implications for the rest of the world.

1.6. Significance of States' Differences

The international system is further complicated by the fact that states differ in systems of domestic governance and in their assumptions about the principles of foreign relations. For example, small and medium European states have for the most part embraced the new principles of the Popular Sovereign Paradigm, even to the extent of accepting some supranational directives and judgements on matters that would traditionally have been clearly within their sovereign rights. While states retain wide sovereign rights, including the right to secession, the EU is a supranational system of legislation and governance, where member states accept the rulings of the European Court of Justice. European states most often also accept the decisions of the European Court of Human Rights. Compared with other regions, Europe represents a wide acceptance of the ideas of universal individual rights and supranational organisations.

Other states do not accept these ideas to the same extent, and work to preserve and strengthen the traditional understanding of sovereignty. Most significantly, China consistently guards the traditional rights of sovereignty closely, both in bilateral and multilateral policies. Its use of the veto in the UNSC is indicative. Since China assumed its seat on the UNSC, it has used its veto cautiously, but increasingly after 2007. In all instances, sovereign rights have been a critical point for China. Its veto of Bangladesh's membership in the UN in 1972 was an attempt to avoid setting a precedence for a province breaking away from a country. It has vetoed three resolutions because of concerns about secession of Chinese Taipei (Taiwan).[25] More recently, China has vetoed resolutions that condemned sovereign states' internal human rights abuses in Myanmar and Zimbabwe, respectively. China has also sided with Russia in vetoing four resolutions on Syria, which, it has argued, would have favoured the opposition over the incumbent regime or which would have referred Syria to the ICC.[26]

The US stands somewhere between Europe and China with regard to sovereignty. It largely accepts and supports universal individual rights, but only rarely chooses to accede to international regimes, including human rights conventions. It guards its sovereign rights very closely, and consistently oppose imposition of supranational authority over any matter. This is

---

[25] China vetoed a resolution in 1997 in order to punish Guatemala for its diplomatic ties with Taiwan/Chinese Taipei and Guatemalan support for membership of Taiwan/Chinese Taipei in the UN. Finally, China vetoed a resolution on Macedonia in 1999 because of the latter's diplomatic relations with Taiwan/Chinese Taipei. LIU Wei, *China in the United Nations*, World Century Publishing Company, Hackensack, 2014, pp. 93–95. List of vetos with links to the draft resolutions at UN web site, available at http://research.un.org/en/docs/sc/quick, last accessed on 1 November 2016 ('Veto List').

[26] *Reuters*, "Russia, China veto UN Security Council resolution on Syria", 4 February 2012 (http://www.legal-tools.org/doc/817589). It should be noted that China accepted the referral to the ICC of the situation in Darfur by the UNSC in 2005 (UNSC Res. 1593, http://www.legal-tools.org/doc/4b208f/), and the UNSC resolution opening for military intervention in Libya in 2011 (UNSC Res. 1973, http://www.legal-tools.org/doc/f4d6ad/).

evidenced in its position towards the ICC, where the US has not only not ratified the Statute of the Court, but also entered into bilateral treaties with parties to the ICC Statute in order to prevent potential indictments of US citizens. At the same time, the US is willing to use the ICC in other situations, as evidenced by the UNSC resolution that referred the Darfur case (Sudan) to the ICC in 2005.

The differences between the states of the world have bearing on the content of the international system. If any international convention, regime or organisation is to be universal, it has to be built on basic principles that encapsulates almost all of the states' perspectives. The absence of one or a few small states to a convention, such as Monaco or Liechtenstein, makes little difference, but the absence of China, India or the US would mean that any pretence of universality is lost.

Therefore, it remains impossible to significantly limit sovereign state rights in any convention or institution that is also to be universal. This is why the UN can be a universal organisation, while the ICC cannot. It is important also to realise that the protection of sovereign rights has no correlation with democracy. As will be discussed, the consistent international policy of the US is evidence of this.

1.7. Influence of States *v.* Non-State Actors and Supranational Entities

The contradictions in the present paradigm of the international system makes it unreliable and unstable. However, they also provide flexibility, allowing states and non-state actors to participate in various aspects of international co-operation despite their diverging perspectives and principles. As discussed in the chapters on international human rights and humanitarian law, the broad participation of NGOs in international negotiations and organisations represents a fundamentally new aspect of the Popular Sovereign Paradigm. This has shaped the contents of the international system, and will continue to do so.

The increased significance of NGOs is also a concern for many state leaders who lean more toward the traditional concept of sovereignty. In the UN main organs, the WTO and other international organisations, the level of NGO participation is a continuous controversy and debate among the state representatives.

There is, however, a limit to how much non-state-actors can influence the present international system. In the end, only states can decide on binding rules that apply to states, including to individuals in them. The possibility for international rule-making lies solely with the states, through agreement by treaty or convention, or with a few supranational organisations, such as the UNSC or the ICJ. These entities, however, remain consistently dominated by states (for example, the UNSC) or have so severe limitations on their mandates (for example, the ICJ), that it would be wrong to assume that they have any significant decision-making power independent from states.

The examples of supranational entities that are independent from states, in their power to independently shape international rules that bind the states, are very few. A case can be made that the international criminal tribunals for Rwanda and the former Yugoslavia have clarified certain developing customary rules of international law, such as the definition of rape as a war crime. However, the scope of the rules formulated by these tribunals is limited, and their universal application are based on expert judicial opinions that set no formal precedence and do not therefore automatically apply in subsequent cases. ICJ definitions of new rules of customary law have greater authority, but, as will be shown, the Court uses this power with extreme caution.

There are no clear examples of supranational institutions that bind all states universally. Even institutions that have less than universal state membership are not usually independent from the states. One possible exception is the ICC, which will be discussed in Chapter 5. Another example is the EU.

The EU certainly has the power to bind its member states on a number of issues, although with three qualifications. First, the future of the EU project is uncertain. At the time of writing, the UK is preparing to leave the Union, a move that could be copied by others. This shows that the states' ceding of certain traditional sovereign rights to the EU are not necessarily permanent, and can be reversed. Therefore, the states remain the constituting powers of the international system, even in the EU.

Second, the states maintain a high degree of decision-making power within the EU. While the European Parliament has gained significance in the past decades, it remains less important than the Commission in terms of decision-making. While the EU commissioners are required to represent the interests of the EU as a whole, each state has a representative on the commission, which serves as a practical safeguard for the individual states' interests.

Third, the Constitution of the EU is an international treaty, decided by its member states. The system is, in general, set up in such a way that the commission cannot deviate far from the sum of policies of the individual member states in its decisions.

Considering these qualifications to the supranational powers of the EU, it may well serve as an example of how far some states are willing to cede their sovereign rights under the present paradigm, including acceptance of common institutions, but with safeguards for sovereignty, including the right to cessation.

Similarly, the European Court of Human Rights is an example of a supranational institution that – through its dynamic interpretation of human rights law – is arguably able to set precedence for new rules. However, this Court remains limited by the states' decisions by treaty in the European Convention on Human Rights, and its decisions must formally be adopted by the states in the domestic system.

All this shows that the states remain the basic foundation for the international system. Within the present paradigm, it is not possible to create a regime in which states permanently cede their rights of sovereignty to a supranational entity, at least not on a global scale. All international conventions and organisations that can make decisions that are binding on states also remain, by design, severely constrained in their mandates and/or state-driven.

1.8.   Key Questions in Subsequent Chapters

In the assessment of the various areas of the international system in the subsequent chapters, emphasis will be placed on the following questions.

- To what extent do the present rules and institutions represent the opposing principles of the paradigm, and to what extent is change possible within that system? For example, an assessment of the UN Charter organs should include discussion on the level of protection of traditional states' rights and the corresponding formal and actual thresholds for reform.
- What are the outer boundaries of possible reform in the international system? Or, what is possible to achieve within the present system, and what requires a paradigm change?

- To what extent do the institutions of the present international system have supranational powers that are both independent from the states and binding on the states? In assessing this, it is necessary to consider the following:
  - Representativity: Are the decision-makers in the international organisation representative as a collective, or disinterested as individuals, or do they merely promote the perceived national interests of their states?
  - To what extent can international organisations base their decisions on information, consultations, evidence and analysis that it can request or receive without state interference?
  - To what extent are non-state actors able and allowed to influence the processes?
  - System integrity: Are there checks and balances that increase the supranational independence of an organisation as a whole? For example, a decision-making entity may be representative of states' interests, but if it is checked and balanced by another entity that is not state-dominated, then the overall system suggests a higher level of supranational independence.

2

Main Organs under the United Nations Charter

2.1. Introduction

No organisation symbolises the present international system more than the UN. In its scope and level, its ambition remains unprecedented and unmatched. The 'UN family' includes not only the main organs of the UN, but also specialised organisations, funds and programmes, such as the UN Development Programme, the World Food Programme, and the Food and Agricultural Organization.

Despite the broad range of activities and entities under the UN, its core is the UN Charter and the main organs. The Charter is one of the most ambitious and influential conventions of all time. One of its central aspirations is to put an end to international wars of aggression. Considering the frequency of war throughout human history, this level of ambition is staggering. It is perhaps the most evident example of how the Popular Sovereign Paradigm differs from the Westphalian Paradigm.

Although failing to fully achieve this objective, the UN has succeeded in securing its position as the most legitimate forum for consideration of global security and international military interventions. It has also outperformed its predecessor organisation, the League of Nations.

The significance of the UN Charter in stating the basic rules and procedures for international military interventions alone makes it the most important international convention under the present international system. At the same time, the inherent flaws and shortcomings of the UN Charter means that it will never fully succeed in its most visionary objective of eliminating wars.

The UN Charter is not limited to idealistic concepts alone. It also embodies the will of the victorious great powers of World War II to persist in a position of global hegemony and to keep potential rivals from threatening their positions. This approach represents continuity from the Westphalian Paradigm and the balance of power tradition. The result is that contradictory principles underpin the UN, similar to the international system in general, where great power rivalry and idealistic concepts are mixed in such a way that the system can be neither effective nor fair. Moreover, in light of increasing great power rivalry in the world at the present, there is a high risk that the system will be effectively paralysed or even collapse before the end of the twenty-first century, absent fundamental reforms.

An important question, however, is whether the UN Charter is actually possible to reform to the extent that may be necessary to save it. This will be discussed below, with a particular view to if and how the UN Charter is founded on the fundamental factors of the Popular Sovereign Paradigm. If it is, then it is all the more unlikely that the Charter can be reformed through a normal procedure of states' negotiations, as reformulation would in fact require a deeper change in the overall international system.

One aspect of the Popular Sovereign Paradigm is that new concepts have been introduced (such as supranational governance) while completely contradicting concepts have been retained (such as full sovereign rights of states). The UN suffers from embodying these contradictions. All UN organs, for example, lack the actual ability to coerce states to adhere to its rules and decisions, even though the UN Security Council can pass legally binding resolutions under Chapter VII of the UN Charter. Moreover, the UN has never been able to build up any military power of its own, and remains dependent on the member states' contributions from case to case. Similarly, the UN is, to a great extent, dependant on voluntary economic contributions from the member states to promote economic and social development. These funds are chronically short when measured against the UN's own planning and ambition. They are also relatively small, compared with the public sector in developed countries. For example, the 2012 budget for Oslo municipality in Norway alone was about three times larger than the general budget of the UN as approved by the General Assembly.[1] UN operations remain contingent on states' co-operation and acceptance of its resolutions, not independent means of enforcement. This is an underlying aspect of all the UN's main organs.

The following discussion goes through each UN Charter organs individually, with a view to assessing their composition, structure and powers according to the basic factors of the Popular Sovereign Paradigm. In all

---

[1] The budget for the UN for the two-year period 2012–2013 was USD 5,512 billion, see UNGA, Programme Budget for the Biennium 2012–2013, A/RES/66/248, 24 February 2012. The budgeted income for Oslo municipality for 2012 was USD 8,204 billion, see Oslo Kommune, *Dokument Nr. 3, Kommunens Budsjett*, p. 60. The exchange rate was 5.98 as of 1 January 2012.

cases, there will also be a consideration of reform-potential under the present paradigm, and which reforms will depend on deeper changes in the international system.

The UN main organs, as stated in the Charter, are the following:

1. The UNSC is tasked with maintaining and restoring international peace and security.

2. The UNGA is an arena for debate and adoption of non-binding resolutions, resulting from the deliberations of almost all states in the world.

3. The ECOSOC is tasked with co-ordination of all matters of international economic and social development.

4. The Trusteeship Council oversees the territories under UN trusteeship, but has been dormant since 1994.

5. The ICJ is the supreme organ for settling legal disputes between states.

6. The Secretariat carries out the operations and functions of the UN in headquarters and globally.

Clearly, some of these organs function better than others. In some areas, for example, in international trade, the UN has a lesser role than other international organisations, such as the WTO. There are historic reasons for this, which will be elaborated in the chapter on the WTO. The present chapter will therefore not discuss the ECOSOC, even though it does have significant functions in the UN system, including elections of various committees and positions of trust. Nor will this chapter discuss the UN Secretariat, except when related to the functions of the other organs. The Secretariat is more constrained in its independence as a decision-making body than the others. The political and financial framework of its operations is fixed by states, through the UNSC or the UNGA.

The Trusteeship Council will be discussed as an example of the developments of the international system according to the fundamental principles of the Popular Sovereign Paradigm.

The most substantial discussion will be on three of the main organs, namely the UNSC, the UNGA and the ICJ. Between them, these three have the decision-making and/or normative force to provide direction for the UN and the present international system, while the capabilities of the other three main organs are more constrained.

Over time, the three main organs have also attained characteristics that are 'state-like'. Most significantly, they produce vast amounts of international law. In particular, the UNGA has characteristics that are comparable to a national legislative assembly, which was not the intention in the UN Charter.[2] To a lesser extent, the ICJ has characteristics of the high or supreme court of a national jurisdiction, while the UNSC has some of the characteristics of an executive branch. There is a limit to how far the comparison with a state can be taken, because the UN remains an international organisation and not a confederation. As a system, however, and particularly when assessing the fairness of that system, the analysis of the UN should take into consideration how the main organs individually influence each other, and collectively, the UN system. In this context, comparisons with the organisation of states will be helpful.

2.2.   The Trusteeship Council and Decolonisation

The Trusteeship Council has lost its relevance, or has achieved its purpose, depending on one's perspective. Its operation was suspended in 1994, but it continues to exist on paper. The Council and its development is closely tied to the process of decolonisation, which again is a consequence of the changing paradigm of the international system. While a basic factor of the Westphalian Paradigm was the inequality between 'civilised' states (almost exclusively European) and others, the underlying principle of the Popular Sovereign Paradigm is equality between all states. In addition, as the concept of a sovereign in the present paradigm is primarily tied with popular will, rather than individual rulers, this renders old forms of colonisation ideologically bunk.

For example, King Leopold II of Belgium ruled the Congo Free State as his own personal property from 1885 to 1908. This area was roughly same as the second largest country in Africa, the Democratic Republic of Congo. Tangier and Bombay were part of Catherine of Braganza's dowry, when she married Charles II of England. Such an arrangement would be absurd in the present age – that a European king should personally rule over Africa's second largest country, or a monarch receive cities through marital arrangements.

---

[2]   Nigel D. White, *The United Nations System: Toward International Justice*Lynne Rienner Publishers, Boulder, 2002, p. 18.

Given the predominance of the concepts of equality and popular will in the Popular Sovereign Paradigm, decolonisation is a logical consequence. It is popular among historians and the general public to credit decolonisation to the economic and military exhaustion of the European colonial states following the two world wars. This, however, cannot fully explain the rapid pace of decolonisation. The colonial powers did not peacefully lay down their claims of dominance in 1945, but fought many wars, including in French Indochina (Vietnam), French-held Algeria, and British-held Kenya (the Mau Mau rebellion).

The economic and military prowess of the colonisers *vis-à-vis* the colonised was, in most cases, still strongly in favour of the former even after 1945. It should not be forgotten that the colonial states did win armed conflicts against national liberation movements also after 1945, such as the Mau Mau rebellion in Kenya. In an array of colonies in Africa, however, the decolonisation came about without large-scale armed conflicts, but through the labours of popular movements and actions and reactions by the colonial powers.

While the UN Trusteeship Council formally oversaw only eleven of the colonies that transitioned into independence, it should also be seen as the embodiment of a new ideal which came to be dominant throughout the international system. Article 76 of the UN Carter, which describes the objectives of the Trusteeship Council, aims at self-government based on the free wishes by the peoples, respect for human rights, and equal treatment.

This ideal can easily be contrasted with the expressed ideals of the statesmen of the Victorian Age. Four-time British Prime Minister William Gladstone, for example, argued in 1855 that the two fundamental reasons for spreading the Empire was to promote trade and to spread British ideology. In his opinion, the reproduction of image and likeness of England was a supreme virtue.[3] The paternalistic perspective was typical of his age. Sharing the goods of civilisation was the epicycle of imperialism, providing a moral veneer to a self-promoting policy. Had this speech been made in 1955 instead of 1855, however, Gladstone would never even have made it into Westminster, let alone Downing Street.

The economics of colonial administration are also revealing for the significance of the paradigm change in the international system *vis-à-vis*

---

[3] William Gladstone, "Out Colonies: an address delivered to the members of the 'Mechanics' Institute, Chester", 12 November 1855 (http://www.legal-tools.org/doc/1aa97a/).

traditional national interest calculations. The economic benefits of the co-lonial adventures of European states are a topic of scholarly dispute. There is a good case, however, for arguing that the returns on investment were in general negative or at least very low. Great Britain's African colonies re-ceived only 5..26% of British exports before 1914, and was the source for 8% of British imports.[4] French colonies were more significant for France. French trade with its own colonies amounted of 28% of total French trade in 1934, but half of that was trade with Algeria alone (that is, 14%).[5] Por-tuguese colonies, again, were more important to Portugal's economy, par-ticularly after World War II.[6]

While proponents of Empire tend to argue that long-term effects of colonial administration (on legal development, free trade and migration) benefited economic growth,[7] the net balance of the colonial adventures of the 1800s and early 1900s were probably at best economically irrelevant for the European colonial powers.[8]

There are today very few still existing examples of colonialism. The transfer of civilian populations into occupied areas is considered illegal un-der customary international law, and under treaty law of Article 51 of the Geneva Conventions, as well as under Article 8 of the Statute of the ICC. The new principles in the Popular Sovereign Paradigm have replaced the old ones, and the Trusteeship Council is likely, therefore, to remain dormant.

However, it is possible to imagine its reactivation. For example, the governance of Gaza in Palestine remains a principled and practical chal-lenge to the international community. Since 2007, it has been *de facto* under administration of Hamas, that is, neither the recognised Palestinian govern-ment (Palestinian National Authority) nor Israel. Moreover, Israel removed its settlers in 2005, although it retains a closure of the land and sea borders,

---

[4] Peter Duignan and L.H. Gann (eds.), *Colonialism in Africa 1870–1960: Volume 4: The Eco-nomics of Colonialism*, Cambridge University Press, Cambridge, 1975, p. 9.

[5] *Ibid.*, p. 10.

[6] *Ibid.*

[7] Niall Fergusson, "British Imperialism Revised: The Costs and Benefits of 'Anglobaliza-tion'", in *Development Research Institute Working Paper Series*, April 2003, no. 2, p. 4 (http://www.legal-tools.org/doc/88d0a3/).

[8] Patrick Karl O'Brien and Leandro Prados de la Escosura, "Balance Sheets for the Acquisi-tion, Retention and Loss of European Empires Overseas", in *IFCS – Working Papers in Economic History*, 1998, p. 1.

---

together with Egypt, which arguably renders Gaza as 'occupied' under the traditional interpretation of the 1907 Hague convention, as well as customary international law. The United Nations Relief and Works Agency provides schooling, health and other services to the majority of Gaza's population, while other UN agencies, such as the UNDP and the World Food programme, also provide large amounts of aid. The case of Gaza, therefore, is one where the UN Trusteeship Council could be asked to take on a role. At present, however, no formal initiative has been taken to this effect. But there may yet be a use for the Council in the future. Its dormant status costs nothing.

2.3. The UN Security Council and Global Peace and Security

In the Charter, the UNSC is envisaged as the only entity that can pass legally binding resolutions. This arguably puts the UNSC in a position of clear predominance over the other organs which require state consent. Because of the near universal state membership of the UN, the binding resolutions of the UNSC is the closest we come to a supranational governance organ.

However, at the same time, the UNSC was, from the outset, carefully crafted so as to constrain its formal supranational powers. The limitations on its ability to reach agreement and enforce compliance are also severe. Its binding resolutions can only be made under Chapter VII of the UN Charter, that is, "Actions with Respect to Threats to the Peace, Breaches of the Peace and Acts of Aggression". In practical terms, the composition of the Council and the rules regarding veto, translates into inaction in all but a few and isolated cases where the P5 members agree.

2.3.1. Composition and Inequality in the Security Council

The UNSC is not an impartial organ. Few would argue that the UNSC is representative, and probably no one would ever argue that it is disinterested. The UNSC was established in 1945 with permanent membership for the five victorious great powers of World War II: the US, the Soviet Union, China, France and the UK. The concept sought to continue the wartime alliance into peace time. This meant keeping the losing great powers out, namely Germany and Japan. Being states with a global outlook, and with global interests, the UNSC permanent members can never be expected to be objective in assessing potential threats to the peace. In this way, the

UNSC represents continuity from the Westphalian Paradigm, where the states were not fully equal.

However, the UNSC is more than the P5members. It also includes 10 other states that are elected by the UNGA. This is in line with the new concept in the Popular Sovereign Paradigm of full formal equality between states. There is a realisation that legitimacy of the UNSC under the present system cannot rely on the great powers' strength alone, but that the community of states must be represented on the Council.

Moreover, the concept of equality between states has grown stronger over time. The precursor of the UNSC, the Executive Council of the League of Nations, was set up with four permanent members (the UK, France, Italy and Japan), and four non-permanent members. The US was intended as a fifth member, but did not join the organisation due to opposition in the US Senate. At the outset, therefore, the great powers had a 50-50 share of the seats in the Executive Council. The composition would change, increasing the number of non-permanent seats to 11 by 1936. The number of permanent seats would also change, with the Soviet Union, Japan and Germany all joining and then withdrawing (Japan and Germany) or being expelled (the Soviet Union).

The Executive Council of the League of Nations was hamstrung, however, by the rule requiring consensus on all substantive matters. After World War I, the traditional view on sovereignty was stronger than today. At any rate, the expansion of the Council is indicative of the increasing emphasis on equality among the states.

The UNSC could be seen as a step backwards, since it had five permanent members and only six non-permanent members initially. However, this can be interpreted in different ways. Most importantly, the creators of the UN viewed the security system under the League as having failed to settle disputes without the use of force. The inefficiency and ineffectiveness of the Executive Council had become increasingly clear throughout the 1930s.[9] It was clear that the UNSC, therefore, would require other powers, other decision-making procedures, and a composition that served to unite the great powers and also include the lesser ones. In this light, it should not be missed that that the League was intended at the outset to have a 5–4

---

9   Christian J. Tams, "The League of Nations", in *Max Planck Encyclopedia of Public International Law*, Oxford University Press, Oxford, 2006, paras. 30–31.

majority in favour of the great powers, while the UNSC was intended to have a 5–6 minority in favour of the non-permanent members.

Since 1945, the issue of inequality – specifically in terms of skewed representativity – in the UNSC has increasingly been highlighted. There are today few, if any, who would argue that the present composition of the UNSC is fair or representative of the general membership or, as regards the permanent seats, of the great powers.

The most frequent argument against the overall composition of the UNSC is that it has become less representative over time when measured against the expansion of the UN membership. In 1945, the UN had 51 members. As of 2016, there were 193 members. The process of decolonisation has been the main driver for the expansion of the membership base. On only one occasion has the UNSC been expanded: in 1965, the number of non-permanent members was increased from six to ten. While this measure did make the UNSC more representative in the ratio between the UNSC members and the UNGA members, it contains only 13% of its members today, while in 1945 it was close to 22%.

Arguments for reform of the UNSC often suggest expansion of the Council to make it more representative, but at the same time there are concerns about reducing the efficiency and effectiveness of the Council.[10] Considering the various reforms in the League of Nations Executive Council, whose lack of effectiveness increased with its expanding membership 1920 and 1936, there are also grounds for this concern. At any rate, the real challenge, in terms of principle, that is confronting the UNSC is not the number of non-permanent seats, but the composition and relative weight in decision-making of the P5 members *vis-à-vis* the others.

2.3.2. The P5 and the Others

Ten non-permanent members are elected to non-renewable two-year terms, and do not have the veto powers that the permanent members hold. The rule of non-renewable alternating seats has two consequences. In principle, it leads to a greater number of states being represented on the Council over time, meaning a greater degree of representativity and equality. However, this is more than offset by the second consequence, that non-permanent members are systematically unable to challenge the dominance of the P5,

---

[10] White, 2002, p. 84, see *supra* note 2; Sabine Hassler, *Reforming the UN Security Council Membership: The Illusion of Representativeness*, Routledge, London, 2012, pp. 53–54.

because two years is too short a time for most countries to significantly influence the direction of the Council. Even if non-permanent states came into their seats with clear objectives of what they want to achieve, it is possible for the P5 to stall reform suggestions until the two-year period is over.[11]

Moreover, co-ordination between the non-permanent members is difficult because they invariably have very different backgrounds, both in terms of cultural traditions, economic development, military strength and – most importantly – foreign policy objectives. Among the non-permanent seats, two are for the Western group (Europe, Canada, Australia and New Zealand), two for Latin America, one for Eastern Europe, and five for the African-Asian Group, of which one is always an Arab Country. In principle, this makes the UNSC more representative of the general UN membership. In practice, it also means that the non-permanent members are not able to co-ordinate effectively to constrain the dominance of the P5. The two-year rotation and non-consecutive terms in practice means that no consistency arises. Long-term patterns of interaction that could lead to consensus are not established.[12]

Finally, even if such consensus among the non-permanent members could be realised, the permanent members will still be able to use their veto power to block reforms that may be detrimental to their own positions on the Council. Mere expansion of the Council will do nothing to change the dominance of the P5 countries. Representation without decision-making power is in fact tokenism.

The arrangement of permanent seats has solid historical reasons. As mentioned, it was – and still is – commonly held that the League of Nations failed because the great powers did not participate: the US failed to join, while the Soviet Union, Japan and Germany only participated for a short time. The necessity of keeping the great powers involved was not lost on the framers of the UN Charter. In order to achieve this, the great powers would also have to receive assurances that their national interests would not suffer from their participation. Their permanent seats and veto power are intended to ensure this.

In this sense, the UNSC composition represents a continuation of the balance of power tradition. No great power can under the UNSC setup

---

[11] For a criticism of the two-year rule, see *ibid.*, p. 51.
[12] *Ibid.*

change the rules or force through a decision to the detriment of another P5 member without their consent, as they would veto it. However, the advantage of the permanent seat goes beyond the power to block resolutions, as the P5 in fact dominate the UNSC in a manner that often sidelines the non-permanent members.

In line with the principle of equality, this UNSC composition is today widely regarded as lacking legitimacy. The continuation of special arrangements for the US, China and Russia will find many supporters, given the desire to keep these states involved in the UN. However, the continuation of the permanent seats for the UK and France is an obvious anachronism. Being world powers in 1945, there is today no reason why these states should hold such prominent positions in the UNSC. Decolonisation has weakened their claims as first-tier great powers, while the economies or population size of states such as India, Japan, Germany, Indonesia, Nigeria and Brazil exceed those of France and the UK. One could perhaps argue that some the permanent UNSC members should represent small and medium states' interests. However, such an argument would not in any case, favour continuation of the seats of the UK and France, considering that both are Western European states. Even if they were not, it would be arbitrary to designate two states to permanently represent the large number of other and more or less similar states.

What is relevant in regard to the international system as such is that while the actual composition of the UNSC is not changing, the *principle* of equality has never seemed stronger. If the UN Charter had been negotiated today, the UNSC composition would never have been accepted. India, for one, would not have accepted a composition that left itself out of a permanent seat. It would probably have been joined by at least Japan, Brazil and Germany. In the lengthy debates about UNSC reform over the past decades, these four countries have all actively campaigned for their candidacy for permanent seats. Furthermore, African countries would make a strong case demanding permanent representation in one form or another. South Africa has long argued for reform of the Council to make it more representative.

There is no longer any ideological basis for reserving powers of decision with only a few European or Western powers. The principle of inequality between 'civilised' (European or Western) states and others has ceased to exist. There are no longer any Gladstonian appeals for such arrangements. This represents a significant change in the international system. The present form of the UNSC persists not as a result of principle, but because of a lack of consensus around an exact new composition. For example, Pakistan strongly opposes India's permanent seat on the Council, as Argentina opposes Brazil's.

In any case, as long as the P5 can veto initiatives for reform, there is little chance of significant change in the absence of immense outside pressure. Paradoxically, while the composition of the UNSC is untenable, it may also prove to be unalterable.[13] All reform initiatives since 1965 have failed. As Philip Alston has noted, never have so many reform initiatives been promoted, by so many, and resulted in so little.[14]

The UNSC thus continues to represent the Popular Sovereign Paradigm: the organ has some supranational powers, that is, to pass binding resolutions under Chapter VII. At the same time, the composition of the Council ensures that its actions will not amount to more than the sum of the policies of the P5 member states. The effect of this is to preserve the traditional sovereign rights of these five states.

2.3.3. The Veto

The dominant position of the permanent members was in 1945 thought to be necessary in order to keep them in the organisation over time. President Harry S. Truman believed that the US Senate would not have accepted US membership in the UN without the veto clause.[15] China has consistently favoured the veto in the UNSC, even from the 1950s, when it was not itself on the Council.[16] It can certainly be argued that a hypothetical loss of veto power would lead the United States, China and Russia to disengage from the UNSC. No such argument can plausibly be made for the UK and France, who are widely seen as no longer justified in their positions in the UNSC

The veto power is formulated as a positive power in the Charter, meaning that all permanent members must concur with the resolution for it to pass, excluding only resolutions on procedural matters.[17] However, the

---

[13] Bardo Fassbender, "The Security Council: Progress is Possible but Unlikely", in Antonio Cassese (ed.), *Realizing Utopia: The Future of International Law*, Oxford University Press, Oxford, 2012, p. 57.

[14] Philip Alston: "The United Nations: No Hope of Reform?", in Cassese (ed.), 2012, see *supra* note 13.

[15] Harry S. Truman, *Memoirs, Volume I: Year of Decisions*, Signet Books, New York, 1955, p. 317 (http://www.legal-tools.org/c4bc98/).

[16] LIU, 2014, p. 56, see *supra* note 25 in Chapter 1.

[17] United Nations Charter, Article 27 (http://www.legal-tools.org/doc/6b3cd5/).

practice that evolved is that the permanent members have to vote against a resolution in order to veto it. Abstentions do not count as veto.

Nevertheless, the veto insures the five permanent members against any collective action that would be to their detriment. As such, it represents continuation from the balance of power tradition. This principle conflicts increasingly with the notion of supranational institutions and rules, as represented by the development of human rights and new international humanitarian law rules focussing on victims and non-international armed conflicts.

The uses of veto in the UNSC dropped significantly after the end of the Cold War. Between 1991 and the time writing, the veto has been used on 29 occasions, and not once by the UK or France.[18] In comparison, the Soviet Union alone used veto 79 times in the first 10 years of the UN.[19] However, as long as the veto remains, it means that one of the P5 states can, in principle, block any motion on which a majority of other states agree. Thirteen of 14 of the vetoes by the United States since the end of the Cold War have been over resolutions relating to the Israeli-Palestinian conflict.[20] Since the veto also applies to Charter reform (Articles 108 and 109), the P5 cannot be stripped of their own veto power within the present system without their own consent.

The veto cements the P5 in their domination over the UNSC. It is increasingly unlikely that the veto rules will change in the foreseeable future. The principles of supranational authority and universal rules are far more advanced today than in 1945, as will be shown in subsequent chapters on human rights and international humanitarian law. Historical developments have therefore increased the stakes for the P5 members. The UNSC veto functions as a conserving factor in a world where states' traditional sovereignty is under pressure. The states that are most sensitive to sovereignty issues, such as China, cannot therefore relinquish the veto without risking severely undermining their own consistent foreign policy of preserving its sovereign rights against, for example, the universality of human rights.

---

[18] Veto List, see *supra* note 25 in Chapter 1.

[19] *Ibid.*

[20] *Ibid.*

2.3.4. The Security Council in Action

The UNSC bases its work on many sources of input. This input is discussed collectively in the Council, but only after being analysed from the perspective within the member states' national diplomatic system. Arguments in the Council are therefore heavily influenced by the members' perceived national interests. The path between the input (evidence and analysis) and output (resolutions) shows how the UNSC, in most circumstances, represent the sum of the member states – primarily the P5 – rather than an impartial position that would be the objective of a full-fledged supranational organ.

The input to the Council in terms of information and analysis is primarily channelled through the Secretariat or the diplomatic and intelligence services of the Council's member states. In addition, the UNSC can establish fact-finding and subsidiary bodies under Article 29 of the Charter. UNSC members are also free to consult with the external experts they deem fit, whether collectively or individually, but this happens on an *ad hoc* basis.

The UNSC may designate a delegation to carry out fact-finding missions. In the course of these missions, the UNSC are generally briefed by high-ranking officials of other UN agencies, commanders of UN forces and occasionally civil society organizations and domestic NGOs. One example is the UNSC mission to Djibouti (on Somalia), the Sudan, Chad, Democratic Republic of Congo and Côte d'Ivoire, from 31 May to 10 June 2008.[21]

Other times, the UNSC requests reports on issues. Council can also be presented with reports initiated by other bodies but addressed to the UNSC. These can be by external experts, like the report following Rwanda in 1994, which was initiated by the UNSG but endorsed by the UNSC.[22] There has been significant criticism of these processes, as many consider the outcomes to be both unclear and ineffectual.[23]

There are two main challenges in the UNSC's consideration of information and analyses. First, there are limited facts and evidence available concerning the situations before the Council. Most of its work relates to

---

[21] Guglielmo Verdirame, *The UN and Human Rights: Who Guards the Guardians?*, Cambridge University Press, Cambridge, 2011, pp. 327–327.

[22] *Ibid.*, p. 328; UNSC, Report of the Independent Inquiry into the Actions of the United Nations during the 1994 Genocide in Rwanda, UN Doc. S/1999/1257, 15 December 1999.

[23] Verdirame, 2011, p. 335, see *supra* note 21.

events in countries on which member states have limited expertise and intelligence. The effect is heightened by the mere distance between the place of the event in question and the venue for the UNSC deliberations, in New York. The distance also affects the flow of information through the Secretariat, as in any diplomatic bureaucracy. The factual basis on which the UNSC takes its decisions does not come close to the extensive fact-base available to governments on domestic issues within their own countries.

Second, the UNSC members filter the facts and evidence available through the sieve of their own national interests. This leads to statements, decisions and resolutions that reflect only some of the available evidence, while other evidence is account.

An example that illustrates both challenges is the genocide in Rwanda in 1994, when the UNSC failed to stop or even obstruct the murder of between 500,000 and 800,000 Tutsis.[24] Limited availability of facts, evidence and capacity for analysis played a part, particularly in the beginning of the crisis. Rwanda was a remote country for most of the UNSC members, which had limited independent quality sources of their own. To a large extent, they had to rely on the information filtered through the UN Secretariat.[25]

The flow of information from the UN Secretariat has been the object of criticism after the crisis. Particularly, the UN force commander on site, Roméo Dallaire, provided the UN Secretary General, Boutros Boutros-Ghali, with both analysis and options from the beginning of the crisis, but these were not presented to the UNSC. Dallaire recommended military intervention to halt the probable coming bloodshed after the death to Rwandan president Habyarimana, and before the genocide began.[26] He also provided relatively detailed plans for military intervention to avoid further atrocities. These recommendations were not channelled through the Secretariat to the UNSC members.[27]

---

[24] Michael N. Barnett, *The International Humanitarian Order*, Routledge, London, 2010, p. 121; Hassler, 2012, p. 84, see *supra* note 10.

[25] Barnett, 2010, p. 119, see *supra* note 24.

[26] *Ibid.*, pp. 131–134; *The Economist*, "Rwanda, remembered; Lessons of a genocide (Lessons from the Rwandan genocide)", available at https://www.highbeam.com/doc/1G1-114671434.html, last accessed on 5 March 2018.

[27] Barnett, 2010, pp. 131–134 and 13–14, see *supra* note 24.

The reasons for this are not entirely clear. It is likely, however, that the distance to the events played a role. The decision-makers in the Secretariat in New York were not in their positions because of any Rwanda-specific expertise. When the local Force Commander provided them with analysis and options, it was difficult to quickly and precisely grasp which parts of this reporting was reasonable and which parts may not have been.[28] The problem will only have been aggravated by the fact that any recommendation to use UN-sanctioned military force would risk the lives of UN personnel in a situation where the member states had little or no direct national interest. In the first phase of the crisis, no states expressed willingness to commit its troops to the UN mission in Rwanda. Belgium, after the death of some of its peacekeepers, in fact announced its withdrawal, and no state offered replacements.[29]

The flow of information could have been improved, and the UN Secretariat deserves criticism for its handling of the situation. However, the challenge of limited information and distance to the events is to a certain degree also unavoidable in the present system. There is no feasible way in which UNSC decisions on Rwanda could have been made on the basis of clear evidence and facts in the same way as a national government normally decides on its domestic policies.

More important than the lack of information, however, was the way the available facts and evidence were handled by UNSC members. Because there were no significant national interests of member states at stake in Rwanda, there was no willingness to commit forcefully to resolve the crisis by intervention. And because of the lack of will, the UNSC members carefully disregarded evidence in their own statements and resolutions. The UNSC, both collectively and individually, did not use the term 'genocide', despite growing evidence of such, because this would only serve to demand action on their part.[30] In this way, the UNSC members deliberately avoided

---

[28] I rely heavily on Barnett's analysis of the internal procedures here. He was close to the deliberations, but this particular point should be seen as an educated guess. It is, however, in my opinion in line with the experience shared by most diplomats having been stationed abroad for more than a few years, about the difficulties of communicating clearly between the field and headquarters. See *ibid.*, p. 134.

[29] *Ibid.*, p. 119.

[30] *Ibid.*, p. 135.

evidence, in order to avoid having to take action that was not in accordance with their perceived national interests.

This tendency to outsmart the truth is not isolated to the Rwanda case. In debates over intervention in the war in Bosnia-Hercegovina, several British decision-makers argued that forceful action would not be prudent, because all sides to the conflict were responsible for atrocities.[31] This despite the fact that by far the most civilians were killed by Serb forces.[32] Another example is the Israeli settlement policy in Palestine. The ICJ, the Security Council and a number of international legal experts consider the settlements as a grave breach of the Fourth Geneva Convention, which is synonymous with a 'war crime'. Even so, the term 'war crime' is never used in official statements by the UNSC, the United States or European states.[33] To use this term would seem to demand action that those states are not ready to take. No such hesitation seems to hinder strong statements when national interests and international law are not conflicting elements. For example, in 1992, the US State Department declared that it regarded the transfer of the Iraqi population into occupied Kuwait as a war crime in its final report to Congress on the conduct of the Gulf War.[34]

The practice of the UNSC in this regard represents continuity from the post-1815 system of great power negotiations. The UNSC operates in

---

[31] Daniele Conversi, "Moral Relativism and Equidistance in British Attitudes to the War in the Former Yugoslavia", in Thomas Cushman and Stjepan G. Mestrovic (eds.): *This Time We Knew: Western Responses to Genocide in Bosnia*, New York University Press, New York, 1996, p. 244.

[32] The CIA has estimated that 156,000 civilians lost their lives in the fighting throughout the war, of which all but 10,000 were killed in territory held by the Bosnian Government or the HVO. Croatian demographer Vladimir Žerjavić has estimated that out of 215,000 killed, 160,000 were Muslims, and the Serbs were responsible for 186,000 of the deaths. See Sabrina P. Ramet, *The Three Yugoslavias: State-Building and Legitimation, 1918–2005*, Woodrow Wilson Center Press, Washington, D.C., 2006, p. 465.

[33] International Court of Justice, *Legal Consequences of Construction of a Wall in the Occupied Territory of Palestine*, Advisory Opinion, 9 July 2004 ('Wall Advisory Opinion'), para. 120 (http://www.legal-tools.org/doc/e5231b/); UNSC Res. 442 (1978) (http://www.legal-tools.org/doc/6a9157/), UNSC Res. 452 (1979) (http://www.legal-tools.org/doc/946db2/), and UNSC Res. 476 (1980) (http://www.legal-tools.org/doc/0b4a51/); John B. Quigley,, "Can Transfer of Civilians into Israel's Settlements Be Prosecuted as a War Crime in the International Criminal Court?", in *Public Law and Legal Theory Working Paper Series*, 2014, no. 256.

[34] US Department of Defense, "Report to Congress on the Conduct of the Persian Gulf War – Appendix on The Role of the Law of War", in *International Legal Materials*, 1992, vol. 31, no. 3, p. 635.

the narrow zone between the old concept of sovereign states as the deciding authorities of the international system, on the one hand, and the new concept of supranational authority, on the other hand. Any extreme on either end is impossible. The UNSC is incapable of rising above the perceived national interests of its members, and particularly those of the permanent ones. If one permanent member perceives a proposed action to be contrary to its own interests, it will counter that move, even if it means deviating from universal ethical principles. On the other hand, the powers of the Council are bound to the new concept of peace as an objective, and of mutual security co-operation to this end. It cannot go beyond these boundaries in the pursuit of their national interest. For example, the P5 cannot decide to appropriate a portion each of Palestine or Western Sahara, in the way that Poland was divided among Prussia, Austria and Russia in the eighteenth century.

Concerted action is only possible when there is room for manoeuvre within the boundaries of national interests and the peace and security mandate of the UNSC. On a few selected issues, such as combatting terrorism, piracy or child soldiers, the UNSC is capable of action, even formulating general rules and follow-up mechanisms. On other issues, such as the armed conflict in Syria or the Israeli -Palestinian conflict, the Council is, at the time of writing, unable to take any strong action. The paradigm underlying the UNSC setup, incorporating contradictory concepts, leaves little room for change in either direction: global governance for the common good does not seem possible, but neither is legitimising permanent territorial expansion by armed force. Where such expansion has been attempted, for example in in Kuwait or Bosnia-Hercegovina, it has been pushed back or remains highly contested.

2.3.5. System Integrity: The Security Council *vis-à-vis* Other UN Main Organs

In the constitutional system common to most democracies, a division of state powers forms a system in which no branch of government can pursue their own interests to the detriment of others. Historically, the fear of power abuse is primarily tied to the executive branch, as kings or dictators might act as tyrants without due regard for the public good or justice. A well-functioning division of power cancan limit this possibility, as mutual checks and balances are placed on the three branches of government, the executive, the legislative and the judiciary.

Similarly, the UN has three organs that in many ways resemble the classic three branches of government. Unlike a democratic constitutional system, however, the possibilities for interaction in the form of mutual control functions, is almost completely lacking in the UN Charter system.

This is a particular challenge for the UNSC, which is the only organ capable of passing binding resolutions. The UN Charter provides no right to appeal or override the Council's binding resolutions. Granted, it does provide the UNGA with a general oversight function, but this is in practice very limited.[35] The closest process in the UN system to a check on the UNSC is the 'Uniting for Peace' procedure, which allows the UNGA, in the event of disagreement in the UNSC and certain other conditions, to recommend action to be taken on matters for the maintenance of international peace.[36] However, UNGA resolutions under this procedure are not binding, in contrast to those of the UNSC.

If the UN functioned as a state system, it would be natural for its highest legal institution, the ICJ, to take on the role of judicial review over the UNSC's actions. However – and for reasons that will be elaborated in the discussion on the ICJ below – the Court does not pursue this course. Thus, no significant checks and balances are in place to restrict or correct the UNSC, if necessary.

The lack of checks and balances also lead to practices that many deem corrupt, and that would, in many national legal systems, be considered illegal. In particular, the practice of vote-trading has been criticised. An example is UNSC resolution 678, which authorised the use of military force in the First Gulf War in 1991. The US offered financial aid to other Council members, specifically to Colombia, Côte d'Ivoire, Ethiopia and Zaire. It also made promises to the Soviet Union and China: to the former, about keeping the Baltic states out of the Paris Summit Conference in November 1990 and to persuade Saudi Arabia and Kuwait to provide it with hard currency needed to make overdue payments; and to the latter, about lifting trade sanctions introduced after the Tiananmen Square incident.[37] While the end result, the resolution and the military intervention, may not be considered to have been an unjust outcome, the process can never be

---

[35] Verdirame, 2011, p. 321, see *supra* note 21; UN Charter, Article 10, see *supra* note 17.

[36] UNGA Res. 377A (1950) (http://www.legal-tools.org/doc/1a21a9/).

[37] Ofer Eldar, "Vote-trading in International Institutions", in *European Journal of International Law*, 2008, vol. 19, no. 1, p. 17.

considered fair. Because of the present setup of the UNSC, however, such practices are almost unavoidable. The lack of any strong oversight mechanism also means that such practices are likely to continue to heavily influence the international system.

The lack of checks and balances on the UNSC is intended and typical of international regimes under the Popular Sovereign Paradigm: there are supranational organs, such as the UNGA and the ICJ, but their powers are limited so as to preserve the traditional sovereign rights. This leads to paradoxical outcomes in many cases. For example, the ICJ can only adjudicate on disputes between states that have accepted the jurisdiction of the Court. In other matters, it can be called upon by the UNGA to deliver non-binding advisory opinions on legal matters. One such advisory opinion is the 2004 Advisory Opinion on the *Legal Consequences of Construction of a Wall in the Occupied Territory of Palestine*.[38] Here, the ICJ concludes that the Israeli construction of the wall on Palestinian territory and the associated regime is illegal, and that the UNSC should consider action to bring an end to the illegal situation. The situation is thus that the highest legal institution in the world has concluded clearly, yet it has no binding effect, and concerted follow-up action from the UNSC remains elusive over a decade later.

The example shows the extent of possibilities under the present paradigm of the international system. The ICJ can give out opinions on issues being dealt with by the UNSC, which will clarify the legal aspects – even to the extent that no serious legally based opposition can be raised – but without this forcing the UNSC to take action. It is possible for the ICJ to take a more active role in clarifying such matters, even to criticise the UNSC when appropriate, but there is no possibility of compelling the UNSC to abide by international law if one of the P5 members chooses to resist.

2.3.6. The Future of the Security Council: Reform, Paralysis or Disintegration?

The fundamental principles on which the UNSC is based are contradictory to such a degree that it is impossible to imagine it as the foundation of a long-lasting and stable international mechanism for peace and security. The setup of the UNSC prevents it from taking any action in situations where significant national interests of the permanent members are at odds. This

---

[38] Wall Advisory Opinion, see *supra* note 33.

means that the conflicts with the largest potential for damage and suffering (that is, between great powers) are the very conflicts that the UNSC is unable to handle effectively. This was of course also the reason why the UNSC was for the most part of the Cold War unable to uphold its mandate as guarantor of international peace and security.[39]

There have been a significant number of reform suggestions and initiatives in the past decades. In particular, in the 1990s, the end of the Cold War gave grounds for optimism about both the UNSC taking on a more active role, and about reforming it to maintain that role better.[40] Most reform suggestions are relatively limited in scope, and seek compromises that could be regarded as relatively feasible within the early post-Cold War context. A few favoured the revival of the Military Staff Committee as laid out in the UN Charter, to assure the possibility of a more forceful UN military organisation.[41] Others suggested that the UNSC should take a stronger interest in preventive measures to stop conflicts from escalating, and that there should be a permanent UN rapid response force.[42] Still other suggestions dealt with inclusion of other members in the UNSC, and some states have actively promoted their candidacy for permanent member, including, India, Brazil, Japan and Germany, as mentioned above.

However, none of these suggestions could fundamentally change the UNSC into a forum that can be sufficiently credible and effective to guarantee international peace and security. This would require much deeper changes in the paradigm of the international system. The protection of the traditional sovereign rights of states is one factor that is impossible to by-

---

[39] Barnett, 2010, p. 45, see *supra* note 24.

[40] Independent Working Group on the Future of the United Nations, *The United Nations in its Second Half-Century*, Ford Foundation, New York, 1995; Boutros Boutros-Ghali, *An Agenda for Peace*, A/47/277, 17 June 1995 (http://www.legal-tools.org/doc/7fc42d/); Commission on Global Governance, *Our Global Neighbourhood*, Oxford University Press, Oxford, 1995; Gareth Evans, *Cooperating for Peace: The Global Agenda for the 1990s and Beyond*, Allen and Unwin, Sydney, 1993. For a discussion and summaries of these, see Barnett, 2010, p. 21, see *supra* note 24.

[41] The Military Staff Committee was envisaged in Article 45 of the UN Charter to be a coordinating forum of the military commanders of the permanent five members of the UNSC. In the Cold War context that followed shortly after the end of World War II, the Committee was not properly realised although the provision for it is still in the Charter.

[42] Fred Halliday, "Global Governance: Prospects and Problems", in David Held and Anthony McGrew (eds.), *The Global Transformations Reader: An Introduction to the Globalization Debate*, Second Edition, Blackwell, Cambridge, 2003, p. 492.

pass under the present system. Despite the fact that popular will is the dominant ideology of legitimate governance, no forceful international regime is based on this principle. At best, one can imagine that the popular will is reflected in the international regimes, such as in the UNSC, as a consequence of the domestic systems of the member states. For example, democratic elections in some countries, or at least broad public consultations in non-democracies, could theoretically form a basis for arguing that the UNSC represents the new sovereign concept, that is, popular will.

However, this line of argument would be flawed. Not all states are representative of their populations or conduct policy consultations with their own people. For example, Libya under Muammar Gadhafi was member both of the UNSC (twice) and of the HRC, despite the fact that the country was autocratically ruled and internal political opposition was severely oppressed. There is no guarantee that such states will not pursue international policies that are directly detrimental to the needs of their own populations. Under the present international system, such injustices cannot fully be avoided, although mechanisms can be introduced to limit the problem.

More significantly, the UNSC is made up of diplomatic representatives of states, not elected representatives of peoples. The diplomats involved are, first and foremost, representatives of the interests of their own states, not of the common good or even the community of states that elected them, in the case of non-permanent members. An alternative system of global governance through elected officials, is not possible at this time. It would require a paradigm shift to make such changes feasible.

Even more moderate reforms, such as elimination of the permanent seats and the veto, would conflict with the present paradigm. Although both measures are damaging both to the credibility of the UNSC as a representative international regime, and to its effectiveness, they are firmly entrenched in the paradigm. A change involving more permanent members, or a change in permanent membership, is probably the most sweeping reform that can be contemplated. Such reforms occurred several times in Executive Council in the League of Nations. In the history of the UNSC, it has only happened once, when the People's Republic of China replaced its predecessor regime (Republic of China) on the Council in 1971. Increasingly, the UK and France's permanent seats are out of touch with the reality of international relations, and at one point – providing the UNSC still exists – it may be likely that they will be forced to give up these positions, for example to the European Union. Although the veto can formally prevent that, the global reality may lead to an unbearable pressure on these two countries to give up their present status. In the same way that the representation of the Republic of China was an anachronism in 1971, the permanent seats of France and the UK will become increasingly untenable.

Other changes within the paradigm are also possible. For example, the possibility for longer and sequential terms for elected members of the UNSC would improve the possibility of all members of the Council to contribute more to the agenda than the situation today allows. No country in the world elects Heads of state for two-year periods without the possibility of renewal. This is because too rapid changes at the top of a government put the system under tremendous strain, and give too little time for reforms to be implemented and tested before the next government comes in with its own priorities. If a country was run by 10 heads of state on two-year, non-renewable terms, the possibilities for good governance would be even lower.

Furthermore, there is some possibility for improvement of the rules for authorisation of international intervention through diplomatic, economic or military means. This need is, to a certain extent, already recognised. In the 2005 World Summit in New York, the state leaders of the world endorsed 'Responsibility to Protect', which provides guidelines for international intervention when faced with mass atrocities – specifically genocide, ethnic cleansing, crimes against humanity and war crimes.[43]

2.3.6.1. Lack of Clarity of Rules

While the agreement on Responsibility to Protect remains significant, its lack of clarity has proved to be crippling.[44] The agreement on the concept consists of three short paragraphs. Compared with any legislation on any topic within a domestic context, the difference in clarity and precision should be self-evident. Since Responsibility to Protect applies to international challenges of tremendous potential impact and complexity, this chasm seems only wider.

---

[43] Outcome Document of the 2005 United Nations World Summit, A/RES/60/1, 24 October 2005, paras. 138–140 (http://www.legal-tools.org/doc/0fc107/).

[44] Fassbender, 2012, p. 58, see *supra* note 13.

The vagueness of the concept means that a variety of interpretations can be justified. This inevitably leads to criticism of the concept itself, hesitation in applying it, and suspicions about possible abuse of mandates given by the UNSC with reference to it. Such suspicions had wide circulation in relation to the intervention in Libya in 2011, which was mandated by the UNSC with reference to Responsibility to Protect. As NATO was seen more and more to work actively for regime change with military means, and under the UNSC mandate many member states openly criticised this as mission creep, unwarranted in the UNSC resolutions.[45]

In other areas that will affect international peace and security more indirectly, such as migration or climate change, rules are not even vague, but non-existent.[46] The lack of rules could be remedied by the UNSC itself had it been willing, but only to a certain extent. Article 34 of the UN Charter gives the Council a wide mandate to investigate any situation that "might lead to international friction or give rise to a dispute".[47] However, the UNSC, for the most part, fails to take the initiative. Clearer rules would also bind the UNSC, including the P5, to take action according to those rules. The lack of rules leaves the UNSC without much clout in areas of high significance to the world, leaving no entity in the UN that can exert executive power over the states through resolutions.

The reason for the vagueness or lack of international rules is that states tend to deliberately keep such regulations unclear and open to interpretation. This is seen as assurance against unwanted transferral of key parts of national sovereignty to international organisations. Particularly, the great powers formulate policy in this way, as they presumably benefit more from an international system that is more or less anarchical than small powers.[48]

However, there is a narrow area in which action is possible. Indeed, the UNSC *has* worked more to improve general guidelines and norms after

---

[45] UNSC Res. 1970 (26 February 2011) and UNSC Res. 1973 (17 March 2011); International Coalition for the Responsibility to Protect, "The Crisis in Libya" (http://www.legal-tools.org/doc/9aedb4/). For more on Responsibility to Protect, see also Henry J. Steiner, Philip Alston and Ryan Goodman (eds.), *International Human Rights in Context*, Third Edition, Oxford University Press, Oxford, 2007, pp. 835–843.

[46] Fassbender, 2012, p. 58, see *supra* note 13.

[47] *Ibid.*, p. 60.

[48] Antonio Cassese, "Introduction", in Cassese (ed.), 2012, see *supra* note 13.

the end of the Cold War.[49] One example is the setting up of a mechanism for protection of Children in Armed Conflict. The UNSC set this up in 2005, and has followed up in resolutions, meetings and diplomatic measures against parties that the Council believes to violate children's rights in armed conflicts.[50] There is a UN Special Representative on Children and Armed Conflict that regularly reports on parties that use child soldiers or perpetrate attacks on schools. The UNSC lists these parties formally, providing incentives for them to enter into dialogue with the Special Representative for improving their practices, with some documented effect. The mechanism, however, is a matter of some controversy among states, and probably represents the outer limits to how far the UNSC can push sovereign rights within the present paradigm.

2.3.6.2. Institutional Checks and Balances on the Security Council

Another measure to increase the credibility and effectiveness of the UNSC would be to increase the possibilities for institutional checks and balances. A procedure to resolve stalemates and to appeal decisions formally, for example, through referral to the UNGA or to the ICJ, is not possible under the current paradigm.[51] Non-binding oversight functions are the maximum that can be achieved. The UNGA already has the Uniting for Peace procedure, and is tasked with general oversight in the UN Charter. However, as the UNGA is not capable of enforcing its will, either formally or practically, its power in such circumstances is limited to making recommendations.

Judicial review of UNSC decisions by the ICJ is also a fairly obvious alternative. There are, however, challenges connected with this, including the very vagueness of the rules for international intervention. Still, a case can be made that the ICJ could take on an increased role going in the direction of non-binding judicial review, which it has so far not done.

It should be noted that the few general rules and mechanisms that have been set up under the UNSC are seldom generated by the UNSC members themselves. Instead, the ideas tend to originate in civil society, or by academics or commissions. The Popular Sovereign Paradigm allows non-state actors to contribute to a much larger extent than in the Westphalian

---

[49] Barnett, 2010, p. 66, see *supra* note 24.

[50] UNSC Res. 1612 (2005) (http://www.legal-tools.org/doc/807dd5/).

[51] White suggests a larger UNGA role in checking the UNSC, see White, 2002, p. 106, *supra* note 2. For legal review by the ICJ, see Robert Colb, *The International Court of Justice*, Hart Publishing, Oxford, 2013, pp. 1205–1207.

Paradigm. The reason is the concept of popular will as basis for legitimate governance, and the increased emphasis on the rights of individuals, not only states. Before the twentieth century, the concept of NGOs participating in the formulation of international law was virtually unheard of. The ICRC, for example, was created by treaty, and has therefore never been an NGO in the sense that is common today.

Under the Popular Sovereign Paradigm, however, NGOs have increasingly come to influence the development of international rules and mechanisms. This will be discussed further in the chapters on human rights and international humanitarian law. Examples in regard to the UNSC include Responsibility to Protect, which was conceived by the International Commission on Intervention and State Sovereignty, in its 2001 report.[52] This was a commission independent of the UNSC.

Such processes are examples of the possibilities under the present paradigm: proposals from commissions or NGO alliances can be refined into new rules or mechanisms through a process in which the UNSC is pressured to adopt resolutions involving further precision of the international system of rules. Such processes can work only when a much broader spectrum of stakeholders in the international system than state representatives is engaged.

The challenge is that such procedures may produce suggestions that the UNSC will find unacceptable, even if they may be embarrassing to oppose openly. Clearer rules may be beneficial to global affairs in general, but not necessarily to the UNSC members. Furthermore, UNSC members would regard many new rules as unenforceable, suspecting that many states would simply disregard the rules, thus leaving the UNSC in a position of not being able to enforce its own decisions.

2.3.6.3. Clearer Rules on International Intervention

In regard to formulation of clearer rules, it has been suggested that the UNSC should systematically build up a series of precedents or general frameworks around its resolutions.[53] This would benefit the UN and in-

---

[52] International Commission on Intervention and State Sovereignty, *Responsibility to Protect: Report of the International Commission on Intervention and State Sovereignty*, International Development Research Centre, Ottawa, 2001 (http://www.legal-tools.org/doc/f96bca/).

[53] Fassbender, 2012, p. 59, see *supra* note 13.

crease fairness and predictability in the international system. However, considering that the UNSC is for the most part unable to effectively address even single issues, such as the conflict in Syria at the time of writing, the build-up of such a system may not be possible for the UNSC on its own. Furthermore, it is likely that the UNSC would become even more inefficient if it was to consider its decisions systematically as the basis for precedents. For example, it is doubtful that the UNSC would have been able to agree on referring the Darfur situation to the prosecutor of the ICC – as it did in 2002 – if it would have set a clear precedent.[54] If so, there would be a solid basis for ICC referral of other cases involving suspicions of breaches of international humanitarian law and human rights law in the future, including by the P5 countries. Had this been considered a possibility in the UNSC debate on Darfur in 2005, the case would not have been referred to the ICC.

In general, the potential for clear rules for international intervention, for formal review mechanisms to check and balance the UNSC, remains very limited under the present paradigm. Under a different paradigm, such as the hypothetical suggested in Chapter 6, the possibilities would be improved. If the international order mechanism is designed in the future to represent a global popular will, then its entities can also be expected to act differently. Under this hypothetical system, clearer rules could be formulated, as they are by national assemblies in constitutional democracies. Furthermore, a full-fledged court system could be introduced, where legal experts could provide judicial review over the acts of the legislative as well as the executive. The combination of clearer rules and system integrity through checks and balances would increase the likelihood of international regimes striving for objectives of common good. The risk of being reprimanded in an appeals or review process should serve to encourage more sobriety in dealing with the facts and evidence in the initial process, and to discourage purely self-serving policies.

Such an international system will easily be dismissed as impossible by many scholars and practitioners alike. However, there is a need to consider that the impossibilities under one paradigm would be feasible, even logical, under another. After all, few would have believed in 1850 that organisations like the UN and the European Union, as they exist today, could

---

[54] UNSC Res. 1593 (2005) (http://www.legal-tools.org/doc/4b208f/).

have been realised.[55] Given the obvious shortcomings of the UNSC, there is a significant likelihood that the present system will not survive in an age when, for example, India, Brazil, Indonesia, and other countries achieve economic and political strength to match their population, or in another major international conflict involving two or more of the most powerful states. In such circumstances, the choice may be between collapse of the system (as was the case or the League of Nations) or fundamental change.

2.4. The United Nations General Assembly

2.4.1. Significance

The UNGA cannot pass legally binding resolutions, unlike the UNSC. However, as the most universal state-member organisation in the world, the UNGA is the primary forum for negotiations over new international treaty law. Examples are plenty-fold, including the International Covenants for Civil and Political Rights and for Economic, Social and Cultural Rights (1966). A more recent example is the Arms Trade Treaty (2013).

Other treaty negotiation processes have commenced in the UNGA too, but then been taken out of the forum in order to reach agreement among a smaller group of states. A recent example is the Anti-Personnel Mine Ban Convention (1997). In 1993, the UNGA adopted a resolution for a moratorium on anti-personnel landmines, and in 1995 a resolution calling for the elimination of such mines.[56] Although not legally binding, these resolutions paved the way for the convention a few years later.

Finally, the UNGA's non-binding resolutions are often interpreted as an expression of the general legal opinion of states, depending on the language of the resolution. As such, the non-binding resolutions can and will, over time, be a significant reference for international courts in assessing whether new rules of customary international law have come into existence. Examples of non-binding resolutions becoming customary international law includes, for example, several provisions in the Universal Declaration on Human Rights (1948), which will be discussed in the chapter on human rights.

---

[55] A similar point is made in Halliday, 2003, p. 490, see *supra* note 42.

[56] Gro Nystuen and Stuart Casey-Maslen (eds.), *The Convention on Cluster Munitions: A Commentary*, Oxford University Press, Oxford, 2010, p. 80.

The UNGA, therefore, is a source of large amounts of new international law. It remains a corner stone of the present international system.

2.4.2. Formal Equality between Sovereign States

As with the UNSC, the General Assembly is clearly not a disinterested body. Each state pursues its national policy objectives in the UNGA, and each are affected, in different ways, by the resolutions that are passed by the Assembly. The UNGA, however, should be seen as representative of the global community of states, as almost all states of the world are members. Moreover, their membership is formally on equal terms, although differences in resources are significant in practice.

At any rate, the UNGA is the most representative organ of states in the world, and clearly more so than the UNSC. The challenge is that the universal membership is strictly limited to states, although the stakeholders of international order is much wider than the UNGA membership. In principle, all individuals, organisations and corporations in the world are stakeholders. The UNGA faces the same problem as other international organisations under the Popular Sovereign Paradigm: the basis is traditional state sovereignty, but the UNGA is also expected to guide the global community toward common good, for all stakeholders (the popular will).

This systemic contradiction is the principled core of a continuous debate in the UNGA about the level of inclusion of non-state entities in various parts of its decision-making process.

Today, the UNGA has a number of non-state observers. These have designated seats in the Assembly and its committees. The ICRC is one example. These observers do not have the full rights of members, and are barred from, for example, sponsoring resolutions and voting on substantive matters. As observers, however, they will be in a position to influence the material content of resolutions though direct access to voting members, as well as access to information on drafts, proceedings, debates, etc. The observers, however, is a very limited group, consisting of international organisations either representing groups of states or founded by groups of states, such as the ICC, the Council of Europe, the World Bank, or and the Arab League.

There are no formal NGO observers. However, NGOs that have attained 'consultative status' with ECOSOC have the right to attend formal

UNGA sessions, including committee meetings.[57] As of March 2017, 143 NGOs have 'general consultative status', which is the highest status.[58] However, the participation of these NGOs in informal meetings and negotiations requires consensus among the state members, and the practice is that NGOs never participate in final negotiations over resolutions. NGOs' most important avenues for influence, therefore, is through lobbying governments on policy issues, and in arranging side-events to formal sessions on selected topics. While informal, the political pressure mobilised by NGOs is critical for achieving substantial movement from the governments on a wide range of issues. For example, neither the 2013 Arms Trade Treaty nor the 1997 Mine Ban Convention would have been possible if not for the concerted and consistent pressure from NGOs.

The UNGA is representative of the stakeholders of its work, only to the extent that the member states are representative of the individuals and organisations within their respective territories. For democratic member states, a higher degree of representativeness can be assumed, although clearly less so than democratically elected representatives would be. A few states represent mainly the interests of their own leaders, such as DPRK. Finally, a number of states fall in-between these categories, where the governments are well-informed about, and, for the most part, also represent the will of their populations, but on key issues work only for the interests of their respective ruling groups.

Another main challenge with representativeness is that each country has one vote, irrespective of population size. This gives, for example, the EU countries – which generally share the same outlook on global values and which co-ordinate their votes as much as possible – an advantage in numbers over, for example, China and India. The latter two each represent roughly twice as many citizens as the EU, but have only one vote. This advantage in numbers is only partially offset by the ability of large countries to rally others around their causes.

The UNGA, therefore, represents continuity from the Westphalian Paradigm in the sense that sovereign states are the deciding authorities of the system. It also, however, represents the new concept of popular will, in

---

[57] A list is of NGOs with consultative status is available at the UN website, NGO branch of the Department of Economic and Social Affairs.

[58] *Ibid.*

which increasing NGO influence is the most important factor, in combination with governments being responsive to this influence and to their domestic population. As an international law maker, the UNGA also functions as a supranational organisation in practice, although only within the boundaries that are not too threatening to the member states' concern over their sovereign rights. Finally, the UNGA clearly embodies the new concept of full equality between states, thus representing a clear break from the Westphalian Paradigm in this aspect.

2.4.3. General Assembly in Action: Sovereign Perspective Inputs, Supranational Outputs

Despite the strict state-centred decision-making process, the UNGA should be credited for seeking out and making use of salient facts and evidence, as well as expert opinions, from non-governmental sources. It regularly requests analyses from the Secretariat on topics of interests, or invites experts to speak at formal or informal events in connection with the Assembly's sessions and, less frequently, requests advisory opinions from the ICJ.

As with the UNSC, member states filter facts and evidence through the sieve of their own national interests. A study of voting patterns in the UNGA for the period 1991–1993 found that states' votes were clearly influenced by their position in the 'North-South' geopolitical stratum, signifying generally their share of power in the international system. States in the North with more power tended to vote against strong resolutions on nuclear disarmament, for example, as well as being more reluctant about resolutions regarding self-determination (Bosnia-Hercegovina, Palestine and South Africa).[59]

However, because there are no members in the UNGA that have higher formal power than the others, unlike the permanent members of the UNSC, this tendency is much less harmful to the fairness of the system. Elected representatives in national assemblies also filter facts in consideration of the interests that they are elected to represent, and tend to speak and vote accordingly. As long as the forum as a collective can be seen to represent the most relevant interests fairly, this will not be a problem in terms of impartiality.

---

[59] Soo Yeon Kim and Bruce Russett, "The New Politics of Voting Alignments in the United Nations General Assembly", in Timothy J. Sinclair (ed.), *Global Governance: Critical Concepts in Political Science*, vol. II, Routledge, London, 2004, pp. 339–344.

The limitations of the system are primarily shown in issues where states tend to have interests that do not necessarily represent the popular will. In particular, this happens in cases where the sovereign right to domestic regulation conflicts with new and universal rights of individuals, such as freedom of assembly, association, and speech. Here, strong action is often not possible. As a consequence of this conflict of principles, the level of inclusion of NGOs is also a continuous issue of debate between the states. On human rights issues, for example, the NGOs lobbying the UN tend to represent the perspective of individual rights more than sovereign rights. Increased inclusion of NGOs will therefore be detrimental to the states most concerned about protection of traditional sovereignty.

Broad consultations among the *state* members are generally carried out by the UNGA. However, there are no formal rounds of hearings on resolutions in which NGOs in general are invited to share their inputs. NGOs will monitor the processes either on their own, or through umbrella organisations, and lobby member states with their input. The level of inclusiveness of NGOs in the UNGA remains below that of the HRC.

The constant and regular reintroduction of resolutions over specific themes goes some way to ensure that there are mechanisms for inputs from outsiders, as well as possible revision by future generations. For example, human rights resolutions on the Rights of the Child are reintroduced every year in the Third Committee of the UNGA. These resolutions are a mix of some new topics and language already agreed from previous resolutions. The downside to this procedure is that it draws tremendous diplomatic resources, with little effect in terms of change. "Agreed language" in UNGA resolutions can be difficult to change, if it is in the interest of some member states to block alternative suggestions. However, it does happen frequently, meaning that the soft law in UNGA resolutions is dynamic and can be altered if changing circumstances require it.

The degree to which the member states consult their domestic stakeholders vary greatly. There are no rules or guidelines for national consultations in advance of, during or after UNGA sessions. Instead, the states decide their own practice. Some member states have rounds with national NGOs, reporting to parliament, or issue publications about national policies in advance of the UNGA. Others do neither of these. There is no overview over the current practice of states, meaning that the extent to which consultations with stakeholders are carried out on a global basis is unclear.

2.4.4. System Integrity: The General Assembly *vis-à-vis* Other UN Main Organs

The UNGA has very few formal checks and balances. There is no judicial review of its decisions, and no entity can overrule any action taken by the UNGA. This is, in one sense, less of a problem in this forum than for the UNSC, because UNGA resolutions are not legally binding. However, the lack of any strong and formal oversight mechanism represents a significant problem for the UNGA, as there is no mechanism that can provide a rebuke when necessary.

Similar to the UNSC, the lack of checks and balances specifically leads to the entrenchment of practices that would be considered to be corrupt in domestic systems. Trading of votes is very common in the UNGA. There is, for example, statistical evidence that the US uses aid to attain supporting votes in the UNGA.[60] In regard to elections, vote-trading is in fact consistently the norm, not the exception.[61] Member states that seek election in the UNGA for themselves, or who have nationals contending for seats on, for example, expert committees, will trade votes with other UN members, typically with the promise of supporting another candidatures in the future. This includes election of non-permanent members of the UNSC and judges to the ICJ.

It should be noted that it is not necessarily the case that vote-trading will lead to bad decisions.[62] Some degree of horse-trading is inevitable and necessary in all politics. However, in the UNGA election system, the horse-trading is endemic, which easily calls into doubt the competence and merits of anyone who is elected by that forum. This undermines the credibility of both the UNGA itself, as well as elected bodies, including the UNSC and ICJ.

While the practice is so widespread, it is also futile for anyone state to simply not participate in the vote-trading system. This would only lead to reduced influence for that state, without causing any systemic change.

The setting up of a strong formal control mechanism to monitor and check the UNGA, for example, through judicial review by the ICJ, is not possible under the present paradigm. This would place too much power

---

[60] Axel Dreher, Peter Nunnenkamp and Rainer Thiele, "Does US Aid Buy UN General Assembly Votes? A Disaggregated Analysis", in *Public Choice*, 2008, vol. 136, no. 1–2, p. 139.

[61] Eldar, 2008, p. 23, see *supra* note 37.

[62] *Ibid.*, p. 39.

with the ICJ and thus undermine the system of sovereign states' rights that is at the core of the UN system.

More subtle or limited means can however, be contemplated. The problem of vote-trading could, for example, be redressed by the adoption of rules about vote-trading by the UNGA. It may even be possible to imagine tasking of a supervisory body with the authority and resources to provide oversight, although probably not to the degree that it can issue penalties for violations. Because of the lack of checks and balances related to the UNGA, this would require a shift in the way of thinking and working in the UN system.

2.4.5. The Future of the General Assembly

Reform of the UNGA is not as pressing a concern as it is for the UNSC. As long as the international system is primarily state-based, there will be a need for a discussion forum in which states can meet and discuss potentially common interests and actions.

Still, a number of reform proposals have been put forward over the years. Among the most sweeping proposals, it is noteworthy that a significant number – perhaps most – relate to the perceived challenge of a lack of democratic accountability in the UNGA. This is an example of the conflicting principles of the popular sovereign paradigm: legitimacy is based on popular will, but the international system is also based on sovereign states, and their formal equality.

Václav Havel, the late President of the Czech Republic, proposed a dual chamber system in his speech to the UNGA on 8 September 2000.[63] In his vision, one chamber would represent states equally, and a second chamber would be elected directly by the global population. These bodies would create and guarantee global legislation, and UNSC would be accountable to both.[64]

Seen from the perspective of the principle of popular will, the benefits would be clear: elected representatives would have stronger and more legitimate mandates, and potentially also more confidence in carrying them out, than diplomatic representatives, due to the former's positions of trust, and the need to publicly showcase results of their work. However, such an

---

[63] Antonio Cassese, "Gathering up the Main Threads", in Cassese (ed.), 2012, p. 648, see *supra* note 13.

[64] *Ibid.*

arrangement would clearly conflict with the fundamental realities of the present international system. If states are, at present, concerned about their sovereign rights to the extent that they are reluctant to let NGOs into UNGA meetings, how can they be expected to reform UNGA to a democratically elected and accountable assembly? The answer is, of course, that they cannot.

A democratically elected world assembly is a concept that would only be possible under a different paradigm of the international system. It would require a clean break with the state sovereignty underpinning the present paradigm.

It is noteworthy that the appeal of a system based on representation and popular will is so widespread and strong, and that – by contrast – the realization that this would require a reshaping of the entire paradigm seems weak. This applies equally to many critics of the reform proposals. Robert Dahl, for example, has argued against democratic global governance because he doubts that the topics discussed in the UNGA will capture the interest of most people of the world to an extent that would make elections meaningful.[65] He argues that as long as the UNGA can only pass non-binding resolutions, the active interest and engagement of the majority of the world's population is likely to remain on a very low level.[66]

Both assertions may be true. They are also irrelevant for the UNGA. Traditional sovereignty is incompatible with global democratic governance. A global democratic assembly with the power to pass binding resolutions is therefore not possible, I submit, under the present paradigm. Elections to a global assembly are therefore not meaningful, and cannot draw on wide global participation, as the assembly to be elected can have no real power within the current order.

Elections to the European Parliament are revealing as regards connection between formal authority and public participation. It has powers that the UNGA does not have, although the EU member states retain the most significant share of decision-making power, including through the Commission. The voter turnout, predictably, lies somewhere between public indifference and public participation in elections to national parliaments,

---

[65] Robert Dahl, "Can International Organizations be Democratic? A Skeptic's view", Held and McGrew (eds.), 2003, pp. 530–541, see *supra* note 42.

[66] *Ibid.*

and it varies considerably throughout the EU. In the 2014 elections, the largest voter turnout was 89.65% in Belgium, while it was a mere 13.05 % in Slovakia. The average turnout in 2014 was 42%.[67] This represents a considerable number of active voters (170 million), but is low compared with most national standards.[68] India, the world's largest democracy by far, achieved a turnout of 66.4% in its 2014 elections.[69] European – and Indian – elections show that number of voters is not an obstacle for a democratic system, but also that public participation and the powers of the elected representatives go hand in hand.

Other proposals for UNGA reform seek to remedy the lack of representativity of the global public in less sweeping ways. One proposal is to set up a Parliamentary General Assembly, which would be complementary to the UNGA. Such an assembly could, its proponents argue, consist of one to three members of national parliaments, who would discuss possible common recommendations.[70] It should be recalled, however, that the UNGA is not the only, nor even the first, experiment in global dialogue. The Inter-Parliamentary Union, for example, is older than the UNGA and still exists. Here, national parliamentarians have come together to discuss global issues for over a century.

There are good reasons why the UNGA has become more significant than the Union as global norm-giver. One reason is that parliamentary representatives are elected on national platforms, not international ones. Most of the time, the mandates from their constituents on international issues are weak or non-existent. An inter-parliamentary assembly, therefore, is not necessarily more representative than the UNGA. Furthermore, it is not necessarily the case that an elected national parliamentarian would take more representative decisions than a diplomatic delegate. Most national parliamentarians spend their time on domestic issues and represent a portion of their constituents and their interests, while the diplomats spend most of

---

[67] European Parliament, "Results of the 2014 European elections", available on the web site of the European Parliament.

[68] Estimated number of eligible EU voters was around 400 million in 2014. Bruni Waterfield, "EU elections 2014: Everything you ever wanted to know (but were scared to ask)", in *The Telegraph*, 12 May 2014.

[69] Bharti Jaini, "Highest-ever voter turnout recorded in 2014 polls, govt spending doubled since 2009", in *Times of India*, 13 May 2014.

[70] Alston, 2012, p. 43, see *supra* note 14.

their time on international issues under the direction of a national government that decides on foreign policy direction for the whole country. From this perspective, the benefits of having national parliamentarians in decision-making positions seem less certain.

Most important, however, is that states remain the fundamental decision makers in the international systems. Individual parliamentarians cannot bind entire populations through international resolutions. States can. Diplomats represent states; parliamentarians represent their parties or their local constituents.

Moreover, a number of UNGA member states are not democratic. For these states, there would be no purpose in sending parliamentary representatives to the UNGA, as opposed to state representatives, as their positions would often be the same, but only the latter wold have formal authority to bind the state.

Another line of reform proposals is to remedy the representation deficit of the UNGA by weighing votes according to population size.[71] For example, China would be given X number of 'vote points', while Denmark has Y.

The issue of weighted voting, however, faces an insurmountable obstacle in the challenge of different models of domestic governance. A system where the votes are weighted on the basis of population size would only make sense if the states actually represent those populations. Otherwise, the new system would be no better – and quite possibly worse – in representing the global popular will. While in principle a dictatorship could represent the will of its population, there are of course no guarantees, and historically too many examples of the opposite. Giving China a voting weight that matches its population size would, according to many, be unacceptable from the viewpoint of Western democratic countries. Weighted voting by population size, therefore, is not possible in the present state of the world, for an organisation that encompasses a universal or near-universal state membership. The basic concept of equality between states, underpinning the Popular Sovereign Paradigm, is therefore likely to persist also as a foundation for the decision-making in the UNGA.

The range of possible reforms of the UNGA under the present paradigm is much more limited. As has been mentioned, the debate among the

---

[71] White discusses this, although he does not propose it, White, 2002, pp. 87–89, see *supra* note 2

member states tends to relate to the level of NGO participation as observers, in some contexts including the right to make a statement, but not to the extent that states should share decision making power with non-state actors.

Increased NGO participation and consultations with non-state actors therefore probably represents the outer boundary of the possible under the present paradigm. To this effect, creative rules and mechanisms can be contemplated. For example, the UNGA could potentially agree on rules – or at least voluntary guidelines – concerning national consultations in advance of UNGA sessions. NGOs themselves could set up an independent body that would monitor states' compliance with such rules or guidelines. If the system could improve the level of states' consultations with its populations, including through national parliaments and local civil society organisations about the issues on the UNGA agenda, it would strengthen the forum in terms of representativity of the popular will. It would also strengthen the awareness of the UNGA and its resolutions throughout the world, leading to a more informed international debate and, over time, potentially greater compliance.

2.5. The International Court of Justice

The ICJ is the judicial arm of the UN system. As such, it is the closest there is to an ultimate arbiter and high court for the state-based international system.

The actual mandate and work of the ICJ is constrained by a number of limitations imposed by the states and by the Court itself. The ICJ is, in reality, only the primary arbiter for *state* disputes, and only when the states accept its jurisdiction. International organisations have no formal standing before the Court, except in requesting advisory opinions.[72] Among other things, this constrains the ICJ's ability to function as a body for judicial review, which would be expected of the highest court in most domestic legal systems based on the division of state powers.

The jurisdiction of the ICJ is limited to disputes between states parties, where both states have accepted the jurisdiction of the Court. The rules are set up in Article 36 of the Statute. Article 36(2) allows states to accept the jurisdiction of the ICJ without special agreement. As of February 2017, 72 states have accepted such jurisdiction, although some have done so with

---

[72] *Ibid.*, p. 119.

reservations.[73] Notably, India and Japan have accepted, but the US, Russia or China have not.[74] Of the P5 states, only the UK has accepted jurisdiction according to this optional clause, in 2014, albeit with some reservations.

2.5.1. Composition of the ICJ International Court of Justice:

Although a court of justice, the ICJ is also an international organisation. As with other such organisations, its statutes represent a compromise between the concerns for states' sovereignty and its degree of supranational authority.

The 15 judges of the ICJ are presumed to be independent legal experts, and therefore disinterested third parties, not state representatives. While the election system is tailored to ensure representation from major legal systems and the world's regions, the judges do not act as spokespersons for their own regions or countries, but serve in their own capacity.

The judges of ICJ are selected through a many-staged process involving the national groups of the Permanent Court of Arbitration, the UNSG, the UNGA, and the UNSC. Lists of nominees are presented by the national groups of the Court, which the UN Secretary-General compiles and presents to the UNGA and UNSC, which again elects the judges in stages. The judges' terms are nine years.[75]

In principle, the election rules ensure that the composition of judges will be broad and impartial as a whole. However, they could also be criticised. As the UNSC is not an impartial body of the international system, an election by that entity will also lack the highest degree of fairness. UNGA members also pursue their own national interests in matters of procedure as well as substance. Empirical evidence suggests that decisions of election of judges are biased first in favour of their country of origin, and secondly in favour of countries that match the economic, political, and cultural attributes of those of the electors.[76]

---

[73] International Court of Justice, "Frequently Asked Questions", available on the web site of the Court.

[74] For a list, see International Court of Justice, "Declarations Recognizing the Jurisdiction of the Court as Compulsory", available on the web site of the Court.

[75] The rules for composition, nomination and election of judges are found in the Statute of the International Court of Justice, Articles 2–19 ('ICJ Statute') (http://www.legal-tools.org/doc/fdd2d2/).

[76] Eldar, 2008, p. 25, see *supra* note 37.

The *actual* composition of the judges in the ICJ shows that the great power influence is even stronger than the formal rules would imply. The practice has been that each of the permanent members of the UNSC are represented on the Court by one of its nationals, usually a person with experience as a legal adviser to the state. Furthermore, Germany and Japan are also usually represented with a judge.[77] This practice of representation has been more or less persistent despite the fact that there are no provisions to this effect in the ICJ Statute and that there is no UNSC-veto in the election of judges, which is clearly a procedural and not substantial issue before the Council.[78]

In this sense, the ICJ bench is not much more representative of the world's peoples and legal systems than is the UNSC. However, other factors in effect suggest a high degree of impartiality and disinterestedness in the ICJ. These factors include that fact that the judges' terms of nine years are long; the 15-judge collective is relatively large; and the persons elected are normally highly competent legal experts. The bench is certainly able to act independently from the sum of the national backgrounds of its judges in adjudication of specific legal cases, even though the practice of great-power representation is not ideal.

In terms of substantial evidence, there is little ground for questioning the impartiality of the Court as a whole, although there are many examples of judges dissenting from decisions in that go in the disfavour of their own country of origin. One such is the dissenting opinion of the US judge Stephen Swebel (US) in the Nicaragua case in 1986.[79] Another is the 1998 court decision, when the US judge dissented to the majority's acceptance of jurisdiction in a case brought by Libya against the US in 1992.[80] While these examples may undermine the confidence in the judge's individual impartiality, it is more significant that the Court, as a collective, did in fact defy a superpower in both cases.[81]

More in doubt, however, is whether the composition of the bench makes it more likely that the general *direction* of the ICJ will lean toward

---

[77] Antonio Cassese, "The International Court of Justice: It is High Time to Restyle the Respected Old Lady", in Cassese (ed.), 2012, pp. 239–249, see *supra* note 13.

[78] White, 2002, pp. 115–117, see *supra* note 2.

[79] *Ibid.*, p. 114.

[80] *Ibid.*

[81] *Ibid.*, p. 115.

legal principles that are shared by these great powers, in the face of alternatives. There should be no doubt that the preference to their own nationals by the more powerful states in the UN system is given on the presumption that these nationals will be sympathetic to their states' points of view. At the same time, it will be difficult to argue that the Court in its rulings is mostly or to a large extent directly biased toward the interests of the more powerful states. One can observe that the Court remains legally conservative, and reluctant to take on more expansive roles which would serve to constrain the UNSC in particular, such as providing judicial review of the UNSC or other UN organs. The most notable example is its refusal to do so in the Lockerbie decision (1998).[82] For this reason, while the ICJ may in itself achieve a high degree of fairness in its procedures, its contribution to the system integrity within the UN system remains limited.

Moreover, as long as the current practice remains, the disinterested impartiality of the ICJ collective of judges can be drawn into doubt, although only to a limited degree. The reason that such doubts are not expressed openly may well be because the Court remains so conservative, and therefore does not expose itself to criticism and public debate in ways that more expansive courts tend to, such as the European Court of Human Rights.

2.5.2. The Court in Action

The level to which the ICJ is able to act as a supranational organisation, independent of the sovereign states that set it up, can be measured against how free the Court is in its own procedures. Its independence would be stronger if it was freer to seek out relevant input and expertise in order to attain basis for strong conclusions.

There are, however, both formal and practical impediments for the ICJ to take salient points of facts, evidence and expert opinions into consideration. The most significant formal obstacle is the limitations on reception of expert legal input from impartial third parties. Highly reputed centres of legal expertise, like the Max Planck Institute of Heidelberg, would be in a position to help the ICJ on difficult points of law, for example, on

---

[82] Verdirame, 2011, pp. 345–346, see *supra* note 21. On the Court's relative conservatism, see Colb, 2013, pp. 1158–1159, see *supra* note 51; Antonio Cassese, "The International Court of Justice: It is High Time to Restyle the Respected Old Lady", in Cassese (ed.), 2012, p. 240, see *supra* note 13.

the existence of a rule of customary law, or if a general norm belongs to the *jus cogens* category.[83] Such input is allowed by other international courts and have proven to be influential and valuable to those courts' work.[84]

The ICJ Statute allows states and international organisations to submit such input only in its work on advisory opinions, which are not legally binding.[85] It is not permissible in contentious cases, which places a limitation on the Court for no clear principled reason.[86] It can be presumed, therefore, that the reason is the desire to limit the independence of the Court *vis-à-vis* sovereign states' interests. A situation in which the ICJ would develop a more dynamic form of legal interpretation – akin to the practice of the European Court of Human Rights, where the text of the European Convention on Human Rights convention is interpreted in light of 'present-day conditions' – could lead to developments in international law where new concepts may undermine aspects of traditional state sovereignty.

Criticism has been put forward regarding the Court's own consideration of relevant external analyses and circumstances. One of the world's foremost experts on international law, Antonio Cassese, argued that the Court is too passive in considering state practice, other courts' views and legal arguments. This leads the Court to legal conservatism, in his opinion, as it does not actively seek to clarify developing principles in customary international law, instead favouring to recite its own jurisprudence.[87]

This passivity is probably not only a matter of will, but also of means. The main practical impediment is the Court's limitations in terms of organisation and capacity for fact-finding. Cassese has argued that, in at least three recent cases, it has become evident that the ICJ lacks the right tools for ascertaining facts.[88]

Although of clear significance to the workings of the Court, the lack of capacity does not necessarily translate into biased decision-making. The restrictions on submission of expert legal opinions to the Court, however, reflects the fact that it is part and parcel of the Popular Sovereign Paradigm.

---

[83] Cassese, 2012, see *supra* note 82.
[84] *Ibid.*, p. 244. Cassese uses the ICTY as an example, where he himself also served as a judge.
[85] ICJ Statute, Article 66, see *supra* note 75.
[86] Cassese, 2012, see *supra* note 82.
[87] *Ibid.*, p. 240.
[88] *Ibid.*, p. 246.

It may change its practice and evolve to a certain extent, but there is a limit to how strong its role can become, considering that the states still hold the key to revision of its Statute.

The most significant of restrictions that protect state sovereign rights is the rule that only sovereign states can appear as parties to cases before the Court.[89] This clause excludes other relevant parties. For example, prior to 2011, the *de facto* government of South Sudan could not bring any dispute with Sudan (Khartoum) to the ICJ. When violent conflict erupted over the contested and oil-rich area of Abyei in 2008, the two sides agreed after negotiations to send the issue to an international legal entity. Because of South Sudan's formal status, however, the issue was referred to the Permanent Court of Arbitration, and not the ICJ.

Other state-like entities are also excluded by the Court's Statute from appearing as parties, such as Palestine. While Palestine is recognised as a state by over two thirds of the UNGA, it is unable to join the ICJ as a member state. The reason is that the Statute requires a Security Council decision for membership, and three permanent members (the US, the UK and France) have not recognised Palestinian statehood. This means Israel has a double protection from legal ramifications under sovereign rights: an Israeli-Palestinian case before the ICJ would require both Israeli acceptance of jurisdiction and P5 acceptance of Palestine as a state. In other words, the highest court on international law in the world is formally not set up to try cases relating to the most well-known armed conflict in the world. It also means that should Jordan and Israel decide to try a case before the ICJ, for example, relating to a dispute over the Jordan River or Dead Sea, Palestine would be unable to intervene, even though it would clearly be affected by a decision.

The ICJ also places upon itself more severe restrictions than are formally required. For example, the Statute allows third states to intervene in cases that are likely to affect them.[90] However, the Court has had a restrictive practice on such third-party (state) intervention. The assumption by the Court is that its decision will take into account the positions of the third state, without it being necessary for that state to actually intervene in the case at hand. This, however, has rightly been criticised as a limiting and

---

[89]   ICJ Statute, Article 34, see *supra* note 75.
[90]   *Ibid.*, Article 62.

unnecessary practice, which excludes relevant stakeholders from consultation.[91]

2.5.3. System Integrity: The Court *vis-à-vis* Other UN Main Organs

As a court that is expected only to serve as an arbiter when states themselves refer cases to it, the limitations on consultations with stakeholders for the ICJ set-up are important, but not crippling. As a court for the international system, however, the ICJ falls far short. The main challenge in this regard is its strict limitation to state actors and its relative disconnect from the rest of the UN system. If the UN had been a national legal system, the high court would be expected to serve as the final adjudicator in all legal matters. The ICJ does however, not have such a role in the UN system. Instead, it remains a court for states' disputes, while international organisations have no formal status and cannot be parties.[92] Therefore, the ICJ has historically not provided significant commentary on, let alone rulings over, decisions by the UNSC or the UNGA. This also means that there is no mature mechanism in the UN where, for example, the UNGA could follow up ICJ rulings with a process to reform international law, if the latter found a resolution to be conflicting with the Charter or a peremptory norm of customary international law.

2.5.4. Future of the Court: Possible and Impossible Reforms

The various shortcomings of the ICJ outlined above are, for the most part, constraints deliberately placed upon it by states that are fearful of losing their traditional sovereign rights. As such, it is difficult to imagine this changing dramatically under the present paradigm of the international system. Furthermore, the threshold for amendments to the ICJ Statute is high: the procedure is the same as for the UN Charter, which means that all of the P5 veto powers have to acquiesce to the proposal in question.[93] In other words, sweeping reform is not coming in the short term. However, there is room for manoeuvre without formal change in the Statute, which can help the Court to live up to its potential under the present paradigm.

---

[91] Cassese, 2012, pp. 242–243, see *supra* note 82.

[92] White, 2002, p. 119, see *supra* note 2.

[93] ICJ Statute, Article 69, see *supra* note 75; UN Charter, Article 108, see *supra* note 17.

As regards reform proposals that fall outside the Popular Sovereign Paradigm, the most significant is that of opening up the Court for non-state actors as parties to contentious cases. One idea is that the ICJ should open up for participation of a broader international society, including intergovernmental organisations, non-state entities like the ICRC, and even some rebel groups.[94] Strong arguments support this proposal: international legal conflicts are not solely caused by states, nor are states the only stakeholders. An almost exclusive emphasis on states, based on traditional sovereignty, is thus not compatible with an approach that takes the totality of stakeholders of the international system into account. As international law has clearly developed increasing protection of the rights of individuals, this further highlights the Courts' limitations.

However, formally opening up for a range of non-state actors would be incompatible with the Popular Sovereign Paradigm. Letting non-state actors appear as parties would represent a formal and permanent undermining of states' traditional sovereign rights. Clearest, in this regard, is the example of rebel groups, which by definition represent a threat to sovereign states. Less clear, perhaps, is the case of international organisations, which remain state-centred and state-driven in most aspects, but also have degrees of independence from states. However, the P5 in particular, will not unanimously allow the ICJ to assume greater powers by letting international organisations refer cases to it. The status of the Court is such that a clear decision will be very difficult to directly oppose, even from a great power, and there will at least be a cost for that power in terms of soft power and credibility loss.

A probable maximum, therefore, is increasing the availability of the Court for providing advisory opinions, which are non-binding. Today, the right to request advisory opinions rests with the UNGA. Other agencies can request advisory opinions only if the UNGA authorises it.[95] However, this leaves the door open for the UNGA to decide to use this mechanism more often. It is thus possible for NGO coalitions, in particular, to lobby UNGA members in order to increase the use of the mechanism. Considering the previous practice of the Court, however, as exemplified in the ICJ advisory opinion on nuclear weapons (1996), such increased use will not necessarily lead to outcomes that the NGO community will consider beneficial. The

---

[94] See White, 2002, p. 241, see *supra* note 2.
[95] ICJ Statute, Article 96(2), see *supra* note 75.

advisory opinion *Legal Consequences of Construction of a Wall in the Occupied Territory of Palestine* (2004) shows that the use of advisory opinions can lead to increased clarity on important legal disputes, although not in itself to actual conflict resolution.

Cassese has argued that groups such as the ICRC, or rebel groups with a certain stability, should be able to request advisory opinions.[96] This would enable them to receive clarifications about the limits of international humanitarian law relevant to their own practice and operations. This would again clarify, and thereby serve to improve, the due consideration given to international law both by non-state actors and international organisations, such as the UNSC. The proposal however, falls outside the present paradigm. States will only allow very small changes in practice to take place, not deeper reforms, if they believe that their sovereign rights can be permanently reduced.

A similar approach should be considered in regard to the proposals that the ICJ should provide judicial review for the UN organs, including the UNSC. In many domestic systems, it would fall under their high courts to undertake review of the legality of decisions by the legislative or the executive branches of government in light of constitutional or equivalent rules.

The reviewability by the ICJ of the UNSC attracted considerable attention in the Lockerbie case (1998). The Court affirmed as a general rule that it does *not* have unlimited powers of judicial review of the resolutions of the UNSC, but also that it is not hierarchically inferior to the UNSC. Therefore, it *does* have the authority to consider and decide on matters that form the object of resolutions by the UNSC.[97] The Lockerbie case was criticised because of the Court's high level of restraint in declining to review the legality of the acts of the UNSC. Despite opinions to the contrary, however, it can certainly be argued that the decision seems to be well in line with the UN Charter and the deliberate limitations placed upon the Court by the states in 1945.

At any rate, it has been argued that the Lockerbie decision also leaves some room for the ICJ to take on a more active role in providing judicial review, without first revising the Court's Statute.[98] It arguably shows that, in terms of judicial review, the ICJ bench has a significant possibility to

---

[96] Cassese, 2012, p. 244, see *supra* note 82.

[97] Verdirame, 2011, pp. 345–346, see *supra* note 21.

[98] Colb, 2013, p. 1157, see *supra* note 51.

shape the direction of the Court though its own practice. Its own restraint is, to a certain extent, caused not by formal limitations, but its own conservative inclination. It could, if willing, be less reluctant in using *obiter dicta* in its rulings to clarify international rules that require such clarification.[99] Furthermore, it can be argued convincingly that the unity of international law will suffer if the ICJ does not become more active in clarifying developing rules of international law. A gap could emerge between the ICJ as custodian of traditional international law – highly conservative and protective of traditional sovereign rights – and the ICC and similar legal organs that may handle the dynamic fields of international law.[100]

If the ICJ should decide to take on a more proactive role in clarifying developing international customary rules, it would also need to change and expand its system of fact-finding and analysis. International law today is a much more intricate and complex system than it was in 1945. The number of treaties, conventions and international organisations have multiplied to an extent that was not foreseeable at the time the ICJ was established. Globalisation has also led to an expansion of both the interrelatedness of international issues of contention as well as in the amount of available information and facts.

The developments in information technology means that state practice is far easier to assess on a global scale today than some decades ago, which opens up opportunities for the ICJ to drive a process for providing precision and refinement of developing customary norms of international law. At the same time, the vast amount of information also implies that resources must be provided for such analysis.

The ICJ was not set up to deal with this, and would require both resources and reform to do it in the future. One suggestion put forth is to set up a fact-finding body in the ICJ, which could consist of one or more judges heading a team of fact-finders.[101] Furthermore, the Court must be made able to request expert input on important issues from external legal scholars and institutions. There is no reason why the highest Court in the world should not be able to request and consider the very best legal analysis. A more

---

[99] *Ibid.*, pp. 1158–1159. An 'obiter dictum' is a statement in a court's judgement that is not directly a basis for the decision, and which can thus not set any precedence, but which may still give theoretical clarification on a legal question.

[100] *Ibid.*

[101] Cassese, 2012, p. 246, see *supra* note 82.

expansive role for the ICJ will, however, be opposed by many states that may feel threatened by it. Therefore, there will be limitations to how far the ICJ can go before the most critical states dissociate themselves from the system or work actively to undermine it.

Finally, the process to elect judges is one area where changes may be possible. Clearly, a system that all but assures that seven out of 193 UN member states continually have their nations represented on the ICJ bench falls short of any requirement of fair procedure. The problem could be solved in several ways. For example, the UN Secretary-General could be given the task of nominating judges for ratification by the UNGA. This procedure is more likely to provide a fair composition of judges. However, this would require statutory change and a power transfer from the UNSC, which the P5 will not accept. The maximum achievable change may therefore be that likeminded states jointly modify the voting patterns, and remove the special status granted to judges coming from specific countries.

3

The World Trade Organization

3.1. Introduction and Historical Background

The WTO came into formal existence on 1 January 1995. It represented a continuation, an improvement, and a replacement of the GATT. While the GATT Council was set up in 1960, this was not an international organisation until it was transformed into the WTO, turning the contracting parties into member states.[1] The creation of the WTO was a significant achievement in the history of international organisation. It represented the fulfilment of a goal that was not possible to achieve even in the 1940s, when the fallout of World War II had made possible other epoch-making achievements, such as the UN, World Bank and the International Monetary Fund.

The idea after World War II was that the UN, specifically the ECOSOC, would be the hub for international trade rules formation. Negotiations on a World Trade Charter and an ITO were envisaged in the Bretton Woods conference in 1944, which set up the World Bank and the International Monetary Fund. ECOSOC adopted a resolution in early 1946, calling for a conference to draft a charter for a global trade organisation. The negotiations continued through 1946–1948. A charter was signed by 56 states in Havana in March 1948. However, the US Congress repeatedly refused to ratify the treaty, mainly over concerns about international involvement in US internal affairs. US President Harry S. Truman finally and formally gave up in 1950. Because of the US failure to ratify, no other state acceded to the treaty.

GATT was negotiated simultaneously, with agreement reached already in October 1947, when eight countries signed the new treaty.[2] GATT came into force on 1 January 1948, with nine members (Cuba having joined in the meantime). By the end of 1948, the number of ratifications had risen to 18, and then to 28 by the end of 1950.[3] Because of the failure to establish an ITO, GATT evolved into a *de facto* international organisation and the

---

[1] Volker Rittberger and Bernard Zangl, *International Organization: Polity, Politics and Policies*, Palgrave Macmillan, Basingstroke, 2006, p. 42 (translated by Antoinette Groom).

[2] The US, the UK, Canada, Australia, France, Belgium, the Netherlands and Luxembourg.

[3] WTO, "List of members and observers", available on the WTO web site.

main arena for international trade negotiations. It is an example of how the international community will find practical ways to organise and co-operate, despite sovereignty concerns, when there is a need and clear mutual benefits for such organisation.

It is also an example of how the paradigm of the international system shapes the modalities of co-operation. GATT was a result of a state-centred and state-driven international order, as in the Westphalian system, but also of the increased significance of popular will as basis for sovereign states' international policies, with a higher emphasis on economic growth than state or individual prestige and traditional sovereignty concerns. Although the efforts of a more substantial superstructure in an international organisation failed, the economic incentives called for at least a binding agreement aimed at increasing trade. The WTO is also an example of implementation of the principle of formal equality between states, although this is more complicated in WTO's actual practice.

The basic principles of the GATT – and subsequently WTO – are equal treatment according to the 'most favoured nation' status provided to all members; non-discrimination between national and foreign products; commitment to lowering trade barriers and tariffs progressively; work for predictability and against 'unfair' practices such as export subsidies and dumping below market prices; and commitment to more beneficial trade rules for developing countries.[4]

By the measuring stick of reduced tariffs and increased international trade, the GATT and WTO have been extremely successful. The trade rounds substantially lowered the average tariffs on goods. Furthermore, the Uruguay Round (1986–1994) addressed concerns about state practise of concealing protective measures in non-tariff trade barriers.[5] That round led to the creation of the WTO, as well as agreements to further reduce tariffs and trade barriers to unprecedented levels.

The average tariff level for WTO members has been estimated at around 22% in 1947.[6] After the Uruguay Round, the average tariffs of the

---

[4] Fatoumata Jawara and Aileen Kwa, *Behind the Scenes at the WTO: The Real World of International Trade Negotiations: Lessons from Cancun*, updated edn, Zed Books, London, 2004, pp. 7–8.

[5] Rittberger and Zangl, 2006, p. 42, see *supra* note 1.

[6] Chad P. Bown and Douglas A. Irwin, "The GATT's Starting Point: Tariff Levels circa 1947", *Policy Research Working Paper* 7649, World Bank Group, 2016, p. 28, available on the

---

largest WTO trading partners were 3.1% (the US, the EU and Japan, based on 1999 figures).[7] As of 2013, the average most-favoured nation tariff of WTO members is around 9%, representing a 15 point reduction since the establishment of the WTO in 1995.[8] The world average tariff has also fallen, from an estimated 5.34% in 1997 to a historically low 2.88% in 2012.[9]

World trade has also grown at a tremendous rate, both in terms of volume and as share of GDP. Despite a slowdown in the years 2012–2014, with growth in world merchandise trade of around 2.5%, world trade has never been greater.[10] This highlights the significance of the international regime for international trade, and its vast and growing importance for the economic well-being of the peoples of the world.

However, it does not necessarily mean, as is widely believed, that the threshold for international armed conflicts has been raised because of mutual economic dependency. Also, in the years leading up to World War I, international trade was significant as share of GDP. Other factors, primarily connected to political and military culture (such as nationalism, great power rivalry, and cult of the offense) were in that case overall more significant than trade relations in the lead-up to the war. What it means, rather, is that the need for a fair, efficient, and predictable international trade regime is more important than at any time in history.

The Uruguay Round also led to agreement on two additional global treaties on trade, the GATS (General Agreement on Trade in Services) and the TRIPS (Agreement on Trade-Related Aspects of Intellectual Property Rights). It also set up the present disputes settlement mechanism of the WTO, replacing the former GATT mechanism.

World Bank web site. A commonly cited figure on average tariffs prior to GATT is 40% (for example by Rittberger and Zangl, 2006, p. 42, see *supra* note 1), but this should be regarded as unsubstantiated. See WTO, *World Trade Report 2007*, WTO, Geneva, 2017, pp. 206–207, available on the WTO web site.

[7]   Brown and Irwin, 2016, p. 28, see *supra* note 6.

[8]   WTO, "Trade and Tariffs", available on the WTO web site.

[9]   World Bank, "Tariff rate, applied, weighted mean, all products (%)", available on the World Bank web site.

[10] WTO, *World Trade Report 2015*, WTO, Geneva, 2015, available on the WTO web site.

WTO had 124 member states at its founding. As of 2016, the total number has risen to 164, including China (2001) and Russia (2012), making the WTO a truly global trade organisation.[11]

The achievement, however, is not without cost. As of 2017, the WTO has for years been virtually paralysed in several respects, significantly in its ability to reach agreement on new general and global trade agreements. There is a deep divide between the perceived interests of groups of member states, particularly between the developed and the developing countries, that prevents new agreements from being concluded.

The consequence is that the global system of international trade is regressing, in the sense that regional and bilateral trade agreements are springing up in greater numbers, making international trade once again more intricate and less predictable. Serious erosion of the most-favoured nation principle is one of the consequences. Also, except for the EU, the regional disputes settlement mechanisms are far weaker than the WTO mechanism.[12] While the WTO, along with the GATT, has been tremendously successful in reducing tariffs and increasing international trade in the past, it is now a sluggish performer that is struggling to defend its continued position as the paramount global trade regime.

The exception to this picture, is the WTO's dispute settlement mechanism. Despite some significant shortcomings, it is widely regarded as a success. The mechanism is mandated to resolve trade disputes between WTO members and approve trade restrictions as sanctions against states that are judged to be in breach of agreement. As of 2015, over 500 disputes have been received by the mechanism for settlement.[13] This can be contrasted with the GATT mechanism, which in its 47-year history received around 300 cases for settlement. The year 2015 was the busiest for the mechanism so far.[14] The dispute settlement mechanism has produced tens

---

[11] WTO, "List of the 128 countries that had signed GATT by 1994", available on the WTO web site.

[12] Debra P. Steger, "Why Institutional Reform of the WTO is Necessary", in Debra P. Steger (ed.), *Redesigning the World Trade Organisation for the Twenty-first Century*, Wilfrid Laurier University Press, Ottawa, 2010, pp. 7–8.

[13] WTO, *Annual Report 2016*, WTO, Geneva, 2016, p. 102 ('WTO Annual Report 2016'), available on the WTO web site.

[14] *Ibid.*

of thousands of pages of jurisprudence in international trade law.[15] In addition, estimates suggest that around half of the disputes are not actually resolved by a dispute settlement panel. Instead, they were withdrawn or settled another way – which can be seen as a good sign of predictability and accountability in the system.[16]

In contrast to the ICJ, any WTO member can bring a case before the WTO dispute settlement mechanism without the consent of the other state involved.[17] Considering the near universal membership of the WTO, this means that most of the world is subjected to an international legal procedure for international trade law. This level of international organization is unprecedented, and beyond that of other areas of international law, perhaps including international criminal law.

The dispute settlement procedure requires that a member's complaint over a potential breach of a WTO agreement is processed through stages.[18] The first stage is consultations, which often leads to an agreement. If no agreement is found, the complaint is put to a panel for adjudication within 60 days after receipt of the request for consultation. The Panel consists of three members on whom the parties agree. If the parties cannot agree, the members will be designated by the WTO Director-General. The Panel receives written and oral statements from the parties, on which basis they adjudicate. The panel procedure is confidential. It is even closed to private parties with direct interest, who are also prevented from submitting material that may have bearing on the case. As such, it represents continuity of the state-centred international system.

The Panel's final report is, in effect, its judgement, which is first shared with the parties, then after two weeks sent to the DSB for approval. All WTO members are represented in the DSB. While panel reports can in principle be overruled by the DSB, this requires consensus, which means

---

[15] John H. Jackson, "The WTO Dispute Settlement System after Ten Years", in Yasuhei Taniguchi, Alan Yanovich and Jan Bhanes (eds.), *The WTO in the Twenty-First Century: Dispute Settlement, Negotiations and Regionalism in Asia*, Cambridge University Press, Cambridge, 2007, p. 32.

[16] *Ibid.*, pp. 31–32.

[17] Yasuhei Taniguchi, "The WTO's Tenth Anniversary", in Taniguchi, Yanovich and Bhanes (eds.), 2007, p. 8, see *supra* note 17.

[18] See WTO, "Understanding the WTO: Settling Disputes: A Unique Contribution", available on the WTO web site.

that there is a *de facto* automatic adoption of the reports by the dispute set-tlement mechanism. This stands in contrast to the GATT disputes settlement mechanism which needed consensus approval, including by the state that was found to be in breach.[19]

Furthermore, there is a process of appeal. A state may appeal the Panel's decision. In this case, the report is not presented to the DSB, but instead to the Appellate Body. This is a unit of seven individuals on four-year terms, selected on the basis of individual competence in international trade law. They are also required to be unaffiliated with governments, and collectively be representative of the general WTO membership. Three members of the Appellate body will hear the appeal, and conclude on whether to approve, modify or reverse the Panel report. The DSB is then required to approve the report from the Appellate body, unless deciding otherwise by consensus.

In the subsequent discussion of the WTO, there will be a separate consideration of the dispute settlement mechanism and the WTO in general. The latter includes the decision-making processes, primarily in regard to negotiations over new or refined global trade rules.

3.2.   World Trade Organization Decision-Making and Negotiations

3.2.1.   Sovereign States' Dominance

The people who conduct trade negotiations in the WTO context are by no means disinterested representatives of a global population. They represent the interests of their states. Participation of non-state actors has increased, but remains more limited than in the UNGA or the HRC. It is significant that, up to and including the creation of the WTO, NGOs were not active participants in the GATT/WTO process. At the time when NGOs partici-pated actively in the process leading to the Optional Protocols to the Ge-neva Conventions in the late 1960s and early 1970s (see subsequent chap-ter), there was virtually no NGO participation at all in GATT, except for that of the International Chamber of Commerce.[20] In the Uruguay Round,

---

[19]   Jackson, 2007, p. 31, see *supra* note 15.

[20]   Steve Charnovitz, "Opening the WTO to Nongovernmental Interests", in *Fordham International Law Journal*, 2000, vol. 24, no. 1, p. 175.

---

leading to the establishment of the WTO, NGOs found it impossible to provide the negotiators with direct input.[21]

This practice was, of course, the source of substantial criticism, and topic of numerous proposals for reform.[22] It led to adoption of language regarding NGO participation in the WTO agreement in 1995, and subsequently, adoption of the WTO "Guidelines for Arrangements on Relations with Non-Governmental Organizations" in July 1996. While these guidelines directed the WTO Secretariat to play an active role in contacts with NGOs, it also concluded that direct involvement of NGOs in the work of the WTO "would not be possible".[23] Instead, the contact with NGOs was relegated to the national dialogues of the members.

The individual and national dialogues conducted by the WTO members are left entirely at their discretion, in accordance with traditional sovereign rights. Domestic consultations between governments and their citizens, parliaments, local NGOs, private companies or research institutions depend on the members' own policies. There are no guidelines for such consultations, for example, in advance of the bi-annual ministerial conferences, where NGOs are also invited.

From 1996, NGOs were invited to attend ministerial conferences, and NGOs have increasingly pushed for possibilities of providing input to the WTO, including in the dispute settlement mechanism. The non-state participation in the WTO, however, remains at a low level, compared with many other international organisations. States are clearly the driving actors.

In WTO, the members' respective ministers of trade collectively form the highest level of decision-making: ministerial conferences (trade ministers) are to be held every two years. Decision-making is by consensus.[24] There are provisions in the WTO agreement (Articles IX and X) for voting, where one member has one vote. These provisions, however, are rarely invoked.[25] Formally, however, it means that there is full equality between the members of the WTO, as is the common norm in the popular sovereign paradigm.

---

[21]   *Ibid.*

[22]   *Ibid.*, p. 177.

[23]   *Ibid.*, p. 179.

[24]   Jawara and Kwa, 2004, p. 13, see *supra* note 4.

[25]   Steger, 2010, p. 7, see *supra* note 12.

However, there is also an *informal* decision-making structure. In addition to the formal ministerial conferences, there are mini-ministerial meetings, which are unofficial and outside the formal WTO-structure. These meetings have important *de facto* decision-making power. Being unofficial, however, there are no procedural rules for representation, decision-making, publicity, information gathering, etc., that would serve to ensure that the meetings are conducted in a fair and transparent manner. The mini-ministerial meetings have been condemned by a number or NGOs for being illegitimate and self-appointed.[26]

Also widely criticised are the former 'green room meetings'. This refers to the practice, now formally abolished, of conducting the most important and sensitive negotiations in the confines of closed door meetings between the EU, Japan, US and selected countries by invitation from the WTO Director-General or the chair of a negotiating group.[27] Despite the abolishment of 'green room meetings', the practice of closed-door discussions persists, where the four most important trading partners play the pivotal roles. These four are the US, Japan, the EU, and China – collectively referred to as 'the Quad'.

The reality of the WTO is thus that, although the institution is formally inclusive and open to members in equal terms, there is an informal structure that exists in parallel, which is restrictive, non-transparent and unequal. Historically, this aspect of the WTO has probably been the main target of criticism. The significance of closed and informal meetings, where large states tend to dominate, is a main irritant of both developing states and non-state critics of the WTO.

The inequality of the informal decision-making process in the WTO cannot be separated from the lack of supranational independence of the organisation. The WTO can be likened to a micro-cosmos of the Westphalian system inside Europe: the formal equality between states, combined with the lack of strong supranational institutions, leads to a situation where the bigger powers dominate the scene relatively unchecked.

If the WTO had some arena like, for example, an executive council elected by the general membership and held to account by it, this problem would have been somewhat alleviated. A more independent secretariat would have had a similar effect. As it stands, however, the only check in

---

[26] Jawara and Kwa, 2004, p. 13, see *supra* note 4.
[27] *Ibid.*, p. 18.

---

the WTO system at present is the dispute settlement mechanism, but this covers only state disputes, and does not directly influence the negotiations or the fairness of new trade rules. As long as the WTO does not have an executive-type body in its formal structure, such informal meetings will continue to be the venues of real power in the WTO. Ironically, a *formally* skewed supranational authority in favour of the strong states (such as the UNSC model) would probably give weaker states more influence in the WTO than the present informal system allows.

The WTO, as a supranational organisation, also remains constricted by the lack of common mechanisms that operate independently of the sum of the states' policies. The WTO functions, as intended, as a member-driven organisation. The WTO Secretariat and the Director-General post predates the WTO, having been established under the GATT organisation. While the work of the Secretariat remains crucial for the WTO, it is lacking in both mandate and ability to carry out the kind of far-reaching and deep analysis that would lead to positive progress in the WTO. This applies both with regard to the need for internal organisational reforms and further development of international trade law. The Secretariat itself does not contest its position, but agrees that the Members are responsible for the content of the WTO, and not the Secretariat.[28]

The present set-up means that the member states must, to a very large extent, rely on their own individual apparatuses to attain the information and analysis necessary to consider consequences of, for example, new rules of international trade. With the current large membership, this translates into an equally wide divergence of views on the optimal rules for international trade. Furthermore, as the membership ranges from members with substantial state resources devoted to fact-finding and analysis – such as the EU and the US – to states with meagre resources by comparison, it also makes it difficult for the entire membership to participate in trade negotiations on common ground.

The problem cannot be solved by information sharing, partly because members base their trade policies on different economic models, and partly because the trade negotiations are interest-driven processes. There are clear incentives for structuring the rules of trade to one's economic benefit, if

---

[28] Carolyn Deere Birkbeck, "Reinvigorating Debate on WTO Reform: The Contours of a Functional and Normative Approach to Analyzing the WTO System", in Steger (ed.), 2010, p. 19, see *supra* note 12.

given the opportunity. The lack of a common mechanism for data collection, analysis and dissemination is therefore an issue of concern.

As with the UN or any other international organisation with state members, there is also a varying degree to which state representatives actually speak for their citizens, or represent the interests of distinct elites or parties. The participation of trade ministers in the General Council further increases the doubts about the representativeness of the WTO decision-making bodies. Having trade ministers as the main representatives in the highest decision-making body (ministerial conferences) may serve to channel discussions more narrowly to consideration of trade interests in isolation, compared with participation of heads of state, prime ministers or foreign ministers alongside the trade ministers. However, trade ministers will be given mandates by their heads of cabinet, and can be expected to represent their countries accordingly. The real concern in this regard, is therefore to what extent governments actually represent their peoples, and to what extent they carry out domestic consultations. Because of the low level of NGO inclusion and the high level of secrecy, there are also fewer safeguards against self-serving policy promotion in the WTO than in, for example, the UNGA.

Between the contrasting principles of traditional state sovereignty and representation of popular will, therefore, the WTO lies closer to the former. The ongoing and controversial debates that surround the WTO on NGO participation, however, give evidence that the organisation is expected by many to include and increase non-state influence. This basic contradiction in the Popular Sovereign Paradigm thus also affects the WTO.

Further, the WTO is clearly inside the Popular Sovereign Paradigm in terms of the principle of equality between states. As in the UNGA and UNSC, however, states pursue their own national interests in the WTO. Due to the secrecy of the negotiations and lack of non-state actors, this pursuit of state interests is comparably less restrained in the WTO. The lack of a formal executive council only adds to the problem, and entrenches the tendency of the WTO to be no more than the sum of the members' policy positions. At the same time, the WTO also represents the adherence to at least basic common rules for international trade and a system of assuring a minimum of compliance with those rules. As such, the system lies outside the Westphalian Paradigm, where a common, global and legally binding trade regime was not a possibility.

It is an interesting anomaly that the membership of the WTO is not strictly limited to clearly sovereign states. For example, Chinese Taipei (Taiwan) is a member, as are Hong Kong and Macao. In this aspect, the WTO is different from most other international organisations. At the same time, these anomalies have limited impact, and can be explained as expedient measures to include significant trading partners that all have a complicated recent political history. The overall picture of an organisation clearly driven by sovereign states remains unchanged.

3.2.2. Special Issues of Cessation of Sovereign Rights in the Trade Area

It is worth noting that the states have been more reluctant to accept transferral of sovereign rights to a supranational institution that deals with trade than they have in regard to peace and security. This was, to a significant degree, a consequence of the tremendous destruction of the two world wars, which highlighted the urgency and importance of a global superstructure aimed at securing international peace. One could further speculate whether there was a window of opportunity in 1945 – when the UN was established and the victorious Allies were co-operating – which was quickly closing from 1946 when the Cold War was becoming a reality. However, already by 1948, few were expecting the Soviet Union to join the ITO in any case, and the ITO would work without the Iron Curtain countries, whose share of world trade at that point was not significant. Furthermore, judging by the debate in the US over ratification of the Havana Charter, which would have led to the establishment of the ITO, it seems clear that the ceding of sovereign rights to decide on trade policies was the main concern of those opposing the treaty in the US.[29]

A further important reason why the ITO failed to achieve acceptance in the US was the opposition by domestic business leaders. The Havana Charter attracted opposition from both protectionists and perfectionists in

---

[29] Maria Sampanis, *Perserving Power Through Coalitions: Comparing the Grand Strategy of Great Britain and the United States*, Praeger, Westport, 2003, p. 95; John Cavanaugh and Jerry Mander (eds.), *Alternatives to Economic Globalization: A Better World is Possible: A Report to the International Forum on Globalization*, Second Edition, Berett-Koeheler Publishers, San Francisco, 2009, p. 65.

the business community.[30] Those who feared economic loss through lower tariffs naturally opposed, while those who stood to gain were critical that the Charter did not go far enough. The US Chamber of Commerce, the National Foreign Trade Council and the National Association of Manufacturers all opposed the Charter.[31] The fears were also framed in terms of loss of sovereignty, with arguments that other countries could make exceptions to the Charter rules on protective trade measures due to special needs and circumstances, such as reconstruction, while the US would be bound. The rule of equal weight in voting in the ITO, which was laid down in the Charter, further increased the fear of US ceding too much power to an international institution.[32] Meanwhile, the American NGOs that supported the ITO often did so without particular enthusiasm, including the labour unions (the American Federation of Labour and Congress of Industrial Organizations).[33]

The case highlights a key feature that restricts the development of supranational institutions under the Popular Sovereign Paradigm: if states that to a high degree already represents the popular will cede sovereign rights to a supranational institution, this can reduce the level of representation of popular will for that state. The reason is that international organisations are state-centred, and only represent the popular will to a limited extent. This is particularly the case with the US, which has a high degree of democracy combined with the economic and military strength to conclude international agreements on favourable terms. It is less of a challenge for small democratic states, which are not able to dictate terms internationally in any case, and thus stand to lose less form joining supranational regimes. All the same, it is clear that the perception of reduced self-determination is a persistent factor in shaping, for example, the opposition towards the EU in European countries.

---

[30] William Diebold, Jr., "The End of the ITO", in *Essays in International Finance*, 1952, no. 16, Princeton University, Princeton, pp. 13–24.

[31] *Ibid.*, p. 15.

[32] *Ibid.*, p. 20. One-country-one-vote without any veto was the rule also in the proposed Executive Bureau of the ITO. A semi-permanent seat arrangement was also proposed, as the eight members with the highest share of international trade were envisaged to be members of the Executive Bureau, to be assessed on a regular three-year basis. Rules in Article 78 of the *Havana Charter* (http://www.legal-tools.org/doc/6ea303/).

[33] *Ibid.*, p. 8.

An unanswered question is why the setting up of a global trade regime seems to be more difficult than, for example, peace and security or human rights. One possible reason may be the high emphasis on economic issues in the present international paradigm, which can be explained as a consequence of the increased significance of popular will and that governance processes are no longer top-down movements only. This may cause a greater public interest and involvement in, and controversy surrounding, international regulations on economic issues.

Another factor may be that the NGO community is more divided over issues of trade policy than, for example, universal individual rights. In the latter area, NGOs have overwhelmingly been on the side of increased protection of victims in war and extension of human rights as universal and legally binding obligations on states. In matters of trade, however, the NGO community is mixed. One example is the US debate on the Havana Charter in the 1940s, where a number of business leaders opposed the Charter. Other examples include European farmers' strong interest in protection of agricultural subsidies *vis-à-vis* developing countries' and poverty-oriented NGOs' interest in reducing those subsidies. The push- and pull-factors over trade issues among non-state actors may therefore be more complex than over, for example, human rights.

At any rate, the WTO works under the same paradigm as the other international institutions, and most of the constraints are similar. The basic contradiction is between the rights of sovereign states and the need for a supranational structure, and between sovereign states and the representation of non-state actors. The difference in the trade area of international relations is mainly that the WTO is more heavily lop-sided toward state sovereignty.

3.2.3. The Disputes Settlement Mechanism: Supranational within Narrowly Defined Limits

Despite clear and significant shortcomings, the dispute settlement mechanism is, by any account, the most advanced feature of the WTO system in regard to supranational authority. The procedure combines features of disinterested and representative parties that have decision-making power over the different stages of the procedure, and is independent of the individual states' policies. It is representative in the sense that the entire WTO membership is involved in the process, through the DSB. As this body administers the system and formally adopts the reports of the Panels and Appellate body, the broad participation assures buy-in from the members into the system as a whole and the outcome of the specific cases.

However, the adjudication itself is performed by persons that are, to a great extent, disinterested. In the first instance, the Panel members are agreed to by the parties or appointed by the Director-General, which assures a high degree of collective impartiality. The most important guarantee of impartiality, however, is the appeals procedure. As a collective of individuals of high legal expertise and independence from governments, the appellate body is as disinterested as can be possible in an international court-like entity. The fact that the membership has almost no formal way of obstructing the disputes settlement procedure is also important to ensure that the process is fair and independent.

The rules about fact-finding and analysis of the dispute settlement mechanism give the panels wide authority in drawing on any external expertise that it deems appropriate. This includes, *inter alia*, requests for advisory reports from an external review group, if one side raises scientific or technical points that require consideration.[34] The rules of the dispute settlement mechanism are, in this aspect, far advanced in terms of independence from the sovereigns as a supranational institution.

However, the submission of unsolicited briefs to the dispute settlement mechanism remain a highly contentious issue. Historically, NGOs have submitted such briefs to the panels, but they have been dismissed in almost all cases. In 2000, the Appellate Body established a procedure for acceptance of such input, following requests for clarification by several members and comments from outsider experts.[35] This move, however, provoked an immediate and negative reaction from many WTO members. Egypt called a special WTO General Council session where many members expressed their dissatisfaction. A main source of the criticism was that the Appellate Body has usurped the legislative function reserved for the WTO members. Shortly thereafter, the Appellate Body rejected all 17 applications for submissions of briefs.[36] Formally, it retains the right to accept such

---

[34] WTO, "Understanding on rules and procedures governing the settlement of disputes, Annex 2 of the WTO Agreement" ('WTO Understanding on Annex 2'), Article 13 (Right to seek information) (http://www.legal-tools.org/doc/c27bae/).

[35] Charnovitz, 2000, p. 188, see *supra* note 20.

[36] *Ibid.*, pp. 188–189.

---

briefs, but the practice is conservative, and there is certainly no *right* on part of NGOs to be heard by a dispute settlement panel.[37]

The example highlights the conflicting principles common to most or all international organisations under the present paradigm: new principles, including the need for some supranational governance for the common good and the significance of the public will, calls for independence of the dispute settlement mechanism in receiving and considering analysis from non-states parties. At the same time, states' concerns about cessation of traditional sovereign rights places limitations on the system.

This conflict of principles underlies other aspects of the dispute settlement mechanism's work. While global trade rules concern a large number of non-state stakeholders, the dispute settlement procedure does not by far facilitate consultations involving those stakeholders throughout the process. The confidentiality of the procedure and the rules preventing private companies from presenting their views to panels, even when their interests are directly concerned, are procedural restrictions designed to protect the position of sovereign states as the sole significant actors. Presumably, the states parties should be expected to carry these viewpoints forward in their own submissions to the panels, but this is not the same as giving direct access. It could be argued that opening up for submissions from private parties could and would lead to a larger case load in the dispute settlement mechanism, risking drawn-out and cumbersome processes. This, however, is an issue of practical capacity, not of principle, which could be solved simply by allocating more resources to the dispute settlement mechanism.

The confidentiality and limitations on submissions from affected parties assure that the dispute settlement mechanism remains fundamentally an arbitral mechanism between states, not dissimilar to the ICJ in this respect. While a significant achievement in the history of international organisation, the dispute settlement mechanism is far from being an international court on trade issues in international law.

The dispute settlement mechanism also represents some of the same internal conflicts as the WTO in general, in terms of formal equality and an unequal reality. The dispute settlement mechanism, while formally open to all members, is in fact a tool primarily for the developed or large states. It is rarely used by the poorest member states. As a consequence, the jurisprudence produced by the dispute settlement mechanism really reflects the

---

[37] WTO, "Participation in dispute settlement proceedings", available on the WTO web site.

concerns only of some of the members. These concerns may or may not be the same as those of the poorest countries.

As of 2015, 205 of the disputes submitted have been initiated by either the EU or US.[38] In its reporting on the use of the dispute settlement mechanism in 2015, the WTO Secretariat pointed out that seven of the 13 new cases that year were initiated by developing countries.[39] What they did not highlight, however, is that those seven members were China, Chinese Taipei (two cases), Indonesia, Pakistan, Ukraine and Vietnam.[40] While technically developing countries – by the definition of the Organization for Economic Cooperation and Development's list of countries eligible for Official Development Assistance – these are not exactly countries among the world's poorest.[41] In fact, only one single dispute out of over 500 was initiated by a country (Bangladesh) on the Organization's list of Least Developed Countries and Other Low Income Countries, the two categories with the lowest per capita gross national income.[42] In all, 358 cases have been initiated by developed countries, the rest mainly by High Middle Income Countries.

The reason is, in all likelihood, the high cost of the dispute settlement process, and possibly the intricacies of the process, which presents the developing countries with a high threshold for instigation of formal complaints.[43] Furthermore, the dispute settlement mechanism has no independent power in enforcing its rulings. Instead, the WTO allows imposition of trade restrictions after a party wins a case. This can be very effective for developed and large developing countries, but is ineffective for small and poor countries.[44] Therefore, the dispute settlement mechanism cannot be said to be a truly global mechanism for justice. While almost all countries in the world have access to it in principle, the cost, time, procedures and

---

[38] WTO Annual Report 2016, p. 104, see *supra* note 13.

[39] *Ibid.*, p. 105. This refers to requests for consultations, which is the first step in the dispute settlement mechanism.

[40] *Ibid.*, pp. 105–106.

[41] OECD, "DAC List of ODA Recipients", available on the OECD web site.

[42] WTO Annual Report 2016, p. 104, see *supra* note 13.

[43] Jawara and Kwa, 2004, p. 13, see *supra* note 4.

[44] *Ibid.*, p. 6.

remedial mechanisms of it mean that it offers little or no protection to the poorest countries.

The generally favourable opinion of the dispute settlement mechanism, therefore, should be tempered with an understanding of its limitations. The dispute settlement procedure is generally impartial and fair, assured not least by its independence and the right of appeal. On the flip side, it is mainly a tool for the wealthier members, not the poorer ones.

The dispute settlement mechanism also has a good average time duration for settling cases (one year without appeal, plus three months with appeal), which compares favourably with other international procedures.[45] For example, the ICJ has an average time of four years (1998).[46] The Inter-American Court of Human Rights has an average case duration of seven years and four months.[47] Compared with domestic courts, the duration is also comparably good in terms of efficiency: a study of the duration of cases in Germany and Chile showed an average duration of five and 16 months, respectively.[48] On the flip side, the efficiency of this system is also a consequence of the inherent limitations of the dispute settlement mechanism. If it was a court for international trade disputes as such, the case load would of course be completely different. By comparison, the European Court of Human Rights is a court for all human rights violations within the territories of the European Council member states, and has currently a backlog of over 100,000 cases.[49] Or, if it permitted submissions of other interested parties than the parties to the dispute, such as private companies with relevant interests.

Furthermore, if the threshold for raising disputes from the poorest WTO members was lower, the case load would also increase. Regrettably, the accessibility is also a further example of the informal reality of the WTO

---

[45] WTO Understanding on Annex 2, see *supra* note 34.

[46] The average length of a procedure before the Court, from the filing of the case to the reading of the Judgment on the merits is nearly four years, according to ICJ, "Press release 1998/14", available on the Court's web site.

[47] Fiona McKay, "What Outcome for Victims?", in Dinah Shelton (ed.), *The Oxford Handbook of International Human Rights Law*, Oxford University Press, Oxford, 2013, p. 944.

[48] Maria Dakolias, "Court Performance Around the World: A Comparative Perspective", in *Yale Human Rights and Development Journal*, 1999, vol. 2, no. 1, p. 104 (http://www.legal-tools.org/doc/ad4a57/).

[49] Owen Bowcott, "Backlog at European court of human rights falls below 100,000 cases", in *The Guardian*, 30 January 2014 (http://www.legal-tools.org/doc/273d09/).

that favours the strong members, despite its formal structure suggesting otherwise. As long as this is the case, the likelihood is that the organisation will continue to wither and become less relevant as the years pass.

3.2.4. System Integrity of the World Trade Organization

There are very few checks and balances in the WTO system. In this area, the WTO should be seen as even less developed than the UN main organs. UNSC resolutions can at least be subjected to a kind of pseudo-review in the UNGA through the Uniting for Peace procedure, and there is at least a hypothetical potential for judicial review by the ICJ, although the court does not pursue this course of action. The WTO, on the other hand, has no review mechanisms. While there is a hierarchy of committees and councils, there are no checks on the system by entities that are independent or even composed of different parties than the committees or councils in question. The Organization's decisions are made by the entire membership, whether in the committees, the councils, in the General Council or in Ministerial conferences, and there is nowhere to refer these decisions in case of wrong-doing or deficiencies. The only option for reviews is by the membership itself, that is, those making the decisions in the first place.

The relative weakness in the Secretariat's mandate, capacity and in-dependence, also means that there is little chance of even differences of opinion within the WTO system. The non-existence of an executive body is an even more important deficiency.

3.3. The Future of the World Trade Organization: Reform Proposals

The internal contradictions of principle that underlie the WTO in its present form are causing a credibility deficit and the situation is unlikely to be com-pletely resolved through reform. The first basic contradiction is between the near exclusive emphasis on states as decision-makers and the need for a supranational institution to increase the uniformity, and thereby the clarity and predictability, of international trade regulations. The second is between sovereign states as sole decision-makers and the idea of legitimacy based on popular will.

The WTO is, as of 2018, in unable to progress further. Specifically, conflicts of interests between groups of developing countries and devel-oped countries have made it all but impossible to move ahead with new global arrangements. The consequence is the resort, instead, to bilateral and regional trade agreements, as mentioned. Among economists, the general opinion is that world trade will in general suffer from this development, in other words, to the common detriment of all.[50]

3.3.1. Fundamental Obstacles to Reform

The woes of the WTO are connected with the contradictory principles that underlie it. If the international paradigm allowed for a supranational entity with the power to bind states to new international trade rules, a common and predictable global system would be possible. However, such a system is most likely impossible under the present circumstances, as states will continue to uphold their sovereign rights in the trade area even more so than in, for example, the peace and security area.

In the absence of a supranational entity with real powers to bind the states, the informal system of decision-making is, at present, unavoidable. The principle of equality is formally implemented in the WTO, but adds to the problem of moving ahead. Getting 164 members to agree on matters of critical importance to their economies is exceedingly difficult. Getting them to agree all at once is nigh impossible.

Furthermore, the secrecy and informal decision-making procedures of the WTO will not change. Because states are unwilling to accept a supranational entity with real powers in the trade area, informal meetings dominated by the large trading partners will continue to be the basic decision-making fora. Furthermore, secrecy will be upheld because there is nothing close to a consensus among states or NGOs about precisely what constitutes good economic policies. To some extent, this is due to competing economic models, but to a larger extent it is due to mutually exclusive economic interests. Fully open and transparent trade negotiations would

---

[50] The argument that clear, predictable and common international trade rules will promote investment and growth seems strongly compelling, if not self-evident. Proving it is of course more difficult, as it requires connecting data from across the globe and isolating factors attributed to various free trade agreements. The research in this area, however, does indicate a 'spaghetti bowl effect' that has a significant negative impact on trade. See, for example, Zakaria Sorghol, "RTAs' Proliferation and Trade-diversion Effects: Evidence of the 'Spaghetti Bowl' Phenomenon", in *The World Economy*, 2016, vol. 39, no. 2., p. 297. The argument can be further strengthened by research on the connection between stability and predictability of the domestic trade rules and the level of investment and growth, where the evidence is strongly compelling, as shown in Aymo Brunetti, Gregory Kisunko, and Beatrice Weder, "Credibility of Rules and Economic Growth: Evidence from a Worldwide Survey of the Private Sector", in *The World Bank Economic Review*, 1998, vol. 12, no. 3, p. 368.

unleash a cacophony of various political and NGO protests that could make progress even more difficult than at present.

Under a different paradigm of the international system, where the state sovereignty issues amount to a reduced factor, publicly elected representatives could determine the rules of global trade. The system that has worked well for economic growth and trade within democratic states is likely to work well also on a global stage. The living standard, poverty rates, and economic well-being of citizens in developed states today can be compared with the same countries several decades ago. The difference is so vast that no further explanation should be needed. On economic issues, conflicts of interests are inevitable. A probably optimum way to move ahead as a collective, then, is to have representatives of those interests work out the rules on which to base economic affairs. Limiting the representatives to states alone makes little sense in a world where non-state actors are the main economic drivers and stakeholders.

A different paradigm may, in the future, allow a system of real checks and balances as well. One could envisage establishment of an executive council with the power to enact sanctions against rule-breakers and propose new rules to the assembly of elected representatives. Moreover, an independent judicial review body could be set up with the authority to comment and criticise any action or decision taken by the other parts of the organisation, on the basis of international trade law.

Under the Popular Sovereign Paradigm, the realistic ambitions must clearly be more limited. There are, however, ways in which some of the most obvious challenges confronting the WTO could be addressed. The most important is to replace the informal procedures with formal ones in order to improve accountability and transparency. Second, to include NGOs, including private businesses, to a greater extent. Third, to increase the independence and capacity of the secretariat in order to give shape and content to the trade negotiations among the members. Fourth and finally, to increase the accessibility of the dispute settlement mechanism to poor countries.

3.3.2. Making Informal Procedures Formal

The informal meetings and opaque decision-making procedures have arguably been the object of the strongest and most principled criticism. For NGOs believing they have a right to provide input, the credibility of the

WTO as representative of a global popular will is low. For developing countries, the WTO procedures are also a source of dissatisfaction, as many have come to feel that the talk of benefits for developing economies is lip service only, and that the large developed countries in reality use WTO to further their own narrow self-interest. As long as the present decision-making procedures endure, the WTO will find it very difficult to move ahead.

Abolishing informal decision-making fora without setting up formal mechanisms in their place will therefore achieve little more than further reduction of the potential for progress in the WTO. There is a need to select or elect a smaller council of members that can be expected to represent the interests of the entire membership, without that membership being part of the complete decision-making process. It has been suggested that such a council should include the large trading partners (the Quad), and representatives of the middle-income members (for example, Brazil) and small/developing members.[51]

This would doubtlessly be an improvement on the present system. A smaller Council mandated to negotiate new agreements – presumably in continuous dialogue between representatives of the Council and the members that elected them – which should be put to the general membership for adoption. In order not to offend sovereign sensibilities, the Council's powers would have to be limited to making recommendations only.

3.3.3. Increased NGO Participation

As regards the NGO participation, several approaches can be contemplated, and the UN's practice is at least one model. For example, inviting NGOs to partake as observers in more events should be possible, although controversial. Furthermore, guidelines for transparency and consultations between members' governments and their respective constituents can be contemplated. Negotiations on trade agreements are generally conducted in secret. Even parliamentarians in democratic states are often kept in the dark until the agreement is complete. This leaves them with a 'take it or leave it' option, rather than having been enabled to provide their viewpoints from an earlier stage.[52] While parliamentarians are kept in the dark, this is even

---

[51] This is suggested in Joseph E. Stiglitz and Andrew Charlton, *Fair Trade for All: How Trade Can Promote Development*, Oxford University Press, Oxford, 2007, p. 169.

[52] *Ibid.*, p. 167.

more so the case with other stakeholders such as NGOs and private companies. Increased transparency and consultations may hamper efficiency, but if managed properly, it would certainly increase the credibility of the international trade regime, and reduce the risk of regress due to popular opposition to multilateral trade regimes.

A limit to the inclusion, however, is natural. Participation of NGOs in the final stage of negotiations of trade agreements will not be acceptable to states. A case can also be made that such participation would make it impossible to reach agreements, due to probable and strong opposition from various interest groups.

3.3.4. Increased Secretariat Capacity and Independence

The independence and capacity of the WTO Secretariat is important in order to assure information dissemination and analysis that can form the basis for a credible process. This would mitigate the present problem of differences in resources available for information gathering and analysis among the WTO members. As the resource gap between the members is unlikely to fundamentally change soon, gathering such functions in an independent secretariat represents one way forward.

It has been suggested that the WTO Secretariat should be expanded to include an independent body, tasked with assessing countries in crisis, and consider and decide on whether to approve imposition of trade restrictions (safeguard measures), and to investigate dumping charges, countervailing duties, and phytosanitary conditions.[53] Furthermore, that a new body within the WTO could be tasked with charting objectively the likely consequences of trade agreement proposals. This would help especially smaller countries with more limited resources to see more clearly the consequences of the trade deals. The body would of course have to operate on the assumption that there is not a 'right model' of economics, but attempt to present a fair view on a broad basis.[54] Such innovations would certainly improve the prospective of attaining a firm and impartial grounds for future negotiations in the WTO on the rules of international trade.

In addition to such tasks, the Secretariat may be given increased responsibility for to set legislative priorities and to propose new rules.[55] This

---

[53] *Ibid.*, p. 170.
[54] *Ibid.*, p. 169.
[55] Steger, 2010, p. 9, see *supra* note 12.

would further improve the basis for decision-making, by focusing the debate on proposals that stem from a common source that the membership can rely on as impartial.

As a starting point, the WTO should establish, through the Secretariat, a common WTO procedure for fact-finding and analysis that may serve the membership as a whole in future trade negotiations. To date, the most significant effort of the Secretariat in this regard is the publication of the annual World Trade Report. While collecting a number of salient fact about world trade, this falls far short of providing a common analysis for going forward in the WTO.

A more independent secretariat would also serve to strengthen the system integrity in the WTO. While the Secretariat may not, in any scenario, be in a position to overrule decisions by member states in, for example, the General Council, a more independent secretariat could at least shed light over consequences of decisions and thus increase the likelihood of revisions when prudent and necessary. The WTO should, ideally, have an independent secretariat with a broad mandate for providing both far-reaching analysis and concrete proposals to the WTO for consideration of its membership.

3.3.5. Increased Accessibility of Dispute Settlement Mechanism

As for the dispute settlement mechanism, it is easy to be blinded by how much better and fairer it is than the GATT mechanism. However, this can overshadow the severe limitations that are also inherent in the present dispute settlement mechanism. The most important is the low accessibility for the poorer countries. One measure that would improve the situation is to set up an independent advisory body that can provide expert legal advice to countries that request it. This would enable poorer countries to use the procedure, and also build capacity in those countries for similar cases in the future. Funding for such an organisation could be made available as official development assistance, provided by developed countries.

The effect of the dispute settlement mechanism would, however, remain of limited value for the poorest countries in the sense that they would still be unable to coerce a rule-breaker through imposition of sanctions. A common obligation by all member states to impose sanctions to a rule-breaking member is not a possibility under the present paradigm, as states will be too keen to protect their own room for manoeuvre as sovereigns.

However, increased accessibility will at least give the poorer members increased possibilities to make themselves heard. This will serve to highlight their central interests and concerns *vis-à-vis* other members and also to shape the developing jurisprudence of the dispute settlement mechanism, which will have implications for future international trade law.

4

The Global Human Rights System

4.1. Introduction

International human rights law represent the most comprehensive system of substantive justice that attempts to be truly universal. Human rights law is, in principle, applicable in all situations in the world, regardless of place, local level of development, domestic legal system or the local political situation. As such, human rights represent an alternative and a threat to traditional state sovereignty, where states can decide for themselves which rules apply on their own territory.

The idea of universal human rights is a critical factor underpinning the Popular Sovereign Paradigm. Unlike other factors, such as the formal equality of states, human rights remain an issue of some controversy. Not all states accept the universality of human rights, while some states accept select human rights but not others.

Some human rights, such as freedom from slavery, have achieved a status of being truly universal, and are considered to be legally binding for all societies in the world. Other human rights are more contested, such as the right to democratic elections. Here, a distinction must be made between the concept of popular will as the legitimate basis of governance, and the practice of democratic elections. For example, communist regimes have been, and are still in theory, based on the concept of popular will, but do not generally practice free elections.

As a whole, human rights can be seen as a kind of *proto-law* for the international system: it consists of general norms that have only recently been developed, or are under development, and that have yet to achieve universal acceptance, let alone implementation. As a legal system, it is fundamentally weak in the sense that many rules are unenforceable at the present, and many of the rules are unclear when compared with national systems of justice.

Human rights law is distinct from all other parts of international law in its broad and universal application. In contrast, international humanitarian law also entails significant rights for individuals, but it is only applicable in armed conflict. Human rights, on the other hand, is applicable regardless of whether a country is at war, at peace or in the midst of a national emergency. The fact that many human rights are *derogable* – that they can be temporarily suspended in times of crisis – is further evidence to this fact: rules about suspension of rights are also rules, meaning that human rights law is applicable at all times. Human rights law is arguably applicable regardless of whether humanitarian law, trade law or other areas of law also applies, although this point continues to be contested by some states.

Human rights are also an innovation in the international legal system since it designates rights to individuals, not states. In this lies one of the most important internal contradictions in the Popular Sovereign Paradigm: states are the deciding authorities, but these powers are encroached by universal individual rights that arguably supersede the states' rights. The struggle of many states to retain sovereign control over which rights it confers to its own citizens is a main theme of present-day international politics.

Under the Westphalian system, international intervention into the domestic affairs of a state was, for centuries, considered illegal from the viewpoint of international law. Only after World War II did this begin to change, and particularly so in the past few decades. International interventions to stop human rights violations have become more acceptable, in some cases even mandatory, for example in response to genocide.

It is worth noting that the Westphalian Paradigm, in 1648, replaced another paradigm of international law, which was also considered by its proponents to be universally applicable, namely the universal law of the Catholic Church. While the states that fought in the Thirty Years' War gained or diminished in power, prestige and territory, the Catholic Church definitively lost the war to the principle of sovereignty.

There is an opposite parallel to the Thirty Years' War today. Traditional state sovereignty has, for a long time, been undermined by the universalistic trend of international human rights. Unlike the Catholic Church of the Renaissance and the early modern era, human rights have developed not as a top-down process to be imposed on the states by Church officials, but in a process of deliberations by the states themselves.

Human rights versus traditional sovereignty is the most critical issue confronting the international system today. It is at the core of many important international conflicts: NATO intervened in Kosovo in 1999 to protect human rights, but was opposed in the Security Council by Russia and

China. The international criticism of China following the Tiananmen Square incident has been a main irritant and cause for colder relations between China and the US. China also remains particularly sensitive of talk of the right of self-determination, as it may have consequences for Chinese Taipei or Tibet. Russia used arguments about human rights abuses to justify its actions in Ukraine in 2014, leading to the annexation of Crimea. It also continually criticises neighbouring countries for abusing the human rights of Russians.

The legal authority to approve international military intervention in a sovereign state rests formally with the UNSC. It can intervene only if it deems the situation to be a threat to international peace and security, according to Chapter VII of the UN Charter. When the situation is an international act of aggression by one state against another, it represents a breach in the agreement *between* sovereign states, and it is, by definition in the UN Charter, a matter of international peace and security. When the situation is primarily *within* a sovereign state, however, international intervention is justified by breach of the contract (whether explicit or not) between a sovereign government and its own citizens. In this case, international human rights are the main measuring stick for the gravity of such breaches, and thus for a case or international military intervention, or *humanitarian intervention*.

The system of international human rights is still being formed. This development has reached a stage where it is no longer possible to imagine a return to the Westphalian Paradigm of full state sovereignty. At the same time, the development is not at a stage where human rights are likely to replace the concept of sovereign control over domestic law. The world is very much in a mixed situation of conflicting fundamental principles.

Human rights in the international system will in the following be assessed in two parts: first, the global rules and then global institutions. The discussion about the rules consider how human rights have developed since 1945, with particular focus on two main conflicts of principles – between the universalistic human rights and the particularistic state sovereign rights; and between human rights and the universal application of religious law. In the latter category, an increased emphasis on religious law has, in particular, been coming out of majority Muslim countries. Finally, a particular focus is given to the right to democratic elections, as an example of a basic human right that is not universally accepted.

The discussion of the institutions centres on the UN HRC – which is the most significant global forum for all human rights, along with the UNGA. For the sake of brevity, the treaty bodies to the various human rights conventions, which deal only with the rights under their respective treaties, are largely left outside of this discussion. Two aspects of the HRC are highlighted: its role in formation and consolidation of human rights norms through negotiations and resolutions; and its mandate to protect of human rights. In regard to the protection, specifically, the UPR of the HRC remains the most ambitious and universal mechanism for ensuring implementation of human rights globally.

4.2. Global Rules of Human Rights

Human rights law is the body of treaties essentially relating to the rights of *individuals* toward their states, and responsibilities of the states to protect, uphold and promote those rights. Notably, some human rights are granted to collectives, such as the right to self-determination of peoples, or the right to freedom of religion that may require a group actions. However, these are either exceptions (such as the right to self-determination), or individual rights that cannot be upheld unless collective rights are also protected (for example, individual freedom of worship cannot be upheld if a religious community is banned). There have also been attempts to include rights for other concepts than individuals or collectives into the human rights category. Most significantly, the OIC has promoted the concept of *defamation of religion* as a breach of human rights, which would entail conceding human rights to 'religions'. This, however, has so far not been accepted as universal human rights norms in any UN resolution due to resistance from other states.

The concept of universal human rights has a long history of antecedents. One early manifestation was the Declaration of the Rights of Man and of the Citizen, passed by France's National Constituent Assembly in August 1789, shortly after the revolution. However, the UDHR[1] should be seen as the basic document and starting point for *global* human rights law under the present international system.

The UDHR was adopted by the UNGA on 10 December 1948. The vote was 48 states in favour, none against, and eight abstentions. The abstentions came from the communist bloc (the Soviet Union, the Ukrainian

---

[1]   UNGA Res. 217A (1948) ('UDHR') (http://www.legal-tools.org/doc/de5d83/).

Soviet Socialist Republic, the Byelorussian Soviet Socialist Republic, Czechoslovakia, Yugoslavia, and Poland) and from Saudi Arabia and South Africa. The stated reason for the communist abstentions was primarily that the Declaration failed to condemn Nazism and Fascism.

However, there was another principled dilemma, which the head of the Soviet delegation laid out in his speech: the rights of individuals, he argued, was not possible to separate from the state that confers those rights as legal obligations.[2] In other words, legal rights cannot exist outside of the state-determined legal system. This position could potentially have led to a communist bloc opposing vote on the Declaration. However, such a course would be incompatible with the communist position that fascism and Nazism *should* be condemned, even though these also were a result of the state legal processes. Therefore, the communist bloc abstained.[3]

This shows that the conflict between human rights norms and rights of sovereign states were inherent from the very beginning of the modern human rights system after World War II. In the following decades, it took on various forms and arguments, but it would persist in shaping and undermining international human rights throughout the Cold War and beyond.

The Saudi Arabian delegation abstained both because of formulations in the Declaration about equal marriage rights, and because of the right to change religion.[4] It is interesting to note that this conflict over rights of women and freedom of religion continue to be main points of contention stemming from parts of the Islamic world to this day. At the time, however, only Saudi Arabia abstained over these cited reasons, while other majority Muslim countries voted in favour, specifically Afghanistan, Egypt, Turkey, Iran, Lebanon, Syria and Pakistan.[5]

Finally, South Africa abstained because it was aware that the US would use the Declaration as basis to condemn practices of racial discrimination in South Africa. This line of opposition toward human rights, on basically racist grounds, no longer exists in the international system. While racism as a sentiment and policy driver can certainly still be forceful, no

---

[2] Peter Danchin, "Drafting History [of the Universal Declaration of Human Rights]" (http://www.legal-tools.org/doc/e06754/).

[3] *Ibid.*

[4] *Ibid.*

[5] *Ibid.* For list of votes, see UN, "Yearbook of the United Nations 1948–1949", p. 535.

country today deploys racism as an argument in negotiations over international human rights treaties. In this aspect, the principle of formal equality of the mixed paradigm has completely replaced the previous Westphalian concept. In fact, even the stated justification of South Africa for its position at the time was that the Declaration was too expansive, and should be kept shorter, while the real motive (protection of domestic racist discrimination) was not explicitly expressed.[6]

In the time after the UDHR, several international human right treaties came into existence. The OHCHR lists nine core human rights treaties as of 2016.[7] It should be noted, however, that two of these treaties have yet to achieve a level of universality similar to the other core treaties, having been ratified by only 49 and 53 states, respectively, so far.

Table 1: Core Human Rights Conventions[8]

Name	Date	Entry into force	Member States	Notable absentees
International Convention on the Elimination of All Forms of Racial Discrimination (ICERD)	7 March 1966	4 January 1969	177	N/A
International Covenant on Civil and Political Rights (ICCPR)	16 December 1966	23 March 1976	168	Saudi Arabia, China (signed)
International Covenant on Economic, Social and Cultural Rights (ICESCR)	16 December 1966	3 January 1976	164	US (signed), Saudi Arabia
Convention on the Elimination of All Forms of Discrimination against Women (CEDAW)	18. December 1979	3 September 1981	189	US (signed), Iran
Convention against Torture and Other Cruel, Inhuman or	10 December 1984	26 June 1987	160	India (signed), Iran

---

6   *Ibid.*

7   OHCHR, "The Core International Human Rights Instruments and their Monitoring Bodies", available at http://www.ohchr.org/EN/ProfessionalInterest/Pages/CoreInstruments.aspx, last accessed on 6 March 2018.

8   Table is compiled from the online UN Treaty Collection. States indicated as 'signed' in the last column have signed the treaty, but not ratified.

Degrading Treatment or Punishment (CAT)				
Convention on the Rights of the Child (CRC)	20 November 1989	2 September 1990	196	US (signed)
International Convention on the Protection of the Rights of All Migrant Workers and Members of Their Families (ICMW)	18 December 1990	1 July 2003	49	No great powers, almost no European states
International Convention for the Protection of All Persons from Enforced Disappearance (CPED)	20 December 2006	23 December 2010	53	US, Canada, Russia, India (signed), China, Australia, UK, South Africa, Indonesia (signed), Iran, Saudi Arabia, Egypt
Convention on the Rights of Persons with Disabilities (CRPD)	13 December 2006	3 May 2008	168	US (signed)

Many of the treaties also have optional protocols, for example for states' acceptance of individual complaints mechanisms. These enable citizens to communicate complaints about their states' human rights abuses to the relevant human rights treaty body for review (such as the Committee on the Rights of the Child would receive communications regarding possible violations of children's rights).

In total, there are nine optional protocols to the nine core treaties, meaning a total of 18 core international human rights treaties, as listed by the OHCHR.[9] The number of states parties to each convention varies widely, as can be seen from the dynamic map that the OHCHR provides on its web site.[10]

---

[9] OHCHR, "The Core International Human Rights Instruments and their Monitoring Bodies", see *supra* note 7.

[10] OHCHR, "Ratification of 18 International Human Rights Treaties", available at http://indicators.ohchr.org/, last accessed on 31 March 2018.

Finally, for some of the treaties that have near universal membership, such as the CEDAW, there are a high number of states that have ratified but reserved themselves against specific provisions.

The universality of human rights, therefore, is a mixed picture. However, it is commonly held by legal scholars that many human rights have achieved that status of customary international law. As such, these rights are applicable also to the states that have not ratified the relevant treaties. This has been argued to be the case for rights in, for example, the Universal Declaration.[11] It is arguably so because state practice, particularly their statements and voting on UN resolutions, show that states consider these rights to be legally binding obligations, even if some states actually continue to violate them.

While this may be acceptable from a legal perspective, it should not be concluded that opposition to the rules on other grounds can be dismissed as irrelevant. The fact that states consider certain rights to be legally binding norms in their statements and voting patterns does not necessarily show a true conviction about the justness of those rules. It may instead only show that the state's representatives are fearful of becoming a target of international criticism.

Furthermore, the voting pattern of a state is not necessarily representative of the actual opinion of its citizens or domestic NGOs. For example, while freedom of religion is arguably a part of customary international law,[12] it is clear that a high number of Islamic legal scholars and practicing Muslims consider apostasy to be a criminal act, and there is significant debate about whether this act is punishable by death.[13] A 2014 survey found that eight majority Muslim countries officially classified apostasy as a capital offense, while a further eight had laws that allowed for prosecution of

---

[11] Jochen von Bernstorff, "The Changing Fortunes of the Universal Declaration of Human Rights: Genesis and Symbolic Dimensions", in *The European Journal of International Law*, 2008, vol. 19, no. 5, p. 913.

[12] Christian Walter, "Religion or Belief, Freedom of, International Protection", in *Max Planck Encyclopedia of Public International Law*, Oxford University Press, Oxford, 2012.

[13] See, for example, S.A. Rahman, *Punishment of Apostasy in Islam*, Second Edition, The Other Press, Kuala Lumpur, 2006, pp. xxii–xxiii, pp. 1–2. The author is a former Chief Justice of Pakistan. He cites Islamic legal scholars who argue that death penalty is right, but he concludes that there is no mention in the Quran about the death penalty for apostasy. See also Magdi Abdelhadi, "What Islam says on religious freedom", in *BBC News*, 27 March 2006 (http://www.legal-tools.org/doc/0b9a00/).

---

apostasy.[14] Although actual executions were limited to one case (Iran) and the number of prosecutions was also limited,[15] it is clear that there is a conflict of principles with local legislation, legal opinion and universal human rights, Therefore, the international rules about religious freedom will not necessarily be considered just or applicable from the perspective of a significant part of the world's population. Similar points can be made about the rights of children and women, as shown in the numerous reservations made by the Arab states that have acceded to the CRC and CEDAW.[16]

4.2.1. How Universal is the Universal Declaration of Human Rights?

The UDHR was primarily the work of a small drafting committee, consisting of nine members of the 18-member Commission on Human Rights, set up by ECOSOC. The process leading up to the formation of the Commission and the UDHR, however, started earlier. In the Dumbarton Oaks conference in 1944, where the basis for the new United Nations organisation was negotiated, it was suggested that the cause of universal human rights should be protected by a Commission of independent and disinterested experts.[17] However, a number of states preferred a commission of appointed state delegates. In the first and second session of ECOSOC in 1946, several delegates presented arguments in favour of independent experts, including the UK and Lebanese representatives. Others, like the Soviet Union delegate, argued in favour of state representatives.[18]

The latter group eventually won, as the ECOSOC, in its second session, decided that the Commission on Human Rights would consist of official representatives of states. As a concession to the former group, it was decided that appointments would be made under consultation with the UN Secretariat before final confirmation by ECOSOC. This was intended to

---

[14] Hanibal Goitom *et al.*, *Laws Criminalizing Apostasy in Selected Jurisdictions*, The Law Library of Congress, Global Legal Research Center, Washington, D.C., 2014, p. 2, available on the web site of the Library of Congress.

[15] *Ibid.*

[16] Notably with the exception of Palestine, which acceded to CEDAW without reservations in 2014.

[17] Tony Evans, *US Hegemony and the Project of Universal Human Rights*, Macmillan, Houndsmills, 1996, p. 86.

[18] *Ibid.*, p. 87.

ensure an equitable geographical distribution of seats and a mixture of expertise in the various fields, which would be necessary for the Commission to carry out its work.[19] It may be the case, however, that the Secretariat did not look deeply into the quality of the representatives, as was argued some years later by Commission member and Director of the Division of Human Rights in the UN Secretariat, John Humphrey.[20]

At any rate, when the Commission was established, its members did include representatives from states with different cultural and legal backgrounds (for example, Egypt, the Republic of China, Lebanon, India, the Philippines, the Soviet Union), but with eight of 18 members representing countries in Western Europe or the Americas, thus also in a sense the 'Western' cultural tradition. In the appointed eight-member drafting Committee, moreover, there was a clear majority of five of eight from 'Western' countries (the US, France, the UK, Chile, Australia, Canada, the Soviet Union, the Republic of China and Lebanon).[21]

From the outset, therefore, the drafting committee was significantly weighted toward the Western cultural tradition. However, other cultural traditions *did* have representation, which represented real opportunities for influence. Furthermore, in the ECOSOC, there was an equal right for all the members to participate in the negotiations leading to the establishment of the Commission. Finally, the decision to adopt the UDHR rested with the UNGA, which was certainly the most representative global forum of its day.

Nonetheless, the Drafting committee's influence of the UDHR was clearly the most important input. There was very little change between the final text adopted in the UNGA and the first draft prepared by the French representative on the Drafting committee, René Cassin.[22] This means that the representativity of the decision-makers at the time of the UDHR should be considered to be primarily the drafting committee, and secondarily the Commission on Human Rights, although it is significant that the many-stage process of adoption of the text included possibilities for other states in the UN to influence the process.

---

[19] *Ibid.*

[20] *Ibid.*, p. 88.

[21] Report of the Commission on Human Rights, ECOSOC Official Records, Second Year, Fourth Session, Supplement No. 3, 1947 (http://www.legal-tools.org/doc/281872/).

[22] Evans, 1996, p. 86, see *supra* note 17.

Finally, as regards representativity, the membership of the UN was small at the time, with only 58 member states, compared with 193 in 2016. Most notably, colonial territories were not members, leaving most of the African peoples to be represented only though their European colonial overlords. Moreover, China was at the time represented by the Kuomintang regime, as there was a civil war in China, with revolutionary change less than a year away. After joining the UN in 1971, China declared its right to a 'clean slate', meaning that it considered itself unbound by international legal obligations entered into by the Kuomintang regime. This meant that neither the UDHR, nor the International human rights covenants (from 1966) were accepted by China as politically or legally binding.[23] China did, however, sign the two covenants later, in 1997 and 1998, and ratified the ICESCR in 2001.[24]

It is probably fair to conclude that the representativity of the decision-makers that formulated and adopted the UDHR in 1948 was limited, at least when considering the global reach of the human rights norms under development. However, state practice in subsequent decades is a good test of how the peoples with less or no representation in 1948 actually viewed the content of the UDHR, when given the opportunity to voice an opinion. Subsequent practice, as documented in, for example, regional human rights conventions or declarations, as well subsequent global human rights conventions, should therefore be taken into account in an assessment of the representativity of the process of formulating the basic human rights norms of the UDHR. This will be discussed below in this chapter.

The drafters of the UDHR were highly competent persons, with different backgrounds, and had a mandate to consult with whomever they deemed relevant to the work of drafting an "international bill of rights".[25] However, because the goal was to formulate a declaration that would be broad and basic enough to be agreed upon by the UN member states, the actual work took more the form of negotiations over drafting than any great outreach.[26]

---

[23] Sonya Sceats and Shaun Breslin, *China and the International Human Rights System*, Chatham House, London, 2012, available on the web site of Chatham House.

[24] *Ibid.*, p. 5.

[25] Report of the Commission on Human Rights, 1947, p. 3, see *supra* note 21.

[26] Evans, 1996, pp. 83–84, see *supra* note 17.

The work consisted more of drafting and negotiations than philosophical or legal discussions. It was a relatively closed process, with little open deliberation, certainly not to the extent of being a global dialogue with broad participation. There was no focus on fact-finding and assessing evidence, but rather a presumption that the negotiations would reveal any significant and reasonable differences of opinion, due to the composition and mixed background of the negotiators. The drafters were more diplomatic negotiators and less public communicators in their capacity as members of the drafting committee.

Testimony to the lack of a broad and open consultation is the failure of informed persons to see he significance of the UDHR when it was adopted. On 13 December 1948, the *Times'* reporting from the UNGA only devoted a few curt lines to the UDHR, as a "bill of rights for those nations who believe in them".[27] In the UK, in fact, neither the Foreign Secretary (Bevin) nor the Prime Minister (Attlee) at the time showed any interest in human rights during the preparation of the Declaration.[28]

It is worthy of reflection that such a historically important procedure was not clearly seen as such by even well-informed foreign policy makers in its own time. It denotes the changing attitude toward the UDHR and human rights in general over the decades after its adoption. At the time, it was made clear by the UN member states that what they wanted and expected was not a formulation of legally binding international norms, but an expression of common moral principles – at the most, *morally* binding principles.[29]

Throughout the work of the Commission, concerns were raised about the legal status of the Declaration. Upon her presentation of the third draft to the UNGA Third Committee in 1948, Commission Chair Eleanor Roosevelt emphasised the non-legally binding status of the Declaration. This reflected the common expectations among the UN member states at the time as well, although some states expressed hope and willingness to reach legally binding norms through treaty formation at a later stage (Denmark, the Netherlands, and New Zealand).[30]

---

[27] *Ibid.*, pp. 93–94.
[28] *Ibid.*, p. 94.
[29] *Ibid.*, pp. 89–90.
[30] *Ibid.*, p. 90.

Because the UDHR was in itself the main goal, and was generally not considered to be more than an expression of common moral principles, there was no need to consider an international system for human rights that included checks and balances and effective implementation as part of the drafting process. System considerations would have to be covered at a later stage, if and when states decided to commit to legally binding treaties on human rights. While the ambition was there in 1948, the broad and legally binding human rights conventions would be negotiated and finalised only in the 1960s in the form of the ICCPR and the ICESCR.

Despite the limitations of the UDHR at the time, it did become the fundamental basis for a system of international norms, many of which are arguably universally legally binding. This, however, was not primarily a consequence of the process leading to the Declaration itself, but of subsequent processes and practices. It is wrong to consider the UDHR as the 'constitutional moment' of the international human rights system, as the constitutions of states are intended as, and actually do form, the basis for a lasting public order. Rather, the international human rights system is more akin to a system of evolving constitutional practice, as is the case with the system of governance in the UK.

To assess the universality of the international system for human rights, therefore, it is necessary to consider the evolving practices of states in light of developments in treaty law and customary international law in the decades after the UDHR.

4.2.2. Human Rights and State Practice after the Adoption of the Universal Declaration of Human Rights

As mentioned, the representativity of the group of states that voted on the UDHR in 1948 was limited by the fact that the UN membership at the time was a mere 58 states, while as of 2017, it is 193 states. Being a declaration and not a treaty, the UDHR was not an instrument to which states could accede in the future, importantly when former colonial states became UN members. However, the practice of the new states after independence suggests most of the UDHR rights have been, and are still widely regarded as, valid binding norms. For Europe and South America, the regional human rights systems are aligned to a very high degree, and in important aspects go further than the global UN system. Furthermore, unlike African coun-tries, European and South American states were well represented in the UN in 1948.[31]

4.2.2.1. Africa

For African states, the African (Banjul) Charter on Human and Peoples' Rights is the most significant example of subsequent state practice in that region.[32] It was adopted by the Organisation of African Unity in 1981, and came into force in 1986. As of 2016, it was ratified by all African countries except Morocco (which is not a member of the African Union) and South Sudan (which is the newest independent African country, gaining independ-ence only in 2011).[33]

The African Charter enshrines many of the same rights as the UDHR. In terms of civil and political rights, for example, the African Charter rec-ognizes the right to freedom from discrimination, equality before the law, the right to life, the right to a fair trial; freedom of association, freedom of movement; political participation and right to property.[34] However, there also differences. For example, the African Charter's formulation about the right to political participation in its Article 13 is different from the formu-lation in the UDHR. Whereas the latter guarantees "periodic and genuine elections which shall be by universal and equal suffrage and shall be held by secret vote or by equivalent free voting procedures", the former stops at guarantee the right to "participate freely in the government of his country, either directly or through freely chosen representatives in accordance with the provisions of the law".[35] The difference is of course that while UDHR

---

[31]   For short comparison between the OAS and UN systems for human rights, see Cecilia Cris-tina Naddeo, "The Inter-American System of Human Rights: A Research Guide", Hauser Global Law School Programme, 2010, available on the School's web site.

[32]   See https://www.legal-tools.org/doc/f0db44/ ('African Charter').

[33]   African Commission of Human and Peoples' Rights, "Ratification table", available on the web site of the Commission.

[34]   Nneka Chukwumah, "The Banjul Charter and Universal Human Rights: A Comparative Analysis", p. 22 (http://www.legal-tools.org/doc/04810f/).

[35]   African Charter, Article 13(1), see *supra* note 32; UDHR , Article 21(3), see *supra* note 1.

---

guarantees democratic elections, the African charter does not explicitly do so.[36] Furthermore, there is no right to privacy in the African Charter.[37]

In terms of reservations, only three have been submitted in reference to Articles in the African Charter, specifically by Egypt, South Africa and Zambia. The most significant in terms for the discussion here is Egypt's, which reserved itself against the Charter's provisions in Article 8, regarding freedom of religion and conscience and Article 18(3) regarding elimination of discrimination of women.[38] For both provisions, Egypt refers to the boundaries set by Islamic law. In this sense, Egypt's reservations in 1981 echoes those of Saudi Arabia in 1948, and on the same basis, that is, Islamic law. This shows a persistent conflict of principles between the system of the UDHR and Islamic law in regard to apostasy and women's equality. At the same time, it is worth noting that no other majority Muslim country in Africa reserved itself against these provisions in the Charter.

In this context, another expression of the relation between Islamic law and universal human rights is found in the Cairo Declaration on Human Rights in Islam. This was adopted by the OIC in 1990, and signed by 55 OIC member states.[39] The Declaration confirms most of the rights of the UDHR, but also clearly subjects human rights to Islamic law in its Articles 24 and 25. The Declaration is notably silent on the right to voluntary religious conversion, although its Article 10 prohibits proselytization away from Islam, when such can be seen as exploiting a person's ignorance or poverty. This should be seen as further evidence that the prohibition on voluntary conversion away from Islam is controversial in majority Muslim states. There was, at the time of the Cairo Declaration, no consensus to explicitly go against the full rights of religious freedom as guaranteed in the ICCPR. The declaration is equally silent on general non-discrimination of women. Its Article 6 declares women to be equal to man in "human dignity", with "her own rights as well as duties to perform". As with religious conversion, however, the declaration does not directly oppose the equality of women as stated in the ICCPR and the ICESCR (specifically Article 3 in either Convention).

---

[36] Chukwumah, pp. 22–23, see *supra* note 34.

[37] *Ibid.* The right to privacy is guaranteed in UDHR Article 12, see *supra* note 1. There are other differences as well, which are not discussed here for the sake of brevity.

[38] African Charter, see *supra* note 32.

[39] Fifty-five states including Palestine, which at the time was recognized as a state only by a minority of the world's states.

The OIC Declaration therefore serves to underscore that there *is* a value conflict between Islamic law and universal human rights, but that there is no explicitly expressed consensus among majority Muslim states to directly oppose the rights previously agreed in the UDHR and the two Covenants.

4.2.2.2. Asia

Asia has not established a common regional human rights platform through a declaration, let alone treaties of common organisations, such as a human rights court. ASEAN, however, established a human rights commission in 2009, for its 10 member countries, namely Brunei, Cambodia, Indonesia, Laos, Malaysia, Myanmar, Philippines, Singapore, Thailand and Vietnam. ASEAN has issued joint declarations on human rights, significantly in 1993 and 2012. The latter was decreed by the 10 member countries on 18 November 2012 at a summit in Phnom Penh. Although none of these countries are global great powers, their combined population run in several hundred million people.

The 2012 ASEAN Declaration contains several interesting points, some of which seem to be contradictory. The Declaration reaffirms the countries' commitment to the UDHR in the preamble and directly in Article 10 regarding "all civil and political rights in the UDHR".[40] It lists several of the rights also in the UDHR, including the rights to life, personal liberty and security, property, a fair trial, privacy, freedom of religion and conscience, assembly, right to vote, and political participation, as well as freedom from slavery, torture, and discrimination including against women.

In its Articles 7 and 8, it states that "all human rights are universal". However, it goes on to write that "the realisation of human rights must be considered in the regional and national context bearing in mind different political, economic, legal, social, cultural, historical and religious backgrounds". Furthermore, in Article 8, it states that limitations on human rights must be subject to "just requirements of national security, public order, public health, public safety, public morality, as well as the general welfare of the peoples in a democratic society". In doing so, the ASEAN Declaration accepts human rights as legal norms, but not of the highest degree. In contrast with the objective of the UDHR, the ASEAN Declaration thus

---

[40] ASEAN Human Rights Declaration, 18 November 2012 (http://www.legal-tools.org/doc/545db2/).

does not consider human rights to be universal at all, or only to the extent that they do not contradict domestic legislation in a number of listed areas, down to and including "public morality". The Declaration is in this regard a clear example of the conflict between sovereign rights and human rights.

For this reason, the ASEAN Declaration was strongly criticised by a wide array of commentators for being an "anti-human rights instrument".[41] The US State Department expressed "deep concerns" about possible weakening of universal human rights and the UDHR. UN High Commissioner for Human Rights Navi Pillay joined 62 local, regional and international NGOs in calling on ASEAN to suspend the Declaration.[42]

Although China was not party to the ASEAN statement, the position of the Declaration could easily have been shared by China. Consistently after 1989 – the year of Tiananmen Square – China has accepted the international human rights system only in the sense of being inferior to domestic legislation. It continually opposes human rights-based criticism of states' internal practices, as a matter of principle.[43] In its voluntary pledge to the UN in 2016, in regard to its candidacy for membership in the HRC, it stated that "China will continue to speak up for developing countries and oppose interference in other countries' internal affairs on the pretext of human rights".[44]

In the Chinese conception of human rights, sovereignty comes first, and is the source and precondition of human rights.[45] Its official human rights policy is that there is a hierarchy of rights, in which social and economic rights come first, and are privileged over civil and political rights. In China's 2016 voluntary pledge, it emphasised that the human rights' cause "must and can only be promoted in line with national conditions and the needs of the people of each country".[46] While the wording itself is fairly open to interpretation, the statement follows the consistent policy of China

---

[41] Mong Palatino, "Human Rights Declaration Falls Short", in *The Diplomat*, 28 November 2012 (http://www.legal-tools.org/doc/b75080/).

[42] *Ibid.*

[43] Sceats and Breslin, 2012, pp. 5–6, see *supra* note 23.

[44] People's Republic of China, "Letter dated 1 August 2016 from the Permanent Representative of China to the United Nations addressed to the President of the General Assembly" ("China's 2016 Voluntary Pledge"), para. 20 (http://www.legal-tools.org/doc/210449/).

[45] Sceats and Breslin, 2012, pp. 6–7, see *supra* note 23.

[46] China's 2016 Voluntary Pledge, para. 22, see *supra* note 44.

in regard to human rights: national sovereignty comes first, and human rights alone cannot constitute a valid cause for international intervention.

As a preliminary conclusion, the universality of human rights as enshrined in the UDHR has a very broad acceptance of the world's states, but with a few notable exceptions. In the following, I will focus particularly on what seems to be possibly the most significant exceptions in this respect: the right to free and fair democratic elections; conflict with Islamic law, particularly shown in regard to women's rights and religious freedom; and the universal applicability of human rights when conflicting with domestic legislation and thus state sovereignty.

Further evidence about the universality of human rights in general, and the mentioned areas in particular, can be found in the processes leading up to the two international covenants on human rights, and subsequent state practice.

4.2.3. Human Rights Treaty Law: The Covenants

If the significance of the UDHR was lost on many in December 1948, this would quickly change. In statements in the UNGA sessions in the years after 1948, states tended to emphasise their long-standing and historic concern for human rights.[47] New constitutional arrangements were adopted by several countries in reference and response to the UDHR, including in Czechoslovakia, Poland and the Federal Republic of Germany.[48] The UDHR was also referenced in treaties and agreements adopted by international organisations, such as the recommendations from the West Indian conference in 1951, the Treaty of Peace with Japan, and the European Convention on Human Rights of 1950.[49]

The UN carried out extensive deliberations and negotiations in order to reach legally binding human rights norms. In contrast with the relatively quick process of the UDHR, the finalisation of the two Covenants, the ICCPR and the ICESCR, took much more time, and was not concluded until 1966. Unlike the UDHR, this process involved years of consultations, and broad and open discussions.

---

[47] Evans, 1996, p. 121, see *supra* note 17.
[48] *Ibid.*
[49] *Ibid.*

The first draft for a legally binding human rights covenant was first prepared by the UN Commission on Human Rights in 1947 and 1948.[50] In the following years, it was passed back and forth between the Commission and the Third Committee of the UNGA, where all UN members are represented. From 1955, an article-by-article debate began, which occupied the majority of the Third Committee's time through many of these sessions.[51] By the time the two Covenants were finalised, the process had been about as exhaustive as is possible in a state-based international system. Therefore, there is no reason to doubt that all UN member states were sufficiently aware of the contents of the Covenants and their legal implications by the time they were opened for signature and ratification in 1966.

The drawn-out process meant that all states involved had ample time to consider all legal aspects, consult experts as needed, and propose possible revisions, before acceding to the treaties. The substantial list of reservations to parts of the treaties is further testimony to this fact.[52]

It is also significant that the list of reservations referring to Sharia law is short: as of 2017, only Mauritania and Bahrain have formal reservations in effect with reference to Islamic Law to the two Covenants. Pakistan did make a reservation on this basis upon ratification, but this was later withdrawn. Egypt declared, upon ratification, that the rights in the Covenants were in accordance with Sharia.[53] This is typical ambivalent diplomatic language, as it does not state clearly which legal system would prevail if a conflict should become clear at a later stage. However, it does not constitute a clear reservation on Egypt's part. The low number of clear reservations based on Islamic law in general presents a weighty argument against any who would argue that the rights in the Covenants are contrary to Sharia and thus to Islamic culture and traditions.

---

[50] *Ibid.*, p. 122.

[51] *Ibid.*

[52] For reservations to the ICCPR ('Reservations to ICCPR') and the ICESCR, see the online UN Treaty Collection.

[53] Reservations to ICCPR, see *supra* note 52. Kuwait declared that certain rights are accepted, but will apply within the limits of domestic law (ICESCR Articles 2 and 3) and Sharia law (ICCPR Article 23). Turkey made a reservation over domestic constitutional law in regard to ICESCR Article 3 and ICCPR Article 27. Israel refers to religious law in regard to marriage rights under ICCPR Article 23.

The right to vote in genuine democratic elections poses a particular problem. The right is enshrined in ICCPR Article 25(b), and has near universal acceptance. The reservations over the paragraph are few and specific. Kuwait excludes members of the armed forces and police from the right to vote; Mexico excludes religious ministers; Monaco refers to its Constitution and the distinction made between Monegasque and foreign nationals.[54] UK has also submitted specific reservations, regarding Hong Kong and Fiji; and Switzerland reserved the right to uphold the practice of voting for certain assemblies by other means than secret ballot.[55] However, none of these reservations aim at diminishing the purpose of the paragraph in ensuring the right to vote in genuine democratic elections.

China, however, has not ratified the ICCPR, meaning that a large part of the world's population is not committed to the convention through their state. From a legal perspective, this is one reason why there is disagreement on whether this right is customary international law.[56] Particularly, one must take into account China's significance, including its population size and its long and independent civilizational and legal history. The fact that other South East Asian countries have not ratified the ICCPR (Myanmar, Malaysia, and Bhutan) gives further weight to the argument both against a customary legal norm and a universal ethical norm.[57] It is further significant that China's present leaders' scepticism toward democracy is not clearly only self-serving. It is, to a large extent, an actual ethical conviction. Furthermore, it is not clear that the people of China disagree with their leaders on this point.[58]

4.2.4. Degrees of Consensus Required for Universally Binding Norms

The procedure for concluding the rules of ICCPR and the ICESCR must be seen as inclusive in the highest degree possible under the present paradigm.

---

[54] Reservations to ICCPR, see *supra* note 52.

[55] *Ibid.*

[56] Niels Petersen, "Elections, Right to Participate in, International Protection", in *Max Planck Encyclopedia of Public International Law*, Oxford University Press, Oxford, 2012.

[57] *Ibid.* Some scholars have argued that the right to voting in democratic elections is teleological, in the sense that it is absolute and universal, but not necessarily to be implemented immediately.

[58] Robert Kagan, *The Return of History and the End of Dreams*, Alfred A. Knopf, New York, 2008, pp. 59–60.

The negotiators were as representative as can be hoped for in a state-based international system, where non-democracies participate, with the significant exception of China's absence. It could perhaps be argued that the ICCPR and the ICESCR are less than ideally universal because they fail to continuously consult the affected parties. Being rules that actually apply in perpetuity, it could further be argued that new generations should also be consulted about the rules. Especially, this would apply to states where the regimes that committed to the treaties in the first place were not representative of their populations at the time, for example, as relatively unresponsive autocracies.

However, the system of the two Covenants is not dissimilar from domestic constitutional systems. There are generally no provisions for renegotiating national constitutions at regular intervals, but instead there are provisions for amendments and revisions, as in the ICCPR. As the negotiations over the ICCPR lasted almost two decades in the first place, it would take an extreme toll on the UNGA to undertake the same procedure again, over the same rules.

In the cases where states have ratified legally binding human rights, such as those in the two covenants, it can be assumed without question that those rules apply to those states. The only questions in such cases would be in regard to interpretation of the rules, where they may be imprecise in content or even silent. In the latter category, the most significant is the lack of clear rules about legal sanctions in the event of human rights violations – up to and including international intervention.

When states have not ratified a convention or submitted reservations, however, the question is whether that state can still be held accountable to that rule, regardless. For example, no one would seriously challenge a UNSC decision to intervene in a state to prevent a genocide, even if that state has not ratified the 1948 Genocide Convention. However, international intervention over, for example, systematic discrimination on basis of sexual orientation is not universally seen as a legitimate cause for international intervention.[59]

---

[59] The example may seem far-fetched, but is in fact an actual and contentious area of policy. In Uganda, parliamentary debate over penalisation of homosexuality has been heated. Introduction of death penalty for 'serial offenders' has been proposed but not gained a majority. In a country with a population of around 37 million (2013), this criminalises possible conduct by an unknown, but significant number of people, potentially running into hundreds of

It is tempting for many to believe that non-acceptance of human rights by certain states is due to self-serving interests of autocracies that have an interest in restraining the freedom of their own people. This, however, is simplistic and certainly not valid in all cases. First off, the US – clearly a democracy – is one of the states that have ratified few human rights conventions. It could be argued, of course, that the US tends to abide by the human rights in those treaties – and promote them internationally – even if they have not ratified. However, this argument only underscores the significance of sovereignty concerns versus universality, which can apply to democratic and non-democratic states alike.

Furthermore, the degree to which democratic representation leads to acceptance of human rights can be questioned, for two reasons: first, although democratic governments are elected by their populations, the diplomats negotiating international treaties are not. Most democratic countries have limited dialogue between the diplomatic corps that negotiates with a mandate from the executive branch and the legislative branch that is the most representative of the people. At least, such dialogue is not continuous and consultative on all matters during the negotiation process. Furthermore, international human rights negotiations are generally not a significant campaign topic in democratic countries, meaning that the elected representatives' mandates on this particular area are limited.[60]

Second, un-democratic states can also be representative of their populations. For example, there can be little doubt that the explicit deference to Islamic law shown by Saudi Arabia in 1948 or Egypt in 1984 would have received broad support in the public, had they been consulted. It could even be speculated if it was the *lack* of representativity that made it possible for the other majority Muslim states to vote for the UDHR and to accede to the African Charter without reservations caused by deference to Islamic law.

More significant for the acceptance of human rights in general, however, are the sovereignty concerns of both democratic and undemocratic states. Viewed from 2017, it is all too easy to lose perspective on the relative

---

thousands. A law introducing life imprisonment for "aggravated homosexuality" was passed in 2013, but later annulled by the Constitutional Court on technical grounds (lack of quorum in parliament at the time of the vote). International sanctions were announced in the interim, including by the US.

[60] There are certainly notable exceptions, for example, Europe in 2015, when the political debate was to a large extent defined by the situations stemming from large migrant inflows.

novelty of international human rights, including the concept of international intervention into sovereign states to protect those rights. Prior to 1945, a government would not have seen it as a violation of international law, if a state conducted persecution or even mass murder of its own citizens in its own territory.[61] At the time, international lawyers considered Stalin's purges in the 1930s as a matter of domestic jurisdiction.[62] In this perspective, what is remarkable is not that many states, such as China, maintain the view that domestic law is superior to international human rights. The remarkable, rather, is that most of the world has changed its mindset so quickly.

Furthermore, international human rights law, as formulated in treaties, is often kept deliberately vague and open to interpretation, in clear contrast with domestic legal systems. States refrain from precise formulations because they want to maintain a degree of discretion in domestic legislation and practice. As multiple states each have their own qualms about precise formulations in different treaty articles that may impede their own room for manoeuvre, reaching full consensus is impossible in all but a few cases, such as slavery and racism.

Finally, it is not uncommon also in democracies that domestic legislation will outrank international treaty obligations. In the case of Norway, the Supreme Court considers both the national constitution and regular national legislation to be superior in case of direct conflict with an international treaty obligation.[63]

The degree to which human rights are universal and binding on all states, therefore, is not simply a matter of democracy or popular will. There are still considerable debate and conflicts surrounding human rights, based on principled arguments relating to sovereignty, but also founded on alternative value systems, be they secular or religious. When assessing how universal and legally binding are human rights, therefore, it is necessary to

---

[61] Anthony D'Amato, "Human Rights as Part of Customary International Law: A Plea for Change of Paradigms", in *Faculty Working Paper*, Northwestern University School of Law, 2010, Paper 88 (http://www.legal-tools.org/doc/302233/). Previously published in *Georgia Journal of International and Comparative Law*, 1995, vol. 25, pp. 10–56.

[62] *Ibid.*

[63] Geir Ulfstein and Morten Ruud, *Innføring i folkerett* [*Introduction to International Law*], Third Edition, Universitetsforlaget, Oslo, 2006, p. 55. However, in the case of human rights law, it is part of both the Norwegian constitution and statutory law, meaning that human rights law is not in direct conflict with domestic legislation. In cases of dispute, the Norwegian government defers in practice to rulings by the European Court of Human Rights.

consider each norm separately. It cannot be assumed *a priori* that human rights norms should automatically be universally accepted if they have been passed in a UN resolution.

At the same time, no law needs universal acceptance to be applicable. If it was not so, any criminal should be excused for their actions if they disagreed with the relevant law. What is required, therefore, is clarity on what it actually takes to make an international norm legally binding on the all states.

4.2.5. Universally Binding Rules as International Customary Law

In international law, the rules for formation of new legally binding and non-derogable rules are in many aspects open to interpretation. New international law can come about in one of two ways: first, by explicit state ratification of a treaty. The rules are laid down in the Vienna Convention on the Law of Treaties (1969). In general, a state will not be bound by treaty law unless it accepts it through ratification. Once party to a treaty's framework, however, different rules may apply. For example, the ICCPR has no exit clause, meaning that states parties are prevented from withdrawing once they have acceded. Furthermore, the ICCPR has its own rules on amendments, which require UNGA approval and two-thirds acceptance by the states parties to the treaty, instead of full consensus.

By this standard, China is not legally bound by the ICCPR, as it has not ratified it, merely signed it. North Korea, on the other hand, *is* bound by it, having ratified it in 1990. This country, in fact, requested to withdraw from the treaty in 1997, but was prevented from doing so after the UN Human Rights Committee considered the request in light of the lack of an exit clause in the convention.

Second, international norms can become legally binding as customary international law. Such legally binding rules come into existence when it is sufficiently documented that they are generally seen by states to be existing and legally binding, and that this is also demonstrated through the general practice of states, such as their voting on UN resolutions. While customary international law is binding also for states that are not party to the relevant treaty, it can be deviated from through explicit actions, such as other treaties or domestic legislation.

Only those rules in customary international law that are classified as *jus cogens* are binding on all states in the world, with no option of deviation. But who decides if a norm is in fact *jus cogens*? It cannot be the UNGA or a world summit of states, because their explicit adoption of a new legal rule would make it treaty law, not customary law. A universally recognised world court could decide on *jus cogens* rules, but such a court does not exist.[64]

The closest institution to such a court, is the ICJ. Granted, UN membership also entails a relation to the ICJ, being the main judicial institution of the UN. However, the ICJ's is not a world court, because its jurisdiction relies on explicit consent by the parties to its jurisdiction, as mentioned in Chapter 2 above.

In any case, the ICJ has remained highly conservative in regard to *jus cogens*, and generally refrains from statements that may establish new legal standards of this category. In fact, the ICJ traditionally goes to significant lengths to avoid commenting on whether a norm is considered *jus cogens*. In its 1996 *Advisory Opinion on the Legality of Use or Threat of Use of Nuclear Weapons*, for example, it coined the term of 'intransgressible principles of humanitarian law' to avoid referring to *jus cogens*.[65] Only in reference to the prohibition on genocide, has the ICJ clearly stated that it is a *jus cogens* rule, although in that specific case, it also concluded that it did not have jurisdiction to rule on it, because of lack of state consent.[66] As discussed in Chapter 3, however, there is an untapped potential for the ICJ to take on a more expansive role. Once a customary rule has been identified clearly by the ICJ, few would seriously challenge it.[67]

The lack of clarity about which rules are *jus cogens*, and the lack of a universally accepted legal institution that has both the authority and the will to decide on whether rules are *jus cogens*, represents a challenge for the universality of human rights. For example, in the wake of the 9/11 attacks, the US launched a significant attempt to water down the international

---

[64] Gennady M. Danilenko, "International *Jus Cogens*: Issues of Law-Making", in *European Journal of International Law*, 1991, vol. 42, pp. 42–43, 65.

[65] International Court of Justice, *Legality of the Threat or Use of Nuclear Weapons*, Advisory Opinion, 8 July 1996, para. 79 (http://www.legal-tools.org/doc/d97bc1/); Andrea Bianchi, "Human Rights and the Magic of *Jus Cogens*", in *European Journal of International Law*, 2008, vol. 19, no. 3. The author refers to the term as a "cacophonic neologism".

[66] Bianchi, 2008, p. 502, see *supra* note 65; International Court of Justice, *Armed Activities on the Territory of the Congo* (New Application: 2002) (Democratic Republic of Congo v. Rwanda), Jurisdiction, Judgment, 3 February 2006, para. 64 (http://www.legal-tools.org/doc/1d7775/).

[67] Cassese, 2012, p. 240, see *supra* note 82 in Chapter 2.

prohibition against torture. It did so, first by attempting to outline a restrictive interpretation of torture, in order to justify the use of harsh interrogation techniques on terrorist suspects.[68] After strong international criticism, it shifted to a line of argumentation that suggested that the UN Convention against Torture was not applicable in times of armed conflict.[69] Such arguments would be difficult to promote, if the prohibition on torture had been previously been clearly established as *jus cogens*.

Regular customary international law, however, applies to a great number of human rights norms. While such rules can be deviated from in treaty, few states actually take this step, because doing so would expose that state to severe criticism both internally and internationally. It does mean, however, that when states have explicitly reserved themselves from specific provisions in human rights conventions, those norms cannot legally apply to that country.

Furthermore, customary international law can be deviated from in domestic legislation. This means that many human rights norms have weak protection, and there are few means of international enforcement on legal grounds, for example, when domestic family law is based on local or religious traditions, as in Israel or Saudi Arabia.

New and unexpected challenges are also arising in regard to the development of binding and universal human rights. One challenge is when people's sentiments change, and previously accepted rights are suddenly called into doubt. An example is the US position on torture, where the 9/11 attacks changed the attitudes in the US, but not as much in the rest of the world. A more persistent challenge to the universality of human rights is the resurgence of religion as a basis for policy in many majority Muslim countries. While only Saudi Arabia abstained from the vote on the UDHR for reasons of adherence to Sharia, several more countries have expressed similar qualms in the subsequent decades.

For example, the Convention on the Rights of the Child remains the most universally accepted of the human rights conventions, with 196 states parties in 2016 – even more than the total UN membership. However, there is a long list of reservations, especially to Article 14(1), which commits

---

[68]   Bianchi, 2008, p. 505, see *supra* note 65.
[69]   *Ibid.*, p. 506.

States Parties to "respect the right of the child to freedom of thought, conscience and religion". Nine states reserved themselves against this paragraph, citing Islamic law as reason.[70] In addition, seven more majority Muslim countries made general reservations to the whole convention with reference to Sharia.[71] Finally, the Holy See also reserved itself against Article 14(1), bringing the total up to 17 states. It is significant that 16 majority Muslim countries have aligned on this point.

This can be compared with the reservations made in reference to Islamic law to article 18 of the ICCPR, which guarantees the freedom of religion. The phrasing in the ICCPR is stronger than in the CRC, given that there is an explicit safeguard of the right to adopt a religion of one's own choice. Under the ICCPR, only three countries reserved themselves against Article 18, with reference to Islamic law, namely Bahrain, Maldives, and Mauritania. All three ratified the ICCPR after 2004, in contrast to other Muslim majority countries, which generally ratified earlier.[72]

The reservations to the CRC, therefore, in all likelihood reflects a changing attitude in those countries, where religious views influence international human rights policy more heavily than in the past. The reservations are, in effect, an attempt to water down and move away from the established international human rights norm of religious freedom, as laid down both in the UDHR and in the ICCPR. This is not dissimilar to the mentioned ASEAN Declaration which also waters down established international human rights.

As there is no exit clause to the ICCPR, the only way to change the norms formally, is to revise the convention. This, however, requires two-thirds majority of the states parties, which will not be possible today even if all majority Muslim countries and the Holy See joined forces in order to do so. At the same time, it is clear that this minority group of states consider the established human rights norm on religious freedom to be an infringement on their own traditional legal system and beliefs. This attitude was not equally strong in the past, when most of the same states accepted the ICCPR without reservations over religious freedom.

---

[70] Algeria, Bangladesh, Brunei, Iraq, Jordan, Maldives, Syria, Qatar, and UAE. See the online UN Treaty Collection.

[71] *Ibid.* Afghanistan, Iran, Kuwait, Mauretania, Saudi Arabia, and Somalia.

[72] International Covenant on Civil and Political Rights (http://www.legal-tools.org/doc/2838f3/).

The process leading to formulation of basic human rights in the ICCPR, however, has been assessed above as fair and inclusive to a high degree and on a global scale. There are also other grounds – legally and ethically – to expect adherence to the rules even by those states that have not ratified the conventions or expressed reservations. This includes the right to religious freedom, up to and including the right of choosing one's own beliefs, irrespective of Islamic law. This right has been accepted by an overwhelming majority of the world's states, representing a clear majority of the world's population. Article 18 in ICCPR has also been formally accepted by the majority of Muslim states. The fact that more states now consider the issue differently than they did a few decades back does not remove the obligation. States that partake in the international system, through UN membership and as states parties to the conventions expressing the most basic norms of that same system, are not ethically or legally free to declare themselves unbound by specific parts of that system. In order to do so, they have to revise the system itself, through the agreed upon rules.

Still, there is an unclear demarcation between human rights norms that should be considered applicable to all states, and those that should not. Rights concerning freedom from slavery are at the one end uncontested, considering that there has been near universal consensus about this norm for a long time-period. Application of the right to non-discrimination to lesbians or gays, however, has yet to achieve anything near the same level of consensus, and remain deeply contested. This is one area where more time is needed before anything like an international consensus can develop.

The two most enduring value conflicts, however, are over democratic elections and Islamic law, respectively, in addition to the overarching disagreement about delimitation of human right *vis-à-vis* sovereign rights. As has been discussed, the right to democratic elections is presently contested mainly by China and a number of states in South East Asia that have not acceded to the ICCPR. This disagreement is substantial to the degree that it is not possible to conclude that the right to democratic elections is universally binding. Time will tell if such a conclusion can become warranted at a later stage in world history.

While a strong principled opposition to election-based democracy remains, it is worthy of reflection how quickly democratic elections as an ethical norm has spread to most of the peoples of the world. Before 1800, virtually no state in the world practiced democratic elections, instead justi-

fying their systems of governance through concepts such as divine provi-
dence. Today, even non-democratic states like Sudan, Iran and the DPRK
do hold elections. Even if those elections are not free and fair, it cannot be
denied that they are held on the presumption that they will bestow legitimacy on the leaders of the states. This shows the strength of the ethical
appeal of democratic elections across most of the globe. Compared with the
world in 1750, it reveals a revolution in political philosophy on a global
scale of which we are still unable to see the full effect.

The basis is the concept of legitimate governance as being based on
the popular will, which is fundamental in the Popular Sovereign Paradigm.
It is feasible, but not inevitable, that this concept will lead to acceptance of
democratic elections as a norm. Communist ideologists, for example, can
argue that a transition period of one-party rule is necessary also on the basis
that the Party represents the popular will.

The value conflict between Sharia and human rights is perhaps
equally strong and principled. However, the starting point is different: while
the norm of democratic elections has never been accepted on a universal
basis, the concern about placing Islamic law over human rights law has
arisen mainly in recent decades. The movement to ensure superiority of Islamic law over human rights law was not predominant in the negotiations,
voting or ratification of the two Covenants or the UDHR. Both of the Covenants tie the states to legally binding norms ensuring, for example, non-
discrimination of women (Article 3 in both conventions), and the freedom
of religion including voluntary conversion (ICCPR, Article18), both with
which Islamic legal scholars often take issue. In more recent conventions,
like the CRC and CEDAW, however, Sharia-related reservations are in
abundance from majority Muslim states. The mentioned defamation debate
in the UNGA is also relatively recent. Therefore, the challenge to human
rights from Islamic law should be seen as a movement to change the existing system, while those seeking to uphold non-democratic systems of governance are in fact seeking to block the imposition of a new norm upon the
existing order in their own societies.

This places the two value conflicts in different categories: those opposing established human rights from the perspective of religious law are
akin to a minority party in a national assembly: they have a right to argue
for their view, but are also obliged to accept defeat by the majority. Those
who have never accepted democratic elections are more akin to a group that
has never accepted the national assembly in the first place. While future

developments may force them to reconsider, there is, at present, no foundation for coercion over acceptance of democratic elections.

Even more significantly, and less clear, is the conflict between human rights as universal and binding and the rights of the sovereign state as the sole legitimate custodian of domestic legal order. Here, the ambivalence has been present from the beginning, with the Soviet Union's position on the UDHR, through the US' and China's non-ratification of the ICESCR and ICCPR, respectively, and the various statements and declarations by other states, such as the ASEAN declarations. It remains unresolved, and there is no likelihood of a resolution anytime soon, as the conflict is part and parcel of the Popular Sovereign Paradigm that underlies and upholds the present international system.

Despite the lack of clarity, it can safely be concluded that a fundamental change has occurred in regard to state sovereignty, which is visible in the present system. The prohibition on genocide faces no significant opposition among any states in the world today. Furthermore, it has been declared *jus cogens* by the ICJ, and is accepted as such by a consensus of legal scholars. This consensus of states and legal experts includes the obligation of intervention in order to stop genocide from occurring. While the UNSC, in practice, may defer from using the term 'genocide' for reasons of political expediency, there is no doubt that such events call for international intervention, and are not a matter of state sovereignty. This is a historical novelty, which was not legally binding before World War II. Even though many states uphold the traditional sovereign rights and resist further encroachment of universal human rights, there is no going back to the Westphalian legal order. The conflict between sovereign rights and human rights will persist as long as the present paradigm of the international system remains in place.

4.3. Global Human Rights Bodies

There is a great number of international human rights bodies. The most significant *global* organisations are the HRC and the OHCHR. In addition, all the main UN human rights conventions have treaty bodies, which assess states parties' implementation of the relevant human rights areas under their mandates. Most of the treaty bodies can also receive complaints from individuals regarding human rights violations by states parties – provided that these states parties have consented to the individual complaints procedure.

Because of the common organisational goal of human rights main-streaming, all UN organisations have to consider human rights in their work. Some organisations have a combined mandate for development and human rights in certain areas, such as UN Women (UN Entity for Gender Equality and the Empowerment of Women) for promotion of women's rights, and UNICEF for children's rights. However, the degree varies to which the UN organisations, funds, and programmes base their work on human rights.

Finally, the UN Charter organs have high significance for human rights, both actual and potential. Of these, the UNGA is the most signifi-cant. The HRC is a subsidiary organ to it, and the UNGA's Third Commit-tee is devoted entirely to human rights work. Furthermore, since human rights require consensus or near-consensus among the representatives of the peoples of the world to be considered universally applicable, only the UNGA has anything close to a composition and mandate that makes such a presumption possible.

There are also a number of regional organisations for human rights, tied to regional treaties. These include the Council of Europe and the Euro-pean Court of Human Rights, the Inter-American Commission on Human Rights, and the African Commission on Human and People's Rights. Asia does not have a regional human rights organisation of this type, nor a re-gional convention on Human Rights. The closest is the ASEAN Declara-tions on human rights, and the ASEAN Intergovernmental Commission on Human Rights. ASEAN members, however, includes only 10 Asian coun-tries in the South-East region. The mandate and powers of the Commission are also much less independent than those of the other regional organisa-tions. Finally, there is not yet any regional human rights organisation for Oceania.

The network of regional and global human rights organisations is in-terconnected. For example, the strength of the regional human rights system in Europe means that most individual complaints are processed through the European Court of Human Rights, and not UN treaty bodies. Furthermore, the lack of judicial review in the UN system permanently restricts the en-forceability and thus the significance of human rights, while at the same time, the lack of clear and precise rule-formulation by the UNSC and the UNGA constrains the possibilities for judicial review, even if, for example, the ICJ had been able and willing to perform it.

In any case, the most important normative fora for human rights rules formulation remain the UNGA and the HRC. As the former was discussed in Chapter 2, this chapter will focus on the latter.

4.4. The UN Human Rights Council

4.4.1. Procedures and Instruments

The HRC was set up in 2006, by resolution of the UNGA. It is tasked with discussing, addressing, reporting and deciding on recommendations on all thematic human rights issues in the world. It is also tasked with mainstreaming human rights in the UN system.[73]

The idea was that the HRC would replace the heavily criticised Commission on Human Rights – established by ECOSOC in 1946 – with a new body that would be better suited to promote human rights. The main criticism of the precursor Commission was that it was too politicised to function effectively. Its block voting patterns led to inaction, including in a lack of response to the genocide in Rwanda in 1994. Before the killings, it received a report alerting it of the potential for mass atrocities, but the Commission took no action.[74] The UN High-level Panel on Threats, Challenges and Change concluded, in their 2004 report *A More Secure World: Our Shared Responsibility*, that the Commission had lost its credibility and required reform.[75]

UNGA resolution 60/251 established the Council formally, and set up its framework for operation. No fewer than 170 countries voted in favour, while four voted against, specifically the US, Marshall Islands, Israel and Palau.[76] Belarus, Iran and Venezuela abstained.[77] The main reason for the US's objection was that it believed the rules of membership of the new HRC would not solve the problems that had undermined the credibility of the Commission. The US representative to the UN expressed these concerns in the UNGA plenary after the vote, saying that the rules were not strong

---

[73] Miloon Kothari, "From Commission to the Council: Evolution of UN Charter Bodies", in Shelton (ed.), 2013, pp. 587–588, see *supra* note 47 of Chapter 3.

[74] *Ibid.*, p. 589.

[75] *Ibid.*, p. 591.

[76] *Ibid.*, p. 592.

[77] United Nations Official Records, General Assembly, 60th Session, 72nd Plenary Meeting, A/60/PV.72, 15. March 2006, pp. 5–6 (http://www.legal-tools.org/doc/d95280/).

enough to prevent states from being elected to the HRC, while actually pursuing an agenda to undermine the new organisation from within.[78] Although membership in the HRC is formally contingent on having a good human rights record, the US and others criticised the text in 2005 for not going far enough. Meanwhile, the African group criticised the text for including this condition for membership at all.[79]

There was also criticism that the HRC would still not have sufficient safeguards against harmful politicisation (African group, Sudan, Cuba, and Pakistan). China argued that there was a significant risk that political considerations would govern the adoption of country-specific resolutions.[80] Finally, a major point of criticism was of the proposed geographical distribution of seats for the UN member states. The Latin American and Caribbean countries group was the only one that raised concerns on these grounds. This group stood to lose 27% of their membership, compared with the Commission.[81]

Despite these criticisms, the adopted rules for the HRC states that it shall consist of 47 member states, elected for three years on secret ballot, with maximum two consecutive terms. Members are elected by the UNGA, by majority vote, but with a geographically-based distribution of seats to ensure equitable regional representation. The requirements for passing a resolution in the HRC is a majority vote and a quorum of one third of the members of the Council.[82]

The HRC also has an Advisory Committee, which replaced the former Sub-Commission. The Advisory Committee consists of independent experts, which are engaged in studies, recommendations and standard setting. It has 18 members. This is intended to be the think-tank of the HRC. Experts are appointed for three years and can have two consecutive terms. The Council elects the members on secret ballot, after nomination by UN member states.[83] Seats are distributed according to regional representation: five from African states, five from Asia, two from Eastern Europe, three

---

[78] *Ibid.*, pp. 6–7; Kothari, 2013, p. 592, see *supra* note 73.
[79] Kothari, 2013, p. 592, see *supra* note 73.
[80] *Ibid.*
[81] *Ibid.*, p. 593.
[82] *Ibid.*, pp. 593–594.
[83] *Ibid.*, p. 595.

from Latin American and Caribbean states, and three from Western Europe and other states. The Advisory Committee meets twice a year, for week-long sessions.[84]

4.4.2. Instruments of the Human Rights Council

The main instruments of the HRC for promotion of Human Rights, besides its resolutions, are the complaints procedure, the UPR and the special procedures.

The complaints procedure of the HRC is based on the procedure of the former Commission (known as the 1503-procedure, after ECOSOC resolution 1503). However, it has been changed in order to be more victim-oriented, transparent and efficient. Anyone can issue a communication with a complaint to the HRC, detailing the violation of a human right. Two working groups deal with the procedure: the Working Group on Communications screens inadmissible petitions, and passes admissible ones to the state concerned for comment. Domestic measures must be exhausted for the communication to be taken under consideration. The communication is then passed to the Working Group on Situations, which considers the case in a private session with the HRC. The Council can then agree to take action through a resolution, appoint an expert, open a public consideration or recommend the OHCHR to provide technical advice and capacity building to the state concerned.[85]

The UPR envisages peer review of all UN member states every four and a half years. The UPR covers all of the human rights obligations that are applicable for the state, including those of the UN Charter and the UDHR, formal treaty obligations, voluntary pledges and even applicable humanitarian law.[86] The UPR takes the form of an interactive discussion with representatives of the state under review and of the 47 members of the HRC, although all UN member states are allowed to participate.

---

[84]   OHCHR, "Background information on the Advisory Committee", available on the OHCHR web site.

[85]   Kothari, 2013, pp. 595–596, see *supra* note 73.

[86]   OHCHR, "Basic facts about the UPR" ('Basic UPR Facts'), available on the OHCHR web site.

In advance, the state under review submits a national report on its human rights record. The other background documents include special procedures reports relevant to the state member, reports from UN human rights treaty bodies, and information from other stakeholders. In the latter category, NGOs may contribute information. Independent NHRIs also provide reports to the UPR, as part of the formal procedure. NHRIs are also entitled to present a statement after the state under review.[87] The input of NGOs and NHRIs ensure that, even though the UPR remains state-driven, it is not exclusively so.

The outcome of the UPR is a country report that summarizes the discussion, and emphasises the recommendations from UN member states to the state under review. The latter has the option of accepting or taking note of those recommendations.[88]

The special procedures are arguably the most significant mechanism in the UN for protection of human rights. The special procedures involve compilation and publication of information on human rights violations by appointed mandate-holders. The Special Procedures are established by the Council through a resolution identifying either a country or a theme of concern. As of April 2013, there were 36 thematic and 13 country mandates approved and in operation. HRC appoints either an expert or a working group, usually of five experts, under the Special Procedure mandates. These are tasked with investigation, reporting, and presentation of recommendations to the HRC.[89]

Reports on human rights violations are intended to be followed up by the HRC, although this part of the procedure is widely regarded as ineffectual.[90] The totality of the special procedure reports, however, represents a significant amount of solid information about implementation of human rights on a global level. For this reason, it has been described a virtual world report on human rights.[91] The impact of the Special Procedures relies

---

[87] Kothari, 2013, p. 603, see *supra* note 73.

[88] Basic UPR Facts, see *supra* note 86.

[89] Kothari, 2013, pp. 594–595, see *supra* note 73.

[90] Bertrand G. Ramcharan, *The UN Human Rights Council*, Routledge, Abingdon, 2011, p. 7.

[91] *Ibid.*, p. 7.

mostly on voluntary acceptance of advice, or adjustments of practice following 'naming and shaming', as the reports will serve to strengthen the pressure on states that violate human rights.

4.4.3. Criticism of the Human Rights Council

Strong criticism of the HRC has been present from the outset. Three common assertions have been that the HRC (1) fails, for political reasons, to take action on many of the worst cases of human rights violations; (2) is biased in its treatment of countries; and (3) is undermined by the actions of some of its members which seek to weaken the Special Procedures.[92] Furthermore, critics argue that politicisation has undermined the HRC from the start; and that national and regional agendas have dominated the Council, particularly on contentious and politically sensitive issues.[93]

In terms of procedure, many still regard the criteria for membership as too soft. That serial violators can become HRC members is a matter of continuous concern for many UN member states.[94] Some have criticized the HRC on the basis of membership of specific states as well, specifically the elections of China, Egypt, Libya, Pakistan, Russia, and Saudi Arabia.[95]

As regards the main innovation of the new HRC, the critics say that the UPR runs the risk of being seen as a sham, because gross violators continue to be treated by their peers with kids' gloves, and there are no strong procedures for dealing with gross violators.[96]

In sum, critics say that the HRC, in its formative years, has failed to fulfil its mandate, particularly in terms of protection, and that it has not succeeded in overcoming many of the shortcomings of the Commission.[97] As a consequence, the reasoning goes, the HRC lacks necessary credibility among states, NGOs and observers, which is hampering its ability to protect

---

[92] *Ibid.*, p. 9.
[93] Rosa Friedman, *The United Nations Human Rights Council: A Critique and Early Assessment*, Routledge, London, 2013, p. 299.
[94] Kothari, 2013, pp. 616–617, see *supra* note 73.
[95] Friedman, 2013, p. 301, see *supra* note 93.
[96] Ramcharan, 2011, pp. 126–127, see *supra* note 90.
[97] Friedman, 2013, p. 297, see *supra* note 93.

and promote human rights. Without reform, it is may face the same legitimacy and credibility deficit as that of the Commission.[98]

Reform proposals, however, mostly suggest only very limited changes. These include reassessment of the size and distribution of the membership. Some argue for a smaller and more efficient council, others argue for universal state membership.[99] Another suggestion is reassessment of the membership criteria to heighten the threshold for membership for the worst human rights offenders.[100]

A third common proposal is to heighten the status of the HRC. At present, it is a subsidiary to the UNGA, and its elevation to a principal UN organ would highlight the importance of human rights in the UN.[101] Finally, a fourth common approach is to increase the participation of non-state actors. This argument is particularly common among NGO representatives themselves, who believe they can contribute to making the HRC more credible, well-informed, objective and effective.[102]

4.4.4. The Human Rights Council and the Boundaries of the Possible

The criticism of the HRC tends to focus on the lack of forcefulness in its work, in making strong recommendations, in enforcing offenders to change, and even in letting offenders take part as members of the Council. The question is, however, whether it is possible for an international organisation, where the states are the driving force and decision-makers, to achieve more than the HRC is presently doing?

As a starting point, there is no doubt that the HRC consists of state representatives on all levels of decision-making, and not objective agents. Granted, disinterested persons do hold important positions, particularly as Special Procedures mandate-holders, and as members of the advisory committee. However, as for the latter, the members are nominated by the states, not disinterested parties. This may seem trivial, but it has the effect that many states will campaign for their own candidates on the basis of their nationality, rather than their expertise. Other countries may not have their own candidates or are simply not as interested, but may be willing to trade

---

[98] *Ibid.*, p. 303.

[99] Kothari, 2013, pp. 616–617, see *supra* note 73.

[100] *Ibid.*

[101] *Ibid.*

[102] *Ibid.*

votes for support to their own candidates in another election. The same procedure applies to the UN human rights treaty bodies, where vote trading among states in advance of elections is a normal procedure.

More importantly, neither the Advisory Committee nor the mandate holders are on the decision-making level in the HRC, as their functions are mainly in advisory and information-gathering capacities. There are also important formal constraints placed on both groups, as the Advisory Committee is not permitted to make recommendations, while the Special Procedures mandate-holders do not actively partake in the interactive dialogue with states under review in the UPR working group sessions.

The HRC is, therefore, for all intents and purposes a state-driven organisation. In terms of representativity, it does not have the unequal practice of permanent representation by great powers, such as the UNSC. The two-term maximum rule of membership (three plus three years) in the HRC ensures rotation in the system. Furthermore, the wide membership (47 members) and regional distribution goes a long way to increase the representativity of the HRC, compared with the UNSC.

The principle of formal equality of states is a basic concept for the HRC. The principle extends very far, in fact, to the extent that non-members of the HRC can participate in consultations, events, and make statements in meetings (after the HRC members), giving opportunities for all UN members to be heard.

The challenge, as with all the UN organisations, is how representative the states are for the peoples in their respective territories. As previously discussed, however, this is an inherent challenge under the present international system, which remains state-centred.

As regards the inclusion of non-state actors, the HRC is generally more positive to NGO participation than most other international organisations. NGOs that have consultative status with ECOSOC have the right to attend HRC sessions and provide written and oral statements to the Council, as well as to organize parallel events to the formal sessions.[103] The level of inclusion is in practice higher than before the UNGA.

As regards the formulation of new human rights norms, however, the process is more limited. Although NGOs sometimes campaign for specific

---

[103] OHCHR, "NGO Participation in the Human Rights Council", available on the OHCHR web site. Consultative status is regulated by ECOSOC Resolution 1996/31, 25 July 1996 (http://www.legal-tools.org/doc/b170c0/).

norms and their formulation through resolutions, the negotiations commence and end with the states. Mostly, the HRC members are themselves the object of bilateral lobbying from the NGOs, but they retain the authority to decide whether or not to heed the advice given, as well as to how closely they will engage in the NGO dialogue.

The procedures allow NGOs to influence negotiations only indirectly. In the scores of human rights resolutions adopted by the HRC annually, most paragraphs contain text that has already been agreed in past resolutions, but with the introduction of some new wording here and there. In these resolutions, the influence of NGOs varies, but is generally very limited. The states do not conduct anything close to broad public consultations about the content of the negotiations. However, well-connected NGOs will tend to get hold of draft resolutions, and be able to lobby members on the content.

On larger issues, when resolutions contain substantially new rules, NGOs often play a greater role. Such resolutions may take years of negotiation before adoption, during which time NGOs can attain information, build up networks, and organise campaigns more effectively around items. This entails at least a possibility for NGOs to mobilise through broad and public debates, although the level to which they succeed will of course vary. After all, public debates about resolutions under negotiation in the HRC are rarely front-page news.

The description of the consultation with stakeholders in the HRC in general for the most part holds for the UPR specifically. NGOs and NHRIs can provide input, but states drive and conclude the process. The level of national consultations with regard to UPR review varies greatly, as some countries have a broad outreach, while others simply prepare their reports in government offices only.

However, the widespread network of NHRIs globally ensures that there will be some form of national dialogue on human rights in most countries. Particularly, this applies to the UPR process and the treaty body review processes, where the NHRIs are expected to present 'shadow reports' on the state of implementation of human rights in their countries. The basis of such reports is generally not limited to the NHRIs' own work, but their dialogues with NGOs that work on human rights locally. While some states have public outreach initiatives in preparation to UNGA sessions, the system for national consultations in the human rights area is much more formalized, sophisticated and widespread. As of April 2016, there were 117

NHRIs in the world, of which 75 have so-called 'A-status', signifying that their organisation and practice is highly professional and independent.[104]

However, nothing of the above takes away the fact that the HRC starts and ends with the state members. NGOs do not participate in the final negotiations on resolutions, and have to rely on lobbying efforts *vis-à-vis* sympathetic state delegates in order to attain information and to influence the content of resolutions. On the dimension between sole state participation and non-state actor involvement, the HRC may be leaning as far toward the latter as is possible under the present paradigm. Initiatives to move this inclusion to even higher levels may be contemplated, but are also likely to be resisted strongly by a number of states that are wary of their sovereign rights and fearful of outside criticism.

4.4.5. The Human Rights Council in Practice

The HRC has been criticised for presumed constraints in regard to its sources of information, and in particular it has been argued that NGOs should be given a greater role.[105] However, this criticism does not hold up when the HRC is compared with other international organisations. In fact, the HRC is to a very high degree well-informed on the global human rights situation. Between the work of the OHCHR and the Special Procedures, there is a wide array of well-documented reports and information flowing to the HRC on a frequent and regular basis. This work significantly also reflects input from a number of non-state actors, including individual testimonies. In addition, the close co-operation with the NGOs and NHRIs means that the HRC gets a far more nuanced picture of the human rights situation in any given country than many other UN organisations have in their respective areas, at least when compared with the UNGA and the UNSC.

While the inflow of information is satisfactory, the processing of that information, however, occurs according the regular procedure in international organisations. Similar to the UNSC and the UNGA, the HRC is also

---

[104] List of NHRIs and their status at, Global Alliance of National Human Rights Institutions, "Accreditation status as of 26 May 2017", available on the OHCHR web site. The status of NHRIs is based on their respective compliance with the Principles relating to the Status of National Institutions (The Paris Principles), UNGA Res. 48/131, 20 December 1993 (http://www.legal-tools.org/doc/fa7c88/).

[105] Ramcharan, 2011, pp. 122–123, see *supra* note 90; Kothari, 2013, pp. 616–617, see *supra* note 73.

heavily influenced by the national political agendas of its members. States are pursuing their national interests in the HRC, as they do in other international organisations.

The problem arises when the interests of a significant number of states converge around areas that lead to a skewed representation of facts. An example is the amount of attention given to human rights and humanitarian law violations by Israel. While it is certainly within the mandate, and indeed obligation, of the HRC to work on violations by Israel, the amount of time spent on this area is well above that given to other situations that also require the Council's attention.[106]

The over-attention to Israel is due in part to the commonly held opinion that alleged Israeli violations are not being effectively addressed by its proper addressee, namely the UNSC. The latter is much more reluctant to take a strong stance towards Israel than the HRC and the UNGA, because of the US's policy on the issue (see Chapter 2). For example, the UNSC has shown itself unwilling to let Palestine join the UN as a member state, despite the fact that over two thirds of the UN members have recognised Palestine as a state and the UN Secretary-General accepts Palestine's accession to UN conventions as a state party.[107] Regardless, when the attention on Israel in the HRC is compared with the attention to other states that violate human rights, there can be no doubt that there is a relative mismatch.

This example of convergence of national interests in the HRC is not the only one. Human Rights Watch accuses China of being a spoiler in the HRC, arguing that it is "blocking greater scrutiny of human rights situations in other countries, including Belarus, Iran, North Korea, Syria, and Ukraine".[108] China, of course, would not agree that it is a "spoiler", but it does state its intention to protect sovereign rights *vis-à-vis* human rights, as shown above. China is certainly able to rally other states to its cause, when

---

[106] Ramcharan, 2011, p. 122, see *supra* note 90.

[107] I refer here to a continuing trend. However, it should be noted that the main Palestinian bid for UN membership was in 2011, when the necessary majority in the Security Council did not materialize. In 2012, the UNGA voted to accept Palestine as a "non-member observer state", by a vote of 138–9, and with 41 abstaining (A/RES/67/19, 29 November 2012) (http://www.legal-tools.org/doc/3a1916/). From this point on, the UNSG has accepted Palestine's requests to accede to international conventions, including the main human rights treaties, as a state party.

[108] Human Rights Watch, "China", in *World Report 2016*, available at its web site.

---

necessary. In a debate on freedom of expression in the HRC on 29 February 2012, China delivered a joint statement on behalf of a long list of countries.[109] It listed many reasons to control, monitor and block Internet sites, arguing that abuses of freedom of expression can encroach on the rights of others. China pointed to expressions favouring terrorism, racism, xenophobia, gaining political advantage, and "violent information that corrupts people's minds", and which may induce them to engage in criminal activities.[110] Critics read this in light of the international criticism over China's domestic practice for censorship of Internet content, and thus as strongly connected to its perceived national interests and protection of its sovereignty.

As long as the HRC remains a state-based set-up that aims to involve all states in a universal discussion on human rights, national interest-based statements are however, unavoidable. In this sense, the HRC has challenges in regard to its members' consideration of relevant facts and evidence, but they are not significantly different from other international bodies. In fact, the inflow of information and analysis from various sources leads to the conclusion that the HRC holds up to a high degree, when compared with, for example, the UNSC, or the UNGA, and certainly the WTO.

As regards the UPR, the written material that forms the basis of the review process is fairly extensive. The state report and NHRI and NGO submissions ensure that a wide array of viewpoints is presented in the process. Furthermore, the special procedures reports are generally of very high quality and bring important analysis to the process.

Despite this, there is a varying degree to which the states under review maintain independent domestic institutions that may report to the

---

[109] The countries were Algeria, Bangladesh, Belarus, Burundi, Cambodia, Congo, Cuba, Democratic People's Republic of Korea, Ethiopia, Iran (Islamic Republic of), Lao People's Democratic Republic, Malaysia, Mauritania, Myanmar, Namibia, Nicaragua, Pakistan, Palestine, Philippines, Russian Federation, Saudi Arabia, Sri Lanka, Sudan, Turkmenistan, Venezuela (Bolivarian Republic of), Uzbekistan, Viet Nam, Yemen, and Zimbabwe. See Permanent Mission of PRC to the UN Office at Geneva and other International Organizations in Switzerland, "Joint Statement at the Panel on Freedom of Expression on the Internet" (http://www.legal-tools.org/doc/e8948c/).

[110] William New, "UN Human Rights Council Rallies On Right to Internet Freedom of Expression", in *Intellectual Property Watch*, 2016.

UPR. For example, China is among the countries that does not have a NHRI as such. This is fully within their sovereign rights under the present system.

Some countries also do not co-operate with the relevant special procedures mandate holders. In the UN Secretary-General's annual report on this issue from 2016, twelve countries were listed as having failed to co-operate as expected with Special Procedures.[111] Because of the basic concept of sovereign rights, there is little that can be done to coerce such states into co-operation in the present system, other than to publicise the fact – which is what the UNSG's list does. When special mandate-holders are prevented from entry, it is common for them to produce reports based on the evidence that they have received. Naturally, the evidence base will be more constrained than it could otherwise have been.

Finally, the state-driven process means that considerations of national policies influence the UPR hearings. However, the broad participation of countries that provide input as peers in the UPR process means that this issue is not a significant challenge to the totality of the UPR, as seen, for example, in the recommendations in the outcome reports. However, the states under review retain the right to work for implementation of the recommendations, as they deem appropriate, or to disregard them. There is no possibility of coercion by the HRC on states, even if human rights violations are obvious, serious and continuous. Granting supranational powers to the HRC has never been seriously contemplated, and will conflict with the popular sovereign paradigm.

4.5. System Integrity: The Human Rights Council *vis-à-vis* the UN System in General

The checks and balances of the HRC lie primarily in its organisational position as a subsidiary organ to the UNGA. It falls to the UNGA to provide revisions of mandate, new directions and review of the HRC. However, the composition of the UNGA is basically the same as the HRC. Even though the HRC formally consists of 47 members, all UN member states that take an interest in human rights discussions can participate in its work as far as they choose to. UN members that are not members of the HRC can still partake in group consultations over draft resolutions – for example those co-ordinated by the EU for its members – as well as speak in the plenary

---

[111] Cooperation with the United Nations, its representatives and mechanisms in the field of human rights, A/HRC/33/19, 16 August 2016. Annual reports can be found on the OHCHR web site.

after the members. There is, in reality, little difference between the HRC and the UNGA in terms of who influences human rights policy. Although the HRC members formally make decisions, this group is so large and broad in terms of regional representation, that it is very difficult to think of issues on which the outcome would be considerably different if voted upon in the UNGA instead of the HRC.

The same can be said specifically in regard to development of norms through adoption of human rights resolutions. Once a paragraph has passed in Geneva, it presents a very weighty argument that it should also pass in New York. Although it does not necessarily have to be accepted in the latter, this is most often the case.

What the HRC does not have is an effective division of powers. The Council itself can be seen as a kind of mini-UNGA. It is too large to be an effective decision-making forum, remaining all but incapable of making precise, sharp and rapid decisions that will lead to effective changes in human rights. Instead, it functions as a testing ground for, and an extended arm of, the UNGA in the area of human rights.

Nor does the HRC answer to any judicial branch that provides meaningful review over its decisions. As has been mentioned, the ICJ does not provide judicial review over UN organisations. Nor is there any global court of human rights that can assess, for example, new rules in regard to established human rights norms, or how norms should apply under specific circumstances. The lack of such an institution is of course not an omission by accident, but a consequence of the states' policy of protecting sovereign rights.

As regards the UPR, there are no checks and balances in the system. There is, for example, no mechanism to ensure that UPR recommendations are implemented by the state under review, other than future UPR rounds themselves. The UPR starts and ends with the states, and there are significant possibilities for states to participate in the UPR while at the same time ignoring important recommendations in the outcome reports.

The alternative to this, that is, an effective enforcement mechanism, is not a possibility. Even in the most developed regional human rights systems, such as those in Europe and Latin America, there is no such mechanism. Insistence on enforcement would alienate so many of the world's states that any pretence of universality would be lost. It would take a paradigm change for this to be instituted.

When the paradigmatic constraints are taken into account, the criticism of the HRC, for the most part, seems misguided, while the overall credibility of the Council stands up well. The broad composition of the HRC, and the inclusive dialogue with NGOs and NHRIs means that the normative outcomes of the HRC procedure generally have high credibility and a high level of universality.

It is important to stress this, because the criticism of the HRC at face value would lead to the conclusion that the credibility of the HRC is low, not high. However, such criticism is in fact often directly parochial, in the sense that its adherents expect all states in the world to fully implement human rights as seen from their own (the critics') perspective. While an NGO is free to work for clearer and legally binding human rights rules, a universal UN organ has to take into account the fact that not all states agree, because the states are the final decision-makers. It is precisely in the arena were all the most important opposing views meet, that universal norms can be agreed upon. If the differences are too great, for example, in regard to China's views on domestic law taking precedence over human rights *vis-à-vis* the EU position, then a clear common position may not materialise. However, this also means that the credibility of the institution is retained also by China.

The criticism of the HRC, therefore, cannot reasonably be directed at the formulation of new norms through resolutions, but rather the failure to clearly protect human rights norms across the globe. In other words, it is the lack of effectiveness that undermines the HRC's credibility. This criticism is, however, to a large part due to wishful thinking about the HRC, and the persistent illusion that it can be what it is not: a supranational organization with wide powers and authority to protect human rights against human rights violators. However, the HRC is not this at all, despite some ambitious formulations to this effect in its mandate. It is rather a common discussion forum that includes so many states that when it *does* agree on a norm, there is reason to consider that norm as universally valid.

Furthermore, the criticism that the HRC lacks effectiveness should, in many cases, be addressed to other institutions. Particularly, there is a lack of action on part of the UNSC in addressing human rights violations, as has been discussed in Chapter 2. Moreover, there is a lack of any global legal institution that can provide legal review over human rights resolutions and adjudicate over issues of possible human rights violations. The latter is due to the basic principles of the Popular Sovereign Paradigm, which are un-likely to change soon.

As with the HRC in general, the broad range of states involved in the UPR is at the expense of effectiveness and efficiency. It cannot be expected under the present system that the UPR will be able to deliver precise and targeted analysis, prioritised recommendations and forceful follow-up.

4.6. Future of the Global Human Rights System

In the international human rights system, the conflicting fundamental prin-ciples of the Popular Sovereign Paradigm are possibly more evident than in any other area. Human rights represent an alternative to traditional state sovereignty, yet it is the sovereign states that determine the content, extent and implementation of human rights. Human rights represent the new con-cept of authority as a symmetrical relationship between the government and the governed, yet states retain the decision-making power. The natural com-promise, as shown in the HRC in particular, is that non-state actors are in-vited to participate and given possibilities for influence, but decision-mak-ing power is ultimately reserved for the states themselves. As a conse-quence, the contest of opposing principles of states' rights and universal and individual rights is most often occurring inside the HRC context, while in the WTO, for example, it is mainly happening outside the organisation.

4.6.1. Paradigmatic Limitations of the Human Rights Council

There are new paradigmatic principles that shape the HRC that are not con-flicting with older concepts. Most evident is the formal equality between the states. This has the combined effect of keeping almost all states in the world inside the organisation, thus making the HRC norm-formation pro-cess highly universal, yet also reducing possibilities for rapid and strong movements, such as radically new norm-formation or strong condemnation of human rights violators, let alone concerted international action against violators.

It should be recognised, however, that the most important function of the HRC – along with the Third Committee of the UNGA – is not to enforce implementation of human rights, but to shape international consensus on human rights norms. These norms develop slowly. It is necessary that all states participate in the process if it is going to lead to universal new norms that are considered legally binding, through subsequent treaty formation or customary international law.

However, there is a limit to how far the norms can develop under the present paradigm. For example, China, the US and many other states have consistently shown that they will not accept international human rights as taking precedence over domestic legislation. This will remain a bridge too far under the present international paradigm. Any significant change would have to come from outside of the institutions of the international system, that is, from changes within the states themselves. This is how the concept of governance by popular will came to a dominant position. It may well be the only way the position of universal human rights can become fully consolidated *vis-à-vis* state sovereignty as well.

4.6.2. Court-Like Entity for Human Rights?

Under another paradigm, a global human rights system could resemble a common domestic system: a court of justice, composed of disinterested experts – may provide effective rulings on actions that violate human rights. The judicial branch would normally also be able to review the laws passed by an assembly of public representatives, as well as the actions of the executive branch. This is far away from the present HRC system, where state representatives struggle to find common ground for passing non-binding resolutions. The UPR similarly depends on state representatives making non-binding recommendations. The court-like entities on the global stage, particularly the complaints mechanisms of the HRC and the treaty bodies, are often closed-door processes, and also pass non-binding rulings and only if the states have accepted to take part.

Realising the boundaries of the possible under the present paradigm is important to sort out the probability of various reform proposals. Most of these stem from a dissatisfaction with the degree of effectiveness of the HRC in taking action against violators and, to a lesser extent, in formulation of new or clearer norms. A smaller Council would arguably be more effective and efficient. However, the experience from the previous human rights Commission shows that this is not necessarily the case. A smaller Council would also be dominated by states' interests.

Bertrand Ramcharan has argued that HRC membership should be expanded to include a group of elected judges or academics, while retaining a majority of government representatives (who should also be judges or academics).[112] Arguably, this would increase the independence of the

---

[112] Ramcharan, 2011, pp. 125-126, see *supra* note 90.

Council, and its ability to take stronger positions *vis-à-vis* violators. However, such a council would easily end up as neither representative nor disinterested. Furthermore, it would alienate the states that are most protective of their sovereign rights, up to the point where they may refuse to co-operate. This again would weaken the notion of a universal norm-giver and - confirmer.

4.6.3. Limiting Membership

Another model, in which the Council would include only representatives of states with a proven and positive human rights record, would also be more apt to present precise recommendations to the UNGA. One proposal is to establish a small group of experts that will screen members on the basis of their human rights record, and clear them as candidates for election to the HRC. Such a group could also be tasked with reviewing periodically the compliance of members of the HRC with their voluntary pledges made upon election to the HRC.[113]

However, such a group would be dismissed by many states – those that would not reach the threshold – as being biased and as an instrument of presumed 'Western hegemony'. It would certainly fail to promote the universality of any new human rights norms that it would formulate.

It would also be a highly difficult practical task to differentiate UN members on the basis of their human rights performance. Some countries, like the DPRK (North Korea), would clearly be disqualified in any credible process. However, it would make little practical difference from the present system, in which DPRK would not have a good chance of being elected. A great number of countries have a mixed record, for example, by scoring low on political human rights and high on economic human rights. Some countries, as mentioned, also disagree on principled grounds with significant parts of the UDHR and ICCPR, for example the right to democratic elections. Furthermore, if ratification of human rights conventions would be the measuring standard, both the US and China would score low.

Limiting the Council to only independent experts would be another way to go about it. Again, such a body would be able to present precise recommendations more than the present set-up. However, it would also reduce the significance of the HRC from an international organisation to a

---

[113] *Ibid.*

high-level panel or even an expert committee. These are plentiful in the UN system, and the addition of another would not make any significant impact.

4.6.4. Merging the Human Rights Council with the Third Committee of the UNGA

A completely different approach would be to merge the HRC with the Third Committee of the UNGA. Many of the functions of the HRC are, at present, in effect preparatory for the UNGA, but with a more extensive programme. The HRC sessions provide a forum for the special mandates and for going more in depth into some themes and countries, which the UNGA has no time for. In principle, a longer session of the UNGA, or regular meetings of the UNGA Third Committee on Human Rights outside of the UNGA session, could serve much the same purpose as the HRC. Merging the HRC with the Third Committee would require some special arrangement for the continuation of the communications procedure and the UPR, but this should not be an impossible obstacle.

The counter-argument against merging the HRC and the UNGA is that there would be no clear benefit to the human rights cause. The norma- tive function is relatively well taken care of in the HRC at the present; at least there is no reason to expect that it would be better taken care of if left solely to the UNGA. The status of the HRC lends higher visibility to human rights than would an expanded Third Committee.

There are limited possibilities, therefore, to change the HRC in a way that would make it more effective and efficient, and at the same time, uni- versally representative. In regard to norm-formation, possibilities for change are few and limited in scope. While NGO participation and national dialogues are well developed in the HRC, there could be a possibility for pushing it somewhat further. States can decide to include NGO participants in their delegations, for example, which is now practiced only very restric- tively. Such participation would not, of course, be akin to direct represen- tation, as states would not allow NGOs to speak for their own policies if contrasting with those of the state. Further inclusion, however, would in- crease the possibilities for public dialogue and awareness, as well as public campaigns to press specific issues.

4.6.5.   Improving the Universal Periodic Review

As regards the UPR, one concrete suggestion is the adoption of mandatory guidelines for national consultations in the UPR process.[114] Such guidelines may improve the level of consultations with stakeholders, although states' practice would doubtlessly still vary greatly.

Another reform proposal is to improve the UPR hearings by allowing the Special Procedures mandate-holders to participate actively in the working groups when states relevant to their mandates are under review.[115] This would aid in the overall analytical approach, and serve to increase the common basis of states' interventions. A further measure in the same direction, may be to task the High Commissioner for Human Rights to report annually to the HRC on the implementation of the UPR recommendations.[116]

A smaller group of disinterested experts tasked with state review would another alternative. This would be similar to the review process under the UN human rights treaty bodies today, the difference being only that the scope of the latter is limited to the specific treaties under which they have their mandate. Those reviews, however, face a problem in not getting the attention they may deserve, either from the states parties (who tend to be late in submitting their reports) or the general public. A general review process of all human rights rules that the reviewed state is obligated to follow, may be more likely to generate greater public interest.

4.6.6.   Enforcement against Human Rights Violators

Human rights implementation can for the most part only progress through the voluntary actions of the states parties. For most human rights violations, the problem is sometimes the lack of knowledge, but very often it is the lack of willingness to act – sometimes by the international community, most often by the responsible government. It is not reasonable to expect that any of the existing mechanisms can take the lead in ensuring actual implementation of human rights in the world, at least not in terms of coercing unwilling governments. Coercion of violators is not possible under the UPR, the treaty bodies, or a general human rights review committee.

Enforcement of human rights compliance by a state beyond 'naming and shaming' is a matter of international intervention into domestic affairs.

---

[114] Kothari, 2013, p. 605, see *supra* note 73.

[115] Ramcharan, 2011, pp. 126–127, see *supra* note 90.

[116] *Ibid.*

Only the UNSC can take legitimate measures to coerce human rights violators, and its formal and actual powers to do so are also highly constrained, as discussed in Chapter 2 above. As mentioned, in only a few instances has it introduced mechanisms for continuous follow-up of human rights violations. An example is its mechanism for children and armed conflict, where the UNSC lists parties involved in use of child soldiers or use of schools for military purposes. Because this is a UNSC procedure, the approach puts pressure on human rights violators to improve their track record in dialogue with the UN in a way that would be difficult for the HRC to achieve.

4.6.7. A Global Human Rights Court

Finally, a natural question is whether there is a possibility for a global human rights court.[117] If an ICC is possible, why not a global human rights court? The existence both of individual complaints mechanisms under the UN treaty bodies and of regional human rights courts in Europe and the Americas can be seen as evidence of this possibility.

Such a court may indeed be possible under the Popular Sovereign Paradigm, but it would not be universally accepted. Furthermore, states would be more reluctant to join it than they have been to join the ICC. The great powers of the world, including the US, China and Russia, will certainly not join such a court, which would limit its universal scope from the outset. Further, the European and Latin-American states that helped to achieve the establishment of the ICC will not necessarily accept a global human rights court. These states already have regional courts that are working well. It is unlikely that other states that do not at present have such regional mechanisms will participate in a strong global mechanism.

Moreover, human rights law is much more extensive than international criminal law. The Statute of the ICC limits its jurisdiction to four categories of crimes primarily connected with situations of armed conflict or attacks against the civilian population, while human rights affect virtually all aspects of governance, in all situations.

Finally, global human rights law is less clearly delimited and defined than international criminal law. Uncertainty about precise rules means a

---

[117] Geir Ulfsten, "Do We Need a World Court of Human Rights?", in Ola Engdahl and Pål Wrange (eds.), *Law at War: The Law as it Was and the Law as it Should Be*, Martinus Nijhoff Publishers, 2008.

perceived risk of a large number of many potential cases, with loss of time and resources and uncertain outcomes for the states concerned.

For these reasons, while a global human rights court is not impossible under the present system, it is unlikely to materialise. From the states' perspective, the benefits are too unclear, and the risks too great.

5

International Humanitarian Law

5.1. Introduction

The last area of the international system to be discussed in this book is international humanitarian law. This area of law regulates conduct in armed conflicts. It is distinct from the law that regulates the right to war (*jus ad bello*). As of 2017, the ICRC lists 75 treaties in its international humanitarian law database.[1] The main treaty-based rules are to be found in the four Geneva Conventions of 1949, including their two first APs of 1977, and the Hague Conventions of 1907 and 1899. Customary international law is also significant. The ICRC study of customary international humanitarian law rules, published in 2005, holds a position of authority. Finally, the development of international criminal law is significant both as consequence and antecedent of evolving international humanitarian law norms.

International humanitarian law is important to any discussion of the international system, for three reasons. First, it is a major part of the body of international rules that regulates the international order. Second, international humanitarian law rules are literally a matter of life and death, as they regulate the conduct in armed conflicts and aim to reduce human suffering in such situations. Third and finally, the evolution of international humanitarian law principles clearly shows a gradually increased emphasis on individual rights and internal armed conflicts, which challenges the traditional dominance of the sovereign states' rights.

International humanitarian law is a branch of international law that was developed relatively early, and certainly precedes modern human rights law. The 1949 Geneva Conventions built upon, expanded, and replaced older treaties. The original Geneva Convention was agreed upon in 1864, then revised and expanded in 1906 and 1929. While the 1864 Convention was concerned with the sick and wounded, the second (1906) concerned armed forces in maritime warfare, and the third (1929) prisoners of war.

---

[1]   ICRC, "IHL Database", available on the ICRC web site.

The latter was the result of a process that followed from the experiences of World War I.[2]

The four 1949 Geneva Conventions represented the then international community's response to what was seen as the exposed shortcomings of international humanitarian law during World War II.[3] The 1949 Conventions payed particular attention to protection of civilians, as compared with the previous conventions, which was the topic of the new and fourth Geneva Convention at the time.

Finally, the two first APs of 1977 focus on the victims of armed conflict. Particularly indicative of the changing realities and perceptions of wars is AP II, which applies specifically to *internal* armed conflicts, thus highlighting a gradual shift from sole focus on international wars to inclusion of rules also for non-international wars. Clearly, this development also speaks to the changing principles in the international system, in particular that of sovereignty *vis-à-vis* the rights of individuals. It is also revealing that AP II (internal conflicts) is far less detailed than AP I. The former has 15 substantive rules, while the latter has more than 80.[4]

In general, the changing Geneva Conventions have evolved to include ever larger groups of persons as bearers of rights or as objects requiring protection. It is a common opinion that this is a consequence of the changing realities of war. The argument is that wars in the modern era have increasingly been at the expense of civilians, in contrast to wars causing deaths mainly of professional soldiers. This is one major difference between World War I and World War II. In recent years, some 90% of victims of armed conflict are reported to be civilians.[5]

However, it is also significant that this change in warfare in many ways go much further back in history than World War II. Cassese points out that already after the French Revolution in 1789, whole citizenries were mobilized for the purpose of warfare, marking a change from the past.[6] As

---

2   Wade Mansell and Karen Openshaw, "The History and Status of the Geneva Conventions", in Sarah Perrigo and Jim Whitman (eds.), *The Geneva Conventions under Assault*, Pluto Press, London, 2010, p. 18.

3   *Ibid.*

4   Jean-Marie Henckaerts and Louise Doswald-Beck, *Customary International Humanitarian Law, Volume I: Rules*, Cambridge University Press, Cambridge, 2005, p. xxxv.

5   Nils Meltzer, "Bolstering the Protection of Civilians in armed Conflict", in Cassese (ed.), 2012, pp. 509, see *supra* note 13 in Chapter 2.

6   Cassese, 2005, p. 400, see *supra* note 4 of Chapter 1.

regards consequences of wars for civilians, there is no reason to start in 1789. Estimates of the civilian death toll caused by the Mongol campaigns under Genghis Khan are disputed and unclear, but unvaryingly run into millions. The effect of wars in Europe on civilians throughout history cannot be doubted either, from the loss of livelihood and death to hunger in the Thirty Years' War, to slave raids by Vikings in England in the tenth century, or by North African pirates in the Mediterranean in the sixteenth century. In other words, the profound effects of war on civilians is not new. Something else must have changed in order for the system of international law to focus more on civilians. Otherwise, this development would have happened much sooner.

Cassese argues further that the framework for international humanitarian law, which was set mainly with the seventeenth century wars between states in mind, has not changed in form even as new considerations have been placed into it. This goes a long way to explain why international humanitarian law conventions remain relatively similar in form, prioritizing states' obligations and rights, but also that new groups have progressively been included in the conventions. Combat privilege, for example, has been extended historically, from regular armies to irregular soldiers and militia (1907), organized resistance movements (1949) and certain national liberation movements representing territorial entities not yet having attained statehood (1977). Extension to non-state belligerents more broadly, however, has not so far been adopted by states.[7]

In terms of victims, the focus on sick and wounded from 1864 has been expanded to include prisoners of war (1929), civilians as protected persons (1949), and specific groups of civilians such as women and children (1977). Finally, the ICC Statute (1998) emphasises the rights of reparations for victims.

However, international humanitarian law remains state-driven and state-centred. Non-state groups have few or unclear obligations and privileges under international humanitarian law. This arguably represents a major challenge in today's international system, considering that there is still a high number of internal armed conflicts, while the frequency of international armed conflicts has dropped.

Another clear challenge in international humanitarian law is that its applicability in armed conflicts has evolved only slowly, while the reality

---

[7] Meltzer, 2012, pp. 515–516, see *supra* note 5.

of armed conflicts has developed more rapidly. There is, for example, no clarity about the applicability of international humanitarian law in internal armed conflicts such as drug wars in Mexico, Colombia and the Brazilian favelas; counter-piracy operations in the Gulf of Aden, and drone attacks by the US as part of its international anti-terrorism campaign.[8]

5.2. Development of International Humanitarian Law Rules: State Sovereignty *v.* Individual Rights

Cassese argues that 'new law' began in earnest with the 1949 Geneva Conventions, which focuses more on victims and less on states than the 'old law' tradition.[9] However, whether the starting point should be seen as 1949, 1945, or even earlier can be debated. Considering the long legacy of international humanitarian law, it is not self-evident that the breaking point should be placed in the 1940s. Regardless, it seems clear that (1) there has been a significant development away from solely focussing on states in international law and more toward individuals; (2) this development has picked up pace after World War II and, in subsequent decades, moved international humanitarian law far beyond the expectations of the previous generations. Furthermore, much of the present body of international humanitarian law has found its form from 1945 onwards, which is a good reason to use this as the starting point.

In the phase immediately following World War II, there were two processes that would shape the future of international humanitarian law. The first was the proceedings under the Military Tribunals set up to try war criminals in Germany and Japan in 1945. The second was the negotiations leading to the agreement on the four Geneva Conventions in 1949. In the assessment of the developing international humanitarian law rules and their relation with the Popular Sovereign Paradigm, it is arguably more relevant to focus on the latter. Certainly, both processes marked a shift in international humanitarian law toward the protection of victims, instead of the traditional state-centred legal tradition.[10] However, the Tribunals differ from the Geneva Conventions in that they were set up by the victorious powers of World War II and tried war criminals from the losing powers. This does

---

[8]   *Ibid.*, p. 510.

[9]   Cassese, 2005, p. 404, see *supra* note 4 of Chapter 1.

[10] Mansell and Openshaw, 2010, pp. 23–24, see *supra* note 2.

not necessarily imply that the Tribunals themselves were unfairly biased and – as such – transitional phenomena in legal history. In fact, the general view is that the processes did respect the principles of fairness.[11] However, the test of whether or not the Tribunals were biased and transitional phenomena lies primarily in the subsequent legal history, as shown in the practice and statements of the wider international community. In this sense, the negotiations over the Geneva Conventions in 1949 are a significant early indicator of the quality of the jurisprudence that came out of the Tribunal proceedings.

5.2.1. The 1949 Geneva Conventions

The 1949 Geneva Conventions were negotiated by states, and built upon drafts prepared by legal experts of the ICRC. These, again, were to a large extent based on the existing Geneva Conventions of 1929 (for the sick and wounded and prisoners of war) and the Hague Convention of 1907 (for the adaptation of Maritime Warfare of the Principles of the Geneva Convention of 6 July 1906).[12]

The 1949 Geneva Convention IV for the protection of civilians in armed conflict was fundamentally new. It built upon the 'Tokyo Draft', from the ICRC conference in Tokyo in 1934, which was revised by the ICRC in London in 1938. The Swiss government had called for a diplomatic conference in 1940, in order to negotiate the new convention, but had been prevented from doing so by the outbreak of World War II.[13] The fact that the process towards a convention for the protection of civilians in war began before the war is one reason why the Popular Sovereign Paradigm can be seen as finding its preliminary form already before World War II.

---

[11] Wolfgang Kaleck, *Double Standards: International Criminal Law and the West*, Torkel Opsahl Academic EPublisher, Brussels, 2015, p. 112 (http://www.legal-tools.org/doc/971c3c/).

[12] Federal Political Department of Switzerland, *Final Record of the Diplomatic Conference Convened by the Swiss Federal Council for the Establishment of international Conventions for the Protection of War Victims and Held at Geneva From April 21st to August 12th, 1949*, vol. I, Bern, 1949 ('Final Record for Geneva Conventions'). The preparatory works of the 1949 Conventions and 1977 Additional Protocols – as well as of the 1948 Genocide Convention – are available in the International Legal Instruments Collection of the Legal Tools Database.

[13] Letter from Swiss Federal Political Department to the states parties to the Geneva Conventions, 11 May 1948, in Final Records for Geneva Conventions, 1949, see *supra* note 12, p. 147.

We cannot know, of course, whether Geneva Convention IV would have been achieved were it not for the tragic events leading up to 1945.

The process was taken up again after World War II with renewed vigour and momentum, in light of the inhuman excesses during the war. A conference of government experts, convened by the ICRC, took place in Geneva in April 1947 to discuss the draft conventions.[14] The drafts were then discussed and amended at the seventeenth ICRC Conference in Stockholm in August 1948. These drafts formed the basis for the diplomatic conference in Geneva the following year.

Fifty-eight states sent delegates to the 1949 Conference.[15] In addition, eight persons participated in the conference as experts, of which five were from the ICRC and a further three represented the League of Red Cross Societies. Finally, five governments and seven international organisations participated as observers to the conference.[16] The Final Act of the Conference and the four Conventions were signed by all 58 state delegates, and a further four governments (Paraguay, the Philippines, Poland and Yugoslavia).[17]

In other words, there was as broad representation by states as would have been possible in 1949. However, the participation of independent experts and non-state organisations was limited to the ICRC and Red Cross societies alone. The general level of representation, therefore, was high only in terms of state participation. Nor were there general consultations with the affected parties other than among and within the states and the ICRC and Red Cross movement. The result is that the Conventions do pro-

---

[14]   *Ibid.*

[15]   Lists of delegates, experts and observers in Final Record for Geneva Conventions, 1949, pp. 158–172, see *supra* note 12. The delegates were from Afghanistan, Albania, Argentine, Australia, Austria, Belgium, Belarus, Bolivia, Brazil, Bulgaria, Burma, Canada, Chile, China (Kuomintang), Colombia, Costa Rica, Cuba, Czechoslovakia, Denmark, Ecuador, Egypt, El Salvador, Ethiopia, Finland, France, Greece, Guatemala, Holy See, Hungary, India, Iran, Ireland, Israel, Italy, Lebanon, Liechtenstein, Luxemburg, Mexico, Monaco, Netherlands, New Zealand, Norway, Pakistan, Peru, Portugal, Romania, Spain, Sweden, Switzerland, Syria, Thailand, Turkey, Ukraine, the USSR, the UK, the US, Uruguay and Venezuela.

[16]   Observers: Dominican Republic, Japan, Poland, San Marino, Yugoslavia, the UN, International Labour Organisation, World Health Organisation, International Refugees Organisation, International Telecommunications Union, Universal Postal Union, and Head Office of International Railway Transport.

[17]   Final Record for Geneva Conventions, 1949, pp. 173–178, see *supra* note 12.

---

vide rules that were then, and continue to be, regarded as fair from the perspective of states, but not necessarily from the perspective of non-state actors.

Perhaps the most glaring gap in the 1949 Geneva Conventions is their strong emphasis on international conflicts between states, and a similar lack of focus on internal armed conflicts and non-state armed groups. Internal armed conflicts are addressed in common Article 3 of the Conventions, which sets up a general obligation of humane treatment, and prohibits only a few specific acts, such as murder, torture, hostage-taking, humiliating and degrading treatment, and summary sentencing.

Not until AP II to the 1949 Geneva Conventions in 1977 would there be a treaty-based international humanitarian law rule-set applicable to internal armed conflicts. However, as will be discussed, this Protocol also falls short for such conflicts, in particular with respect to the status, privileges and obligations of non-states parties to a conflict. For example, rebels lack combatant status, which would grant immunity from certain acts during armed conflict and status as prisoner of war upon capture by enemy forces.[18] Furthermore, rebels who *de facto* control territory are not clearly obliged to follow international humanitarian law rules as are governments.[19]

In the case of Gaza in 2017, for example, Hamas has *de facto* control over the territory from the inside and exercises *de facto* government functions. Meanwhile, Israel and Egypt exercise all but full control over the boundaries by land, sea and aerospace, including all movement of goods and people in and out of Gaza. From an international humanitarian law perspective most states therefore regard Gaza as occupied (by Israel), even though it is clearly evident that this is a situation of mixed authority and control. Because of the state-centred focus of international humanitarian law, including the Geneva Conventions, the present rule-set is inadequate to define precisely, let alone give clear direction to, the conduct in armed conflicts such as the one in Gaza.

The representative background of the framers of the Geneva Conventions has probably significantly influenced their scope. Under the Popular Sovereign Paradigm, states can be expected to support international law

---

[18] Sandesh Sivakumaran, "How to Improve upon the Faulty Legal Regime of Internal Armed Conflicts", in Cassese (ed.), 2012, pp. 525, see *supra* note 13 in Chapter 2.

[19] *Ibid.*

that protects individuals, in particular states that conduct extensive political consultations with its own citizens. But states do not represent rebel groups, and can hardly be expected to represent their perspectives on international law. Only states that do not harbour fear of internal rebellion can reasonably be expected to consider international law accommodation of significant rights to non-governmental armed groups. With no place at the table, even in the consultations process, non-state armed groups are unlikely to be adequately considered in the formation of international humanitarian law, even if they have considerable influence over the conduct of hostilities.

The process leading to the 1949 Geneva Conventions was based on firm ground in terms of facts, evidence and analysis. The process marked the temporary culmination of a process that had evolved over almost a century, from the process leading to agreement on the first Geneva Convention in 1864, to a number of international humanitarian law conventions. The experience of World War II and the evidence presented before the International Military Tribunals are significant components in the process leading up to 1949. The draft conventions had been discussed for over a decade (the Tokyo Draft was formulated in 1934), although the process was catastrophically interrupted by World War II.

The rules regarding sanctions for breaches of the Geneva Conventions are particularly vague and weak, as can be expected of states wary of sovereignty issues. In essence, they leave it to the states parties (called High Contracting Parties in the Geneva Conventions) and the parties to a given armed conflict to work out how they choose to execute the contents of the Conventions. While the states parties are required in general to carry out sanctions toward anyone who breaks the convention and to pursue litigation in their domestic legal systems in such cases, the provisions are general. There is no follow-up or even monitoring mechanism that does no rely on the states parties themselves. Should there be a dispute over an alleged violation of the Conventions, it is for the involved parties to decide on a mechanism of inquiry or designation of an umpire to establish the facts. In effect, this means that states parties may get away with breaches, should they choose to simply ignore the Conventions.[20]

---

[20] The rules are set out in the common articles under "Execution of the Convention", in the case of Convention (IV) Relative to the Protection of Civilian Persons in Time of War, Articles 146–149 (http://www.legal-tools.org/doc/d5e260/).

A domestic legal system would have a firm legal follow-up mechanism in place, where courts of justice would adjudicate over disputes and decide on sanctions. In the case of international humanitarian law, such mechanisms have for the most part either been absent, or strongly restricted by sovereign states. Before the establishment of the ICC in 2002, the only global court-like institutions mandated to deal with international humanitarian law violations were the Permanent Court of Arbitration and the ICJ. Both require consent from the parties to the conflict for jurisdiction to be activated. The ICJ also requires that the parties are states, which exclude all non-state groups from being able to refer a case to the Court.

Furthermore – and despite the focus on victims of war in the Geneva Conventions – there is no global legal institution to which complaints of abuse can be petitioned by individuals. Nor has there been, before the ICC, a global institution able to prosecute individual perpetrators responsible for war crimes or to decide on compensation for the victims. In other words, the implementation of the 1949 Geneva Conventions was left completely in the hands of sovereign states. No institution was set up to provide any checks on the practice of the states, certainly not with the powers to decide on sanctions and not even to monitor their compliance. Not until the establishment war crimes tribunals in the 1990s (in relation to the conflicts in Rwanda and the former Yugoslavia) did this system begin to change.

In conclusion, the 1949 Geneva Conventions represented a significant achievement in the development of international humanitarian law, and thus the international system as a whole. However, a state-centred process resulted in rules that largely ignored the significance of non-state actors and internal conflicts. A general lack of consultations outside of the states and the ICRC and Red Cross movement left no room for actors other than states to participate in shaping or reformulating the rules. Finally, the sovereign state tradition is inherent also in the limited stipulations regarding implementation and execution of the Conventions. There was no mechanism outside of the states themselves, let alone a mandate to decide on facts, conflicting interpretations, or sanctions in the event of breaches of the Conventions.

5.2.2. The 1977 Additional Protocols

The process leading to agreement on the two first Protocols additional to the Geneva Conventions was also primarily state-driven, but it included a large number of non-state actors. As is evident from the official records of the process, NGOs played an important role in lobbying for effective language in the Protocols. They had achieved a high level of NGO co-ordination, in order to improve their prospective influence. Several memoranda were submitted by NGOs as well as governments and various expert groups to the conference, and circulated to the delegates.

One of the memoranda provided detailed suggestions for stronger language in the draft protocols, and was co-signed by 45 NGOs. Among them were Amnesty International, International Confederation of Free Trade Unions, International Commission of Jurists, International Alliance of Women, International Federation for Human Rights, International Federation of Free Journalists, and various veterans' organisations and faith-based coalitions representing Christians, Muslims and Jews.[21] Many of these organisations were also represented in the process as observers, either in their own capacity or as members of the Working Group for Development of Humanitarian Law.

The level of consultations with interested parties outside of the states, was thus considerable – much higher than in 1949. Doubtlessly, this is one reason why the Protocols succeeded to enshrine rules for the protection of individuals and vulnerable groups in armed conflict to a greater extent than had previously been achieved.

The level of representation on the state level was also higher. As many as 126 states were represented at the first session in 1974, 121 states at the second in 1975, 106 in the third in 1976, and 109 in the fourth and final session in 1977.[22] Furthermore, the UNGA adopted 23 resolutions in the period 1968–1975 relating to human rights during times of armed conflict, showing that the consultations among states went well beyond the process in Geneva and the years 1974–1977.[23]

---

[21] "Memorandum by non-Governmental Organizations on the two draft Protocols to the Geneva Conventions, 1949 – Supplementary to Memorandum of 31 December 1973, 27 April 1976", in Federal Political Department of Switzerland, *Official Records of the Diplomatic Conference of the Reaffirmation and Development of International Humanitarian Law Applicable in Armed Conflicts, Geneva (1974–1977)*, vol. IV, Bern, 1978, pp. 207–218 ('Memorandum by NGO'), see *supra* note 12.

[22] Federal Political Department of Switzerland, *Official Records of the Diplomatic Conference, Geneva (1974–1977)*, vol. I, Bern: 1978, pp. 4–7, see *supra* note 12.

[23] For a list, see *ibid.*, pp. 3–4.

Significantly, the conference also invited national liberation organisations to participate in the deliberations. Eleven such organisations were invited to participate, including the African National Congress, Palestine Liberation Organization, and Zimbabwe African National Union.

Finally, and similar to the 1949 process, a number of inter-governmental and international organisations participated as observers. The ICRC participated in an expert capacity, having also drafted the two APs.[24]

Several limitations in terms of representation and consultation in the 1949 process were therefore much improved in 1977. The resulting Protocols represented a new and unprecedented step in the widening of international humanitarian law to include non-state actors, in particular the rights of individuals as actual or potential victims of armed conflict. However, states did have the final say, remaining the constituting powers of the international system. The most far-reaching proposals from non-state actors, therefore, were not included in the final document. For example, the NGO-coalition had proposed an explicit ban on incendiary weapons and land mines, which were not reflected in the Protocols.[25]

In contrast to the 1949 Conventions, the 1977 process also resulted in a mechanism for implementation, although this was far from a full-fledged court of justice which would have been natural in a domestic system of justice. An international Fact-Finding Commission was established through Article 90 of AP I.[26] This Commission was intended to enquire into allegations of grave breaches of the Geneva Conventions or AP I. The Commission also has the mandate to enquire into other situations, when requested by a party to the conflict. However, the Commission cannot work unless consent is also granted from the other parties to the conflict.

State acceptance of the competence of the Commission requires a declaration by that state to the Swiss government, the depository of the Conventions. As of January 2017, 76 states have made such declarations.[27] Most are small or medium powers and from Europe or Latin-America.

---

[24] *Ibid.*, pp. 7–8.

[25] Memorandum by NGO, p. 209, see *supra* note 21.

[26] Protocol Additional to the Geneva Conventions of 12 August 1949, and relating to the Protection of Victims of International Armed Conflicts, 8 June 1977, Article 90.

[27] International Humanitarian Fact-Finding Commission, "The IHFFC in a few words" ('IHFFC Article'), available on the Commission's web site.

There are some notable exceptions, such as Russia, Democratic Republic of Congo, United Arab Emirates and Tajikistan.[28] The Commission was officially constituted in 1991, when the required number of 20 state declarations was reached.

The Commission has yet to be called upon.[29] One reason for this is the requirement for state consent for it to be able to carry out its functions. Its potential impact is also limited by the confidentiality of its proceedings and conclusions. Only if the parties consent, could it make its conclusions public. As a consequence, the actual power of the Commission to enforce compliance of states to the rules is severely curtailed. It cannot be seen as a supranational entity in the sense of having significant powers independent of the sovereign states.

As for AP II, there is no such implementation mechanism at all. This Protocol represented a significant leap forward in setting up rules for internal conflicts. Before 1977, the only treaty law applicable to such conflicts was common Article 3 of the 1949 Geneva Conventions, which was, as we have seen, severely limited. At the same time, AP II fell short of the original ambitions. Out of 47 articles proposed by the ICRC, only 28 were adopted.[30] Among those dropped were articles regarding methods and means of warfare, instead regulated through the general principles of Article 4 of AP II. Furthermore, the applicability of AP II, as defined by Article 1, is narrower than that of common Article 3. The latter deal with all non-international conflicts, while the former specifies additional provisions, such as that the non-governmental armed groups must be under responsible command and exercise a degree of territorial control.

The original ICRC draft restricted the scope of application of AP II less. It did contain a phrase regarding responsible command, but not in regard to the degree of territorial control.[31] The most revealing deletion from the draft, however, was the proposed Article 5, which would have placed

---

[28]   List of ratifications and signatories available from the ICRC, "Treaties, States Parties and Commentaries", available on the ICRC web site.

[29]   IHFFC Article, see *supra* note 27.

[30]   Protocol Additional to the Geneva Conventions of 12 August 1949, and relating to the Protection of Victims of Non-International Armed Conflicts, 8 June 1977 (http://www.legal-tools.org/doc/fd14c4/).

[31]   ICRC, *Draft Additional Protocols to the Geneva Conventions of August 12, 1949: Commentary*, Geneva, 1973, p. 132 (http://www.legal-tools.org/doc/a1b7c6/).

---

equal rights and duties on all parties to internal conflict. The concern was that without such a provision, the insurgent parties would only be lightly bound by the Protocol.[32] This concern was correct. However, states' fears in regard to sovereignty overrode the concern. In 1977, as today, most states were not ready to admit rights to insurgents on a general basis.

5.2.3. How Universal are the Geneva Conventions and Protocols?

The four 1949 Conventions have been ratified by 195 states, which exceeds the number of members of the UN and includes all the great powers.[33] There are relatively few reservations to the Conventions. The bulk of these stem from former and present communist states that reserved themselves from the specific provision, common to the four Conventions, that enables the state detaining, for example, prisoners of war to designate a 'protecting power' (state or humanitarian organisation) to monitor the compliance of the detaining state with the Geneva Conventions. Communist states argued, not without merit, that this could be abused by the detaining state in order to designate a 'puppet' as a protecting power.[34] The communist states therefore insisted that designation of a protecting power cannot be made without the consent of the state of which the detained or protected persons are nationals.

Other significant reservations concern Article 68(2) of Geneva Convention III about the death penalty, where among others the US and Pakistan, among others, have made reservations. Some other countries made reservations that are not shared by any other high contracting party.

At any rate, the universal acceptance of the four Geneva Conventions leaves most discussions about the binding nature of the Conventions unnecessary, except the two points mentioned, regarding the death penalty and the protecting powers. There are provisions in the Conventions regarding withdrawal from the treaties, however. If a state attempted to withdraw,

---

[32] *Ibid.*, p. 135.

[33] ICRC, "Lists of the ratifications", available on the ICRC web site. The ICRC also considers Niue to be covered by the conventions, even though it has not specifically ratified them. This is the reason why the number of states parties is often listed as 196 instead of 195.

[34] ICRC, *Commentary to I Geneva Convention*, ICRC, Geneva, 2016, Article 10 (http://www.legal-tools.org/doc/587f06/).

there would be a compelling case for considering the rules of the Conventions as customary international law – even to the level of *jus cogens* for some provisions.[35]

The ratifications of the first two APs have also reached a very high number, but not universal. AP I has been acceded to by 174 states, while AP II stands at 168. In regard to AP I, notable absentees include the US, Israel, Iran, Pakistan, India, Indonesia and Turkey. In regard to AP II, the list also includes the DPRK, Angola, Vietnam, Iraq, Syria and Mexico. However, China, Russia, all European states, all South American states and all African states except Angola, Somalia and Eritrea have ratified both APs.[36]

This means that the degree to which the rules of the APs are universally binding is more difficult to assess than for the Conventions. One could argue that the non-ratification by the US, India and Indonesia accounts for a such large part of the world's population that there can at least not be any *a priori* strong conclusions about the universal legal or ethical applicability of the rules, before other factors, including state practice, are taken into account.

There is a significant number of reservations to the APs. Most of these reservations apply to AP I, which is also more detailed and widely ratified than AP II. In total, around 150 unilateral declarations have been made by states in regard to the signing or ratification of the two APs. It can be argued that around 30 of these constitute actual reservations.[37] The reason for the imprecise figure is that several of the declarations are vaguely or ambiguously worded.[38] In almost all the cases, the declarations do not reserve against the main content of specific articles, but provide additional conditions of a limited nature.[39] The most significant challenge for the APs, therefore, is that many states have not ratified, including some great powers.

---

[35] Theodor Meron, "The Geneva Conventions as Customary Law", in *The American Journal of International Law*, 1987, vol. 81, no. 23, p. 50.

[36] For Europe, one exception is Monaco.

[37] Julie Gaudreau, "The reservations to the Protocols additional to the Geneva Conventions for the protection of war victims", in *International Review of the Red Cross*, 2003, vol. 85, no. 849, pp. 26–27.

[38] *Ibid.*

[39] *Ibid.*

As regards whether the rules of the APs should be seen as customary international law, the most comprehensive study to date is the above-mentioned 2005 ICRC publication, mapping customary rules applicable in international and non-international conflicts.[40] The study is widely cited, and has become a main source of reference for customary international humanitarian law. However, its methods and conclusions are not universally accepted. Significantly, the US has expressed strong criticism of both the methodology and conclusions of the study.[41]

As a comprehensive study of international humanitarian law rules and state practice on a global scale, it is of course possible to find arguments that the ICRC study is insufficient as a basis for drawing strong conclusions, with the US criticism as one example. More broadly, the lack of consensus shows a persistent limitation of the international system: there is no willingness among states to agree on a comprehensive legal system for armed conflicts, nor a world court that can clarify the customary rules. Therefore, the developing analysis of international humanitarian law – necessary in order to achieve greater clarity – falls to a great extent to legal scholars. On some issues, practice by international tribunals is also a significant guide, although it does not set formal and binding legal precedents.

In conclusion, international humanitarian law is a coin with two sides. On the one side, there *are* international humanitarian law rules in existence that are universally binding on states. The international system is not a lawless society in which states are free to do as they please. A state cannot invade another state and carry out a mass murder of civilians without facing legal repercussions for violating well-known and universally accepted laws. On the other side, the rule-set is deliberately ambiguous in many aspects, and is rudimentary or silent in others. In general, the more a rule may infringe on traditional sovereign rights, the more likely it is less clear or non-existent. International humanitarian law rules for non-international conflict are particularly rudimentary or lacking, both in treaty law and customary law.[42]

---

[40] Henckaerts and Doswald-Beck, 2005, see *supra* note 4.

[41] John B. Bellinger III and William J. Haynes II, "A US government response to the International Committee of the Red Cross study Customary International Humanitarian Law", in *International Review of the Red Cross*, 2007, vol. 89, no. 866.

[42] On the rudimentary rules in APII, see Jean-Marie Henckaerts, "Study on customary international humanitarian law: A contribution to the understanding and respect for the rule of law in armed conflict", in *International Review of the Red Cross*, 2005, vol. 87, no. 857, p. 189.

Sovereign states being the decision-makers and sources of authority in the international system is not likely to change in the foreseeable future. It is fundamental to the Popular Sovereign Paradigm. Non-state groups will continue to have few or no privileges in the international system, unless they reach a level of power and influence that they can be elevated to statehood. An example is the Sudanese People's Liberation Army/Movement and the formation of South Sudan as a state. Another, though less clear, is the Palestinian Liberation Organization and the formation of the Palestinian state, although this has yet to be universally recognized. Groups that, for different reasons, do not reach this threshold, like Hamas/Gaza, will remain isolated in the international system. While individual groups can change status and join the state community, there is no possibility for a systemic change that would allow non-state actors to participate and become decision-makers alongside states in general. The principle of equality in the international system is tied to the states only, and does not extend further.

5.2.4. The International Criminal Court

Other international humanitarian law conventions than those mentioned above mostly have a more specific focus, as they typically aim to regulate specific methods or means of warfare. Examples include the manufacture, stockpiling and use of chemical weapons, cluster munitions, land mines, and proliferation of nuclear weapons. Others aim to regulate specific areas, such as protection of cultural property or criminal repression.[43]

The most ambitious of these legal instruments is the Rome Statute of 1998, which set up the ICC. This can be seen as the extension of more limited international humanitarian law processes in the 1990s, where local or regional international tribunals were set up to provide justice in regard to crimes perpetrated during armed conflicts. The International Criminal Tribunals for Rwanda and for the former Yugoslavia were both historic achievements and precursors for the general and permanent ICC.

The ICTY and ICTR have made decisions and passed judgements that have taken international humanitarian law forward in terms of increased precision and identification of new or emerging rules. As has been discussed above, states have remained reluctant to agree on precise and far-reaching treaty law in many areas of international humanitarian law, including specific sanctions in the event of international crimes. Therefore, the

---

[43] For a list of international humanitarian law conventions, see *supra* note 1.

practice of the Tribunals has been highly significant in filling in gaps in international humanitarian treaty law through interpretation and clarification of customary norms. For example, the ICTY's initial judgement and appeals judgement in the *Furundžija* case are considered to have established the definition of rape as crime against humanity.[44] The 1990s tribunals were significant milestones in the development of international humanitarian law.

The Tribunals were however, limited to the specific cases of Rwanda and the former Yugoslavia. In specific cases of armed conflict, a convergence of interests of the great powers, including in the UNSC, is often possible. However, the ICC is a general project that aims at universality. While resembling the Tribunals, its level of ambition and potential significance goes much greater. Furthermore, it represents a definitive leap in terms of implementation of international humanitarian law. As mentioned, the implementation of the Geneva Conventions has been left almost entirely to the states themselves, with the exception of the toothless international Fact-Finding Commission under AP I. By contrast, the ICC is a full-fledged international court of justice.

The ICC was set up based on its Statute which was adopted in Rome in 1998 and entered into force in 2002 when the first 60 states had acceded. The material jurisdiction of the ICC ranges over four categories of crimes, specifically genocide, crimes against humanity, war crimes, and the crime of aggression.[45]

A draft statute was prepared by the International Law Commission. Upon request by the UNGA, the Commission presented a draft in 1994, after some time of work.[46] This draft attracted numerous comments and criticisms both from states and NGOs generated during meetings under the UNGA in 1996, 1997 and 1998. This process led to a draft consolidated text that formed the basis for the 1998 Rome negotiations, which left open several important and contested issues.[47]

---

[44] Cassese, 2005, p. 193, see *supra* note 4 of Chapter 1.

[45] Rome Statute of the International Criminal Court, Articles 5-8 ('Rome Statute') (http://www.legal-tools.org/doc/7b9af9/).

[46] David Wippman, "The International Criminal Court", in Christian Reus-Smit (ed.), *The Politics of International Law*, Cambridge University Press, Cambridge, 2004, p. 151.

[47] *Ibid.*, pp. 151–152.

At the opening of the Rome conference, therefore, there was no certainty about the final outcome, including how strong and independent the new court could become. For example, the US reportedly believed at the time that it could achieve a text that it might accept and even ratify. In the end, however, the US voted against the Rome Statute, alongside China, Iraq, Israel, Libya, Qatar and Yemen.[48]

It is significant that the Rome Statute was opposed by the US and China, and, to some extent, also Russia and India.[49] It shows that the ICC is not a product of self-interested great power calculations. On the contrary, its creation was an event that occurred, to a large extent, in spite of those interests. This renders the so-called 'realist' tradition of international relations at a loss in explaining the ICC, because there is no way it can be seen as an instrument of power projection by the world's most powerful states.[50]

Those entities that pressed the hardest for a strong and independent ICC were the NGOs. Around 300 NGOs were present in Rome for the negotiations and engaged actively in lobbying the state delegates.[51] These served to create sufficient pressure on the negotiating states to ensure an outcome in line with their objectives.[52] However, the NGOs also found sympathetic ears among a significant number of states, without which no amount of NGO advocacy would have been able to produce results. These states were primarily, but not exclusively, European.[53] Germany played a particularly important role on the side of a strong, universal and independent court.[54]

Significant in this regard are the rules of the Rome Statute regarding the opening of investigations. The P5 states originally all supported the position of having the UNSC as the exclusive trigger mechanism for the ICC.

---

[48] *Ibid.*, p. 152.

[49] *Ibid.*

[50] *Ibid.*

[51] NGO observers regulated under Rule 63 of the Rules of Procedure, in United Nations Diplomatic Conference of Plenipotentiaries on the Establishment of an International Criminal Court, Rome, 15 June – 1 7 July 1998, Official Records, Volume II: Summary Records of the Plenary Meetings and of the Meetings of the Committee of the Whole, A/CONF.183/6, p. 60 (http://www.legal-tools.org/doc/253396/).

[52] Wippmann, 2004, p. 164, see *supra* note 46.

[53] *Ibid.*, p. 160. Senegal was one of the non-European states in this group.

[54] *Ibid.*, pp. 160–161.

This position was heavily criticised by many other states, including India.[55] The P5 consensus included France and the UK, which tended to see the process though the presumption of having great power interests. However, during the negotiations, the UK defected from this position. This served to place even greater pressure on France, which also followed suit.[56] In the end, the text of the Statute deviated far from the original P5 position. While there is in the Statute a provision for the UNSC to refer a situation to the ICC, situations can also be referred by states parties to the Statute. In addition, the ICC Prosecutor can initiate investigations into situations on his or her own.[57] The latter provision was opposed by China, among others.[58]

The result is that the independence and jurisdiction of the Court is far greater and wider than the great powers would have preferred. In addition, the UNSC mechanism for referral of situations, rather than constraining the Court, in fact adds to its universality, because it allows the UNSC to refer situations in states that are not parties to the Statute. An example is the mentioned referral of the situation in Darfur in 2005.

It is of course not surprising that the NGOs were the most active proponents of having mechanisms to open investigations independently of the UNSC, including on the Prosecutor's own initiative.[59] In principle, the independence of the ICC could have been taken even further. Germany argued in Rome for universal jurisdiction, meaning that the Court should have jurisdiction regardless of state consent and the nationality of the accused. However, most states were not ready to abandon the system of state consent to jurisdiction.[60]

Nevertheless, the level of independence is without doubt testimony to the changed self-perception of many states concerning their own sovereignty and the universality of the rights of individuals, which would not

---

55 Rahmat Mohamad, "An Afro-Asian Perspective on the International Criminal Court", in Morten Bergsmo, CHEAH Wui Ling, SONG Tianying and YI Ping (eds.), *Historical Origins of International Criminal Law: Volume 4*, Torkel Opsahl Academic EPublisher, Brussels, 2015, p. 733.

56 Wippmann, 2004, pp. 166-168, see *supra* note 46.

57 Rome Statute, Articles 13–15, see *supra* note 45.

58 Mohamad, 2015, p. 735, see *supra* note 55.

59 Wippmann, 2004, pp. 168–169, see *supra* note 46.

60 *Ibid.*, p. 171.

have been possible under the Westphalian Paradigm. It also reflects the significance of active participation by non-state actors in diplomatic negotiations. In this aspect, the Rome negotiations are similar to those in Geneva in 1974–1977, and differ from, for example, those in Geneva in 1949.

Still, the universality of the ICC is hampered by the lack of ratifications by a number of states, including great powers. The US voted against the treaty, and has subsequently worked to constrain the Court, even though most of its allies have ratified.[61] The US policy toward the ICC has been seen by some as being contrary to the Clinton administration's overall attitude towards human rights. This attitude was arguably consistent with the idea for the Court. The US also supported both the ICTY and ICTR.[62] However, the US resistance is no doubt in line with its persistent reluctance to ratify any treaty that may lead to a loss of even limited aspects of its state sovereignty. Without an effective veto over the opening of cases before the Court, ratification by the US was not, and is not, realistic. In this aspect, the Rome Statute is evidence that without the veto in the UNSC, the US and other great powers would likely have disengaged a long time ago, or not joined in the first place.

The US also harbours the realistic fear that the ICC can be used against it by critics or rivals in the international system. With around 200,000 troops regularly stationed abroad, and frequent involvement in armed conflicts around the world, the US is arguably more exposed than any other country to potential cases before the ICC.[63] The American attitude toward the Court, however, is mixed. It does agree to a large extent to the general principles behind it, that is, that the four categories of crimes are criminal acts and should, in principle, be punished. It has also used the Court in situations where it deemed it prudent, such as Darfur.

In Rome in 1998, 120 states approved the Statute.[64] As of January 2017, 124 states had ratified. The list includes all South American states and almost all European states, with the exception of Belarus, the Holy See, Monaco, Ukraine and Russia. The US and India have not ratified, nor have Indonesia or Pakistan. Almost no Arab state or South East Asian state have ratified, with the exceptions of Tunisia, Palestine, Jordan, Cambodia and

---

[61] *Ibid.*, p. 151.

[62] *Ibid.*

[63] Figure from *ibid.*

[64] *Ibid.*

the Philippines (which signalled its intention to withdraw in March 2018). Most of the world's population, therefore, remain outside the ICC's jurisdiction.

The actions of the Court and its Prosecutor have so far underscored the independence of the Court, as far as we know from publicly available information. Its issuance of an arrest warrant for the President of Sudan, Omar Al Bashir, in 2009, could on the face of it be seen an example of this. Already, there was a widespread criticism that the Court placed an unfair emphasis on situations on the African continent. Taking the step to indict a President in an African country would normally not have been risked if the Court was unduly influenced by worries about states withdrawing from the Rome Statute. A further litmus test of the independence of the Court will come in its handling of the situation in Palestine, which acceded to the Rome Statute in 2015, with the risk of alienating the US further.

The Court is also supranational to a high degree, as it is capable of making binding decisions and acting independently of states. The Court is composed of 18 judges that are nominated and elected by the states parties, according to the Statute on the basis of their legal expertise. There are criteria for geographical and legal systems' representation, but no permanent representation of specific states. The collective of judges, therefore, can be presumed to be as fair as can be possible in the present international system. This places a very high responsibility on each of the judges.

As regards the consideration of relevant evidence, information and expert analysis, the ICC Rules of Procedure and Evidence are significantly broader than those of the ICJ.[65] The independent role of the ICC Prosecutor, and the possibility for various non-states parties to provide evidence and information to his or her Office, give further assurance that the Court will in fact be able to receive the information necessary for a fair procedure. There are of course also provisions ensuring the rights of the defendants to a fair procedure and legal representation in both the Statute and the Rules. The existence of an appeals process increases the fairness of the system, in providing a check on the trial chamber and a route for overturning possible errors in judgements.

---

[65] Rules of Procedure and Evidence of the International Criminal Court, 9 September 2002 (http://www.legal-tools.org/doc/8bcf6f/).

While arguably highly supranational, the ICC is not universal. The number of states not having ratified remains significant. On the scale between state sovereignty and supranational authority, the ICC leans towards the latter. Similarly, its emphasis is on the universal rights of individuals more than the sovereign rights of states. For these reasons, the Rome Statute is unlikely to achieve universality akin to, for example, the four Geneva Conventions or the UN Charter.

5.3. The Future of International Humanitarian Law and the International Criminal Court

If one takes the view that development of international law is linear – in the sense that new rules build on and replace old rules and thus shape the system perpetually – then it would be natural to assume that international humanitarian law will progress to include more precise rules for protection of individuals, for rights and obligations of non-state armed groups, and for international co-operation to ensure that the law is implemented. It is the main argument of this book, however, that the international system has boundaries that set limits to how far any such linear development can be taken. Specifically, sovereign states remain the driving force and source of authority in the system, and they will continue to preserve these rights for themselves. New concepts that conflict with traditional sovereignty will continue to create new rules, but only within limits.

For example, the concept of equality between states requires that Northern, Western, Southern and Eastern states will be held to international humanitarian law rules. However, non-state actors, such as armed rebel groups, will not be given an equal share of influence as decision-makers when new rules are negotiated. The new concept of governance by popular will requires that NGOs be consulted and included to a certain degree in formulation of new rules. However, they will not be given authority to decide on any substantial matter, which is a right reserved for the states alone.

The limits of the possible is shown in the process leading to the two first APs of the 1949 Geneva Conventions: NGO pressure and small and medium states can align and push for more precise rule-formulation. However, the more intrusive these rules are on traditional sovereignty, the less likely they are to gain universal consensus. Great powers and the states most fearful of losing sovereign rights – such as states susceptible to armed conflict – will refrain from joining.

It should be noted, however, that the lack of *formal* universal commitment may not necessarily be decisive. When a significant number of states commit to new rules, it also produces an opinion of justice or of law (*opinio juris*) that affects outsiders as well. For example, while Israel has not joined the Convention on Cluster Munitions, it has not used such munitions after the adoption of the treaty. Doing so would inevitably lead to strong criticism, even if the source would be moral indignation and not legal obligation. The effect, then, is to change the practice of states, which again may lead to the new rules attaining the status of customary international law.

Some restraints, however, are likely to remain. A full symmetry of legal rights and obligations of states parties and non-states parties to an armed conflict is not in the realm of the possible under the present paradigm.

The ICC is an institution of particular interest. It is an international organisation that has global reach and is supranational in the sense that it has the possibility to act and decide on matters independently of the states. This is rare. At the same time, it is not universal, due to the number of states outside the Rome Statute. Nor is it likely to become so. The states parties are, to a great degree – although by no means exclusively – located in regions where the impact of the Court is likely to be limited in the foreseeable future. While European and South American states may participate in international military operations abroad, such participation is likely to be of narrow scope in the near and medium term. The possibility of war in Central and Western Europe is relatively remote, and was even more so in 1998, when the Rome Statute was negotiated. In other words, the risk of joining the ICC for many of the states that did so, was limited. The risk is higher for most of the countries that have not joined, due to more likely, and more significant, involvement in armed conflicts.

Furthermore, the great powers have very few incentives to join the institution. The high degree of supranational powers of the ICC make their ratifications less likely. The possibility of the ICC becoming a universal institution are therefore remote. However, it is likely to produce jurisprudence that will have universal influence. The ICTY jurisprudence, for example, has affected international opinion about customary international humanitarian law rules, despite its formal limitations. The ICC will doubtlessly have similar influence.

Here again, however, the limitations that are likely to remain in place also in the future are uncovered. The Court does not have unlimited powers to act independently. Its Statute and jurisdiction over the four categories of crimes are the most obvious limitations. However, states also retain the right to withdraw from the Rome Statute. There is thus a safeguard for regaining the sovereign rights that have been ceded to the ICC. The fundamentals of the international system, therefore, have not changed with the agreement to set up the ICC. Rather, the Court is the most important example so far of diplomatic brinkmanship under the present international system. As such, it is a mile stone that can potentially take international humanitarian law and international criminal law to new and unprecedented levels. But it cannot transcend the limitations imposed by state sovereignty as a fundamental principle in the international system as it currently exists.

6

What the Future Holds

6.1. Benefits of the Paradigmatic Approach

It has been the aim of this book to assess the limitations and possibilities of the present international system in light of the basic principles that underpin it. I have labelled these principles collectively as the Popular Sovereign Paradigm. I have argued that, while various reforms and actions may push and pull the international system in different directions, there is no possibility for overstepping the boundaries of this paradigm. In order to do so, the paradigm itself would first have to change.

The approach to the international system as a paradigm is different from the main traditions of international relations theory, namely (neo)realism, (neo)liberalism and constructivism. I have argued, in the introduction, that realism falls short of explaining the international system because there is no possibility of explaining systemic changes. In fact, changes – such as the setting up of the United Nations in 1945 – tend to be dismissed as more or less inconsequential, insofar as power remains the ultimate broker and the international system remains anarchic.[1] As argued in Chapter 5, however, such an approach struggles to explain, for example, the formation of the ICC, which was opposed by the great powers of the world. Furthermore, it fails to explain why wars of territorial conquest were normal procedure in the past, but are today rare and rendered illegal when they do occur.

Liberalism and constructivism, on the other hand, are often at a loss in explaining the permanence of central features of the international system. If it is possible to give shape and direction to the international system, why is it near impossible, for example, to reform the UNSC? Council reform remains elusive in spite of a broad and general consensus – even among most states – that the present setup is neither representative, nor fair, nor effective, nor efficient.

The paradigmatic approach provides the possibility of explaining both permanence and change. By pinpointing the fundamental principles

---

[1]   Hurrell, 2007, p. 296, see *supra* note 1 in Chapter 1.

that underpin the system, it is possible to explain the limitations of reform and permanence of certain features. The most prevalent is the continuance of sovereign states as the main actors and decision-makers in the international system. It is also possible to explain why the international system is able to set up institutions and rules for itself now, which were impossible before World War I, such as the United Nations, the WTO, and not least global human rights and international humanitarian law rules and institutions that define universal rights of individuals and non-state groups *vis-à-vis* states.

It can be speculated whether one reason for the differences in the realist, liberalist and constructivist traditions is a tendency to focus on only one or a few of the paradigmatic principles. The Popular Sovereign Paradigm retains sovereign states as the main decision-makers. This is a feature that is common with the Westphalian Paradigm. Focus on this feature alone would suggest a continuance of the entire international system, which is a central line of though in (neo)realism. It is not difficult, either, to find examples of unscrupulous self-serving state behaviour that disregards international law. However, the existence of criminal acts does not mean that there are no laws. For example, few would seriously argue that the genocide in Rwanda should not have been stopped by international intervention because of a lack of national interest of potentially intervening powers.

The Popular Sovereign Paradigm, however, also features new fundamental principles: sovereign states are no longer persons; popular will is the dominant ideological foundation for legitimate governance; authority is no longer a top-down process only; and states are formally equal. These features all represent changes from the Westphalian Paradigm. A focus on either one of these principles suggests that the international system can take on a completely different shape than it currently has: it could suggest that popular elections to the UNGA would be possible; that the veto in the UNSC could be removed; that the ICC jurisdiction could be universally accepted; and that the ICJ could be transformed into a world court with wide and independent powers over states. There are, however, reasons why such ideas have not materialised, nor are likely to do so in the foreseeable future.

6.2. Possibilities and Impossibilities in the Present International System

An alien visitor to Earth, or a time-traveller to our present time, would probably see the constraints and contradictions of the international system more clearly than we are able to, being situated in the middle of it. Alf Ross, in his 1950 book *Constitution of the United Nations*, laid out an allegory that is still compelling: the world is like a densely forested area with scattered houses, which is prone to frequent fires. Instead of taking the logical step of organising a joint fire brigade, the houses agree only that each and every one will fight the fires individually and with their own means. Rich house owners manage to put out their fires, while the poorer ones burn up. The only degree of co-operation that they have managed to create is a group that can conclude that a fire indeed has broken out and authorise individuals to take action against it. However, even this is dominated by the few and rich who have the final word in most, if not all, matters.

While seductively persuasive, the allegory is also faulty: unlike fires, armed conflicts are not one-sided affairs that are simply a matter of stomping out. Often, all sides to a conflict are convinced about the righteousness of their cause, and can present at least some legitimate grievance to back up their claims. Furthermore, unlike fires within a community, conflicts affect states and peoples in different ways. It is logical to organise a fire department for a small community, but not a global fire department that is tasked with putting out all fires on the planet.

Still, the allegory speaks to the contradictions in the UN system in regard to maintenance of peace and security, which are also evident in other areas of international relations. There is a general and principled agreement about objectives – in this case the avoidance of war and unnecessary human suffering – but an inability to organise in a manner that would effectively deal with erupting crises.

Ideally, perhaps, the international system would borrow more from the best practice of governance within states. A triangular division of the powers of government, with a judicial branch, an executive branch and a legislative branch, has proven to be a historically stable construct. A similar design for the international system would doubtlessly be more effective than the present system in which individual states very often can and do block efforts at co-ordinated action. Furthermore, a global system of governance that is based on democratic elections to a World Assembly would far better represent the global popular will, and would be more forceful in providing precise rules for the globe.

None of this is possible under the present paradigm. For the changes to materialise, the fundamental principles of the international system would have to change. The continued basis on sovereign states as the decision-makers prevent any such thing from being realised. The possibilities for reform of the international system must, therefore, aim at improving the system within the boundaries that are at present not possible to cross.

A number of reform ideas have been presented in this book. One general conclusion is that increased inclusion of NGOs in the international system will tend to lead to greater changes than any decisions on which the states alone can agree. The gradual enlargement of international humanitarian law and human rights rules since 1945, for example, has coincided with increased involvement of non-state actors. While states will not surrender their position as decision-makers, there is room for increased involvement though various means. For example, national dialogues between states and NGOs regarding international affairs before, during and after UNGA or HRC sessions, is possible. States can also include NGO representatives into their delegations more often, thus giving them access to first-hand information, enabling them to achieve both greater understanding and potential influence in the future.

Another possibility that applies across sectors, is to increase the independence of those international organisations – or parts of international organisations – that may provide guidance to the common good, unbiased by particular state interests. An increased independence and mandate of the WTO Secretariat, for example, would most likely aid the member states toward a more common understanding and basis for future agreement. Agreement on rules for vote-trading in the UNGA system would also increase the likelihood of more competent and legitimate representation on various committees or positions of trust. Finally, some unwritten agreements about skewed state representation, such as the P5 representation on the ICJ bench, can be undone.

None of this would fundamentally change the international system, but it would strengthen its credibility as representative of a global popular will, and increase the possibilities of supranational governance.

6.3. Area-Specific Reforms

In the case of the UN Security Council, its composition and the veto has long been the object of criticism and reform ideas. The skewed representativity, however, is mostly by design. The permanent membership and veto rules ensure that the victorious powers of World War II remain in a position of global hegemony, but it also ensures the survival of the Council as a global decision-making forum, by keeping the great powers within the UN. An alternative model, without the veto, would never be accepted by the US and China, in particular. The ICC is an example of an institution without a veto, and where the great powers do not participate.

The most that can be hoped for is probably a change of practice in the medium to long term. If the global security environment improves significantly – and there is a greater degree of trust between the P5 countries – a temporary moratorium on use of veto might be contemplated. In the short term, however, there are no possibilities for this to be agreed.

Over time, the composition of the UNSC may also be possible to change. Since 1945, all but two initiatives have failed, namely the change from six to ten non-permanent seats, and the entry of the People's Republic of China as a permanent member instead of the Republic of China. As the positions of the UK and France are likely to become increasingly untenable in the face of rising great powers, like India, changes in the UNSC composition may become possible in the medium or long term. The European Union may come to assume France's permanent seat, whereas the UK seat will come under increasing pressure.

For the UNSC, it is also possible to continue to develop clearer rules and more permanent mechanisms in the areas where there is considerable consensus among the P5 members. The recent history of the UNSC is illustrative of the possibilities and constraints. The UNSC has managed to establish both better rules and enforcement mechanisms in regard to armed parties that use child soldiers. UNSC listing of such parties encourages them to engage with the UN system to agree on policy changes in their organization, and thereby be removed from the UNSC list. It is an imperfect system, but better than no system at all.

The constraints are shown in the history of the concept of Responsibility to Protect. It came about as a consequence of two main factors: the moral outrage over the failure to act to prevent the genocide in Rwanda, and the relative rapprochement of the great powers after the Cold War.

However, the actual agreement on the Responsibility to Protect in the Out-come Document of the World Summit in 2005 also shows the constraints: the text is short, and thus not fully clear, remaining open to interpretation. Furthermore, it is not legally binding. This means that even the end of the Cold War and the genocide in Rwanda were not sufficient factors to lead to the establishment of clearer rules for international interventions in face of mass atrocities. Even the short and non-binding text from 2005 fell into disuse and lost credibility in particular for China and Russia after the inter-vention in Libya in 2011. This is indicative of the comparably less condu-cive international environment at the present.

The international security environment also makes it less likely that the ICJ will receive any significant overhaul of its Statute designed to strengthen its mandate in the near future. However, the Court can decide on its own to comment more on UNSC resolutions in relation to established international law, and take a more active stance in determining the status of developing rules of customary international law.

If the ICJ decided on such a course, there is little that states are likely to do about it, other than voice protest. An outright activist policy by the Court is not a possibility due to statutory constraints and the limitations of international law in general, but the Court can through its own actions steer a somewhat different course.

In elections of the ICJ judges, moreover, the present Statute is not an obstacle to changing the practice of representation from the P5 countries, Japan and Germany. The UN members could change this simply by voting differently. The risk of disengagement from the great powers from the ICJ is not significant should the composition of nationals on the bench change. After all, among the P5 countries, only the UK has formally accepted the ICJ's jurisdiction over states' disputes. Moreover, the US has already once decided not to implement an ICJ decision – in the Lockerbie case – and there is no international enforcement mechanism that would prevent this from happening again. Changing the practice of great power representation, however, would increase the ICJ's credibility, and there is also a fair chance that it would lead to a more engaged and active Court.

Finally, the UN General Assembly could make more frequent use of its right to request advisory opinions from the ICJ. This would potentially serve to clarify important aspects of international law, including developing customary rules.

The reform potential for the UNGA itself is even more constrained. Introduction of new mechanisms, rules or guidelines for strengthening the level of consultations between the UNGA as such, or its individual members, and non-state stakeholders can be contemplated. One example is to pass a resolution providing guidelines for national consultations between UN member states' governments and public representatives prior to, during and after the UNGA sessions.

Another possibility is the contemplation of guidelines or rules to regulate vote-trading, in order to raise consciousness about the issue, avoid at least extreme excesses and raise the overall integrity and credibility of the UN elections system.

Similar to the UNSC, the World Trade Organization also has a skewed system of influence. Unlike the UNSC, however, this is not the result of institutional design, but the lack of it. It has resulted mostly from failure to reach agreement, and learning to live with an incomplete institutional setup. Ironically, the credibility for the WTO is arguably lower than that of the UNSC, as a consequence of the informal and opaque decision-making processes. The lack of an executive council and a more independent Secretariat allows informal structures to become more important, which give rise to suspicions, disgruntlement and a degree of paralysis. A formal decision-making structure would be preferable to the present one, even if it was skewed in favour of some states, as it is in the UNSC.

The frustrated development of the WTO is already clear, which is at least one factor that may lead to deeper reforms than may be possible in the UN main organs. There is clearly a need to make changes in order to get the WTO back as the pivotal organisation for global trade. Restoring faith in the system from the developing countries is critical. This can be achieved, at least in part, by strengthening the independence of the Secretariat and tasking it to develop analysis about probable consequences of various trade rules. Clearly, independence and openness of the Secretariat for different economic models is critical for such analysis to be received in good faith.

Furthermore, the establishment of a WTO executive council may be contemplated. This would replace many of the heavily criticised informal fora with a formal one. It would also lead to increased representativeness in the decision-making procedures, as a more systematised practice of consultations between elected executive council members and the general membership is likely to develop.

Finally, the dispute settlement mechanism of the WTO should be made more accessible for poorer countries. This can be accomplished through grants by developed countries to be used for legal assistance to poorer countries. Concretely, a trust fund and secretariat could be set up for this purpose, with joint representation on the board by developed and developing countries.

As regards the UN HRC, the reform potential in the short term is limited. There is little appetite for it, considering that there has been a significant reform in 2005. The HRC system will need to run for more years before any push for reform can be considered. In the meantime, measures can be undertaken in order to raise the level of national consultations between states and their populations in national dialogues. One way to improve this is to pass a resolution about guidelines for national consultations in advance of UPR hearings. Another is to devote more time and money to strengthening NHRIs across the globe, and establishing such institutions where none presently exist.

In effect, the HRC is at present a forum of universal state representation, due to the openness of the procedures also for non-member states. This is necessary and positive if the goal is to function as a universal norm-giver. However, the Council struggles under the misconception that it can somehow also assure universal compliance to human rights – even in cases where the UNSC is not willing or able to do so. There is, however, little that can be done by the Council itself to ensure such implementation. As with the other international organisations, the untapped potential lies in including NGOs and impartial experts (such as special mandate holders) even more closely, although the HRC is in fact ahead of many others on this point.

Similar to the HRC, the ICC is a relatively new institution, which probably has to function for a longer time period before reform potential becomes clearer. As has been discussed, however, its formal setup entails a greater degree of independence from states, and supranational powers, than any other international organisation that has a global reach. It is therefore not very likely that it can be further strengthened in this regard without it causing a backlash *vis-à-vis* states that may withdraw from the Statute.

International humanitarian law, in general, is likely to experience a development similar to that of recent decades, of increasing international legislation of specific areas. The Arms Trade Treaty, Convention on Cluster Munitions and Anti-Personnel Land Mine Ban Convention are examples.

Other regulations can be contemplated. One candidate is incendiary weapons, which are subjected to particularly weak international treaty legislation, and which has lost military significance compared with the 1970s.[2]

Furthermore, international humanitarian law rules may develop further in regard to privileges and obligations of non-state armed groups, although only to a certain extent, as this will be strongly resisted by many states.[3] The conflicting principles of the Popular Sovereign Paradigm will, in this case, come to the surface: the consideration of individuals' rights and the concept of popular will clash with the concept of sovereign states as the sole decision-makers. A likely result is a continued ambiguous status for insurgent armed groups, although clearer rules can be contemplated, especially in the form of sub-universal rules – that is, agreed to by only a part of the international community, such as the Convention on Cluster Munitions.

6.4. *Quo Vadis*? Risk of Rupture or Disintegration

The internal tensions of the Popular Sovereign Paradigm imply that stable and fully amicable relations in the international system are not possible, for the time being. The global institutions are not strong or independent enough to effectively govern international relations, so as to maintain co-operation and peace for the common benefit of the peoples of the world.

Let us consider some factors that show frailties in the present system, and which may lead to its rupture or disintegration of that system. It should be noted, however, that such developments would not necessarily lead to a paradigm change. In the past, post-conflict phases have more often than not led to a continuation of the pre-existing paradigm, than to change. Examples include the end of the Cold War and the Napoleonic wars.

An armed conflict between two or more of the world's great powers is one scenario that might lead to a rupture in the international system. The

---

[2]   The Convention prohibiting Certain Conventional Weapons (CCW), CCW Protocol III prohibiting Incendiary Weapons, 2 December 1983 (http://www.legal-tools.org/doc/22c3ef/), regulates incendiary weapons, but goes no longer than customary international law, and in some cases even falls short of it. See Stian Nordengen Christensen, "Regulation of White Phosphorus Weapons in International Law", in *Occasional Paper Series*, Torkel Opsahl Academic EPublisher, Brussels, 2016 (http://www.legal-tools.org/doc/6acbe4/).

[3]   Cassese has suggested that such rules are seemingly under development as customary international humanitarian law, see Antonio Cassese, "Should Rebels be treated as Criminals? Some Modest Proposals for Rendering Internal Armed Conflicts Less Inhumane", in Cassese (ed.), 2012, p. 519, see *supra* note 13 in Chapter 2.

UNSC will never be able to resolve such a situation, meaning that it would expose the weakness of the present setup.

There is little doubt that the potential for such conflicts exist. Most likely, the main actors in the twenty-first century great power politics will be the US, China, Russia and India, with Japan, Pakistan and the EU in supporting roles. Major questions include whether China's rise will lead to military confrontations; or if Russia's foreign policy will threaten the territorial integrity of neighbouring countries. And consequently, whether the international system can survive these developments.

China's rise since 1978 has been peaceful, but scholars differ in opinions on whether this may change in the medium to long term.[4] China's leaders consistently stress their peaceful intentions. The 'New Strategic Concept' announced in 1997, rules out military threat as useful in international relations.[5] At the same time, China's leaders also believe that increasing wealth will create increasing competition, including possibly, but not necessarily, military confrontations.[6]

What is certain is that there are potential flashpoints. The most significant is with the US over Chinese Taipei, but there are also others, including with India over disputed territory. Conflict with Russia is less likely, although not unthinkable, considering inflow of Chinese money and influence into traditionally Russian-dominated Central Asia. It is, however, at present not possible to make firm predictions about any of this.

More certain is that Russia will continue to challenge US hegemony throughout the world, and primarily in its immediate neighbourhood. The significance of the events in the Ukraine since 2014 should not be missed, as they may show a Russia more interested in hard power projection abroad than in economic gains.[7] This arguably separates Russia from the other

---

[4]   For an example of a 'peaceful rise' argument, see FENG Huiyn, "China's Strategic Culture and Foreign Policy", in Emilian Kavalski (ed.), *The Ashgate Research Companion to Chinese Foreign Policy*, Ashgate, Farnham, 2012, p. 47; for an example of the argument that China is behaving according to nineteenth century great power politics, see Kagan, 2008, pp. 27–34, see *supra* note 58 in Chapter 4.

[5]   HENG Yee-Kuang, "The 'New Security Concept': The Role of the Military in China's Foreign Policy", in Kavalski (ed.), 2012, p. 105, see *supra* note 4.

[6]   Kagan, 2008, pp. 24–25, see *supra* note 58 in Chapter 4.

[7]   Agnia Grigas, *Beyond Crimea: The New Russian Empire*, Yale University Press, New Haven, 2016, p. 29.

---

great powers in the world, including China, which places a higher emphasis in its economic performance as basis for its internal legitimacy.[8] Russia also challenges the established rules about territorial sovereignty to an extent that is detrimental to the latter's perceived core interests. Russia is therefore the player in the international arena that most clearly separates itself from the others, and has the most potential to effect deep change the international system.

However, Russia's power is less than it may seem. Its military strength, while considerable, is less than that both of the US and China, and clearly less than NATO combined. Its soft power is limited, reaching few outside Russian speaking communities abroad, and is restricted even among those. Russia's soft power is comparably lower than that of the US and the EU, and also behind that of China and India. It cannot be compared with the soft power of communism during the Cold War. Finally, Russia's economic power is also limited. It is not in the first tier of world economic or trade powers, falling far behind the US, China and Germany. Russia is, at present, only the eleventh largest merchandise exporter in the world.[9] Its ability to affect the international system is therefore limited, although its position in the UNSC is one of influence, and its conflicts with the US in particular can paralyse that forum over a number of situations in the coming years.

Military conflicts between great powers, however, may not be the highest risks to the international system. Although such conflicts would be the most disastrous, the probability of them incurring is far less than other risks that may undermine the system. More probable is the risk of disinte-gration of the system as a consequence of the global fora losing ground to sub-global alternatives. Such fora do not aim at universal global member-ship, but are limited to either certain regions or states with perceived com-mon interests. The WTO is the clearest example of a global forum that is

---

[8] It is a common argument that the Communist Party of China's legitimacy is contingent on economic growth, although the emphasis varies. For example, Michel Cormier argues that economic growth is the critical factor, in Michel Cormier, *The Legacy of Tiananmen Square*, translated by Jonathan Kaplansky, Fredericton, Goose Lane, 2013; Kingsley Edney and HE Baogang argue that nationalism and economic growth are equally important: "The Rise of Nationalism an China's Foreign Policy", in Kavalski (ed.), 2012, p. 83, see *supra* note 4.

[9] WTO estimate for 2014, see WTO, "Modest trade recovery to continue in 2015 and 2016 following three years of weak expansion", in *WTO Press Release*, 14 April 2015, available on the WTO web site.

being gradually overtaken by regional and bilateral trade agreements. Russia and China are clearly pursuing courses that aim to bring smaller countries closer to themselves, both in economic and in political terms, through various mechanisms and new instruments, such as the BRICS development bank, and the One Belt initiative. These initiatives have the upside of potentially generating economic growth and trade in a system where the global institutions are falling short. At the same time, they also represent a risk that the global architecture can become less relevant and effectively be replaced by regional ones.

Also in terms of human rights, the future of the international system is uncertain. China is asserting itself more as a leader of likeminded states on issues that it considers to be important, and which opposes the traditionally hegemonic views. China and South East Asia is also the region in the world with the most outspoken and principled opposition to the universality of human rights and the right to democratic elections. Many majority Muslim countries also pursue international policies that are shaped more by religious convictions than has been the case in the past, and which represent an alternative to the established human rights, particularly in regard to religious freedom and women's rights.

The current setup of the HRC is so ineffectual in terms of enforcement that it does not pose any threat to strong states that disagree on certain human rights. Its work will nevertheless be affected in the sense that new universal norm-development will be more difficult to achieve in the coming years. It should be noted, however, that this is not particularly different from the situation during the Cold War, when human rights development did progress despite the opposing views of communist and democratic countries.

The trend of establishing sub-global fora for co-operation, such as the BRICS or the Shanghai Cooperation Organisation, is significant, and is likely to continue. Russia and especially China see this to be a useful way to increase their countries' international status and influence. The Western countries, under US hegemony, already have a number of older and more well-established fora, such as NATO and the G7.

These sub-global constructs are more than mere co-operation organisations. They are also entities that can potentially bestow legitimacy on international policies. What NATO did in Kosovo, after failing to receive a mandate for military intervention from the UNSC, can in principle be emulated by the Shanghai Cooperation Organisation in another situation. However, in being sub-global and in having no formal legal mandate to approve international intervention, neither one can bestow legitimacy equal to the UNSC. Still, they would appear more legitimate than actions that are unilateral or by *ad hoc* 'coalitions of the willing'. As the democratic states of Western Europe and the Americas, along with Japan, South Korea and Australia in particular, continue to drive most of the agenda in the global organisations, China and Russia are likely to continue to develop sub-global alternatives.

This trend is similar, but stronger, in international trade. In this area, the tendency of seeking sub-global, regional or bilateral trade agreements is clear for all to see. As progress through the WTO has proven exceedingly difficult, sub-global agreements are an unavoidable development.

Finally, in human rights, similar trends are so far not very clear. The reason is most likely that the HRC and treaty-body system in the UN is not able to enforce its own rules, and also allows disagreeing states fully to participate. The need for regional organisations is therefore less than in security and trade. However, some trends do increase the likelihood of disintegration also in the global human rights system. The two most significant are the re-emergence of religion in the majority Muslim states leading to conflicts of values between human rights and Islamic law; and the growing confidence of China and South East Asia, where democratic rights face significant and principled opposition.

The tendency of seeking sub-global unity is likely to undermine the global system. The existing global organisations will be faced with a catch-22 situation: the system will need deep reform in order to effectively handle increased great power rivalry. Such reforms, however, will be prevented by those powers. As a consequence, the relevance of, for example, the UNSC or the WTO will continue to erode and risk being *de facto* replaced by alternative and sub-global fora.

It has been suggested by some, that in light of developing great power politics combined with increasingly ineffective global institutions, there should be a push to establish a co-operation organisation for democratic states. This idea has been developed along many lines, as a "League of Democracies" or a "Concert of Democracies".[10] As the thinking goes, this

---

[10] Kagan, 2008, pp. 97–98, see *supra* note 58 in Chapter 4; G. John Ikenberry and Anne-Marie Slaughter, "Forging a World of Liberty Under Law: U.S. National Security in the 21st Century", in Final Paper of the Princeton Project on National Security, *The Princeton Project on*

could serve to reconcile differences and increase likelihood of consensus on key international issues. It could draw together nations such as Japan, India, Australia, EU members, and Brazil. Such a forum could, its protagonists argue, bestow legitimacy upon actions that autocracies would block in the UN, like the NATO intervention in Kosovo in 1999.[11]

However, these proposals are not necessarily helpful to the cause of the democratic states, and may therefore not be realised, for two reasons. First, there is only one democracy that actually has clear global security interests, and that is the US. All other democratic states have mainly or only regional interests, which also differ widely. Consider, for example, the security interests of Mongolia, being located between Russia and China *vis-à-vis* those of Argentina or South Africa. Furthermore, India is clearly a democracy, but has steered away from alignment with any of the superpowers. It could be argued that it now stands to reap benefits of its relatively independent position *vis-à-vis* the US, China and Russia, being able to cater to all sides. India therefore has in the short term little to gain from joining a close-knit league of democracies. Only if at some point a serious worsening of relations with China should occur, would India's full alignment with the US, under an international organisational setup, become a possibility. It is therefore relatively simplistic to believe that the shared value of democracy is enough to unite the broad spectrum of states that are currently governed according to this system.

Second, the democratic states are the hegemons of the existing international system. Three of five permanent UNSC members are Western democracies. While a great number of UNGA members are autocratic, the democratic member states are generally richer and more active in taking initiatives, including through resolutions. The same is the case for the HRC. If it holds, as protagonists of democratic states' co-operation assume, that democratic states in fact do have common interests, those interests would continue to be best served if the present global fora remain universal, global and functioning.

As for those global fora that are not functioning well, there are already a number of organisations with *de facto* exclusive or nearly exclusive democratic membership – for security, there is NATO; for human rights,

---

National Security Papers, The Woodrow Wilson School of Public and International Affairs, Princeton University, Princeton, 2006, p. 7.

[11] *Ibid.*

---

there is the Organization of American States and the European Council. For climate change, the nature of the subject means that global organisation is necessary and alternative sub-global organisation would make little sense. For trade, there is the EU and NAFTA.

Having a league of democracies merely to approve economic or military sanctions against non-democratic states would also have limited value. Economic sanctions may just as well be achieved if the US and the EU agree to such sanctions, as over Russia's actions in the Ukraine in 2014. As for military sanctions, NATO is already in existence. It is difficult to imagine that this organisation would be equally effective if other large democratic states, such as Japan or India, would join as members, considering diverging security interests stemming from geostrategic placement and foreign policy trajectories.

A new league of democracies as a meaningful international organisation may yet materialise, but there is, at present and in the short term, no clear need for it, nor any particularly significant interest that could be served by it. A more likely development, in the deterioration scenario, is a retreat by the US from global regimes such as the WTO and UNSC, and into sub-global or bilateral ones. The need for new regimes is not necessarily pressing. NATO, for example, offers a well-tested organisation that has succeeded in holding off war in Europe since 1945. In the short run, regional or bilateral trade agreements can give the US and the EU the material benefits comparable with global institutions.

6.5. Paradigm Shift: Rupture or Evolution

One remaining problem is what causes paradigm shifts in the international system. Looking at the history of such changes, it seems that large-scale cataclysms have been significant in bringing about change. These were the events immediately before the breakthrough of the Westphalian system at the close of the Thirty Years' War, and the Popular Sovereign Paradigm after the world wars of the twentieth century.

However, there were also evolutionary developments that underpinned the previous paradigm changes: the Thirty Years' War and the Westphalian Paradigm were preceded by increased independence of secular princes in Europe and the Reformation, *vis-à-vis* the ideologies of the Catholic Church and the Holy Roman Empire. Without these developments, the Westphalian Paradigm would not have been possible. The world wars were preceded by changes of equal magnitude, most importantly, the spread of the idea of popular will and replacement of personal sovereigns with impersonal state institutions. While the world wars were clearly catalysts for change, there would not have been a paradigm change if not for the change in the ideological foundations. It is also true, as Cassese agues, that from the 1800s, entire populations were mobilised for war.[12] This undoubtedly gave strategic military advantages to popular will-based governments (for example, France, the UK, the US and Prussia/Germany), which were able to mobilise broader popular support than absolute monarchies (for example, Tsarist Russia and the Ottoman Empire).

At present, the conflicting principles of the paradigm are connected to the concept of state sovereignty, as contrasted with full implementation of the concept of popular will and individual rights. The resulting space for international governance is too narrow for a stable international system to be a likely consequence. This is not to say that the concept of state sovereignty will, at some point, no longer be a factor. As of 2018, the trajectories of the international policies of the world's great powers are arguably pointing toward a strengthening of the sovereignty principle. The point is merely that the present system is not stable, and will change at some time in the future.

Whether this occurs as a consequence of a new international catastrophe or an evolutionary process is not possible to say definitively.

The definitive changes, however, will not occur in the international system itself, but in the factors that underpin it. Neither the Reformation, nor the idea of popular will, spread as a consequence of the international system, but rather they did so in spite of it. Similarly, it seems a safe assumption that changes in the Popular Sovereign Paradigm are likely to be caused by developments within states, peoples and economies, not by international reform efforts.

It could be argued that the European Union represents an example of an evolutionary change in the international system that is of the scale of a paradigm change. It certainly shows that it is possible for states to converge around such a system for mutual benefit. Europe used to be composed of small states vying for influence in a zero-sum game of power politics. Physically crossing state borders in Europe was difficult due to formal constraints and checks. Anyone who has travelled between states in most other parts of the world will be familiar with long lines for passport control, exit

---

[12] Cassese, 2005, p. 400, see *supra* note 4 of Chapter 1.

fees, entry fees, insurance fees, etc., which are incomparably more difficult than border control internally in the EU today. International trade in Europe used to be hampered with high tariffs and restrictions. The common market has removed those obstacles, and Europe has prospered economically to unprecedented levels.

Finally, irreconcilable enemies have become close partners of co-operation. The rise of nationalism in Germany from the 1800s was, to a large extent, anti-French. It received its largest early mobilisation power during the Napoleonic occupation and the Rhine crisis in 1840. Anti-German sentiment in France has been equally strong, especially following the occupation of Alsace-Lorraine from 1871. And, not least, the two world wars involved millions of deaths on both sides, causing deep mutual hatred and resentment. Few could have imagined in 1945 that these countries in a few decades would become close allies in the same Union, with citizens free to travel back and forth almost without restrictions. If this is possible for two of the most bellicose states in modern history, it is possible for others as well.

The potential for such a development on a global scale, however, is constrained by a number of factors. Particularly, as has been mentioned, the more powerful states have more to lose if they cede sovereign rights to supranational institutions. Their relative influence will diminish, while their relative gains may be uncertain. A global system that is effective, efficient and just requires a minimum of universal rules. Furthermore, it requires a minimum of institutions that can develop and revise those rules, execute certain tasks, and judge on the basis of those rules. This is not possible without states ceding some traditional sovereignty to supranational institutions.

Moreover, the EU is not necessarily a stable construction either. States retain their sovereign rights in many aspects, most importantly in the right to secede from the Union. Also, the democratically elected European Parliament has only limited powers, while the European Commission retains a higher share of decision-making authority than executive branches in EU member states, internally. In the Commission, all member states have one representative. Finally, changes on the constitutional level of the EU requires consent of the sovereign states, and cannot be decided by supranational mechanisms.

However, there are also other examples in history that involve cessation of traditional sovereign rights to a supranational entity. The history of

German unification is one such. To a significant extent, the unification of Germany came about through developing economic ties between the North German states under the common customs union (Zollverein) from 1834. The creation of the North German Confederation in 1866, which was the basis for the German Empire from 1871, did not come about by conquest. Although it may not have been possible without the Prusso-Austrian war of 1866, the non-Prussian states that joined the Confederation did so on the presumption that it would be to their benefit.

The significance of this should not be missed: the model statesman of the realist tradition, Otto von Bismarck, achieved the unification of Germany not only by holding off rival great powers, but also by appeal, based on the presumption of mutual benefits between the states that joined the North German Confederation and outweighed traditional concerns about strict Westphalian sovereignty.

6.6. Future Paradigms of the International System

A compelling question is what a future paradigm of the international system might look like. Regrettably, answers other than speculative ones are unlikely to be reached. It is not possible to predict the future. The only safe assumption is that the present system will not last forever. If there is indeed a paradigm that exists and upholds the present international system, and this is founded on certain irreconcilable internal principles, then it follows that this system is bound to change in time.

Many alternatives can be imagined. One such would be a return to the Westphalian order, where traditional sovereignty and balance of power-politics prevail, while presumptions of universal individual rights and prohibition on war not in self-defence are abandoned. Another would be a unified world order, which both Immanuel Kant and John Rawls have imagined to be dystopian, as either a global dictatorship or a civil strife-ridden global empire.[13] Or, one could imagine a paradigm in which the new principles in the present paradigm have come to replace the traditional ones. This would entail a system that is not based on the principle of sovereign states as decision-makers, but in which a global popular will would be manifested in universal institutions.

---

[13] John Rawls, *The Law of the Peoples, with the 'Idea of Public Reasoning' Revisited*, Harvard University Press, Cambridge, 1999, p. 36.

Because the Popular Sovereign Paradigm contains contradictory old and new elements, it is natural to imagine the continuation of the new and removal of the old. With this as a starting point, a future paradigm of the international system may be imagined as follows:

1. All matters of importance are decided through mechanisms designed to reflect the popular will, including in global affairs. While most issues are decided locally, by municipalities or similar entities, these do not have any traditional sovereign rights, but act in accordance with the global framework.

2. Global institutions decide on the universal rules that apply throughout the world. These institutions are representative of the peoples of the world, but have a number of limitations that safeguard against majority power abuse against minorities and the possibility for revisiting important issues through, for example, legal institutions. The global rules are general and limited to those concerns that cannot safely be left to the local authorities, for example, prohibition on genocide, torture, war of aggression, forcible annexation of territory, commitments for the global environment and climate, assurance of the conditions for free and fair trade, and right to a fair trial.

3. Use of force is a matter of police action, whether on an international or a local scale, the rules for which are decided by the representative authorities, and checked by impartial courts of law.

4. Rules apply universally, with no difference between regions of the world, save for rules necessary to safeguard the system itself, for example, by protection of minority rights.

5. Local authorities are representative, and have a high degree of autonomy, save on matters of identified common concern. The actual representation may not necessarily be through elections, but require a degree of political participation that assure that the individual is the basic entity in the decision-making apparatus and on equal terms with other individuals, save for personal abilities and merit.

6. Authority is based on a system of fairness and impartiality, where broad political consultations are mandatory before important decisions, and corruption or abuse of power is illegal and subjected to checks and balances.

Certainly, new and unforeseen factors can and will also be introduced in the future. The obscurity of the future can be illustrated through an historical example. Immanuel Kant wrote his essay *On Perpetual Peace* in 1795. A key point for Kant was that "[n]o State shall intermeddle by force with the Constitution or Government of another State".[14] The example used is when a country is divided between two separate groups, both claiming the right to govern the whole. Kant believed it would be unacceptable for another state to intervene.[15] Such a notion would have been possible to defend cohesively in the 1800s, but is today completely out of touch with the general world opinion of justice. The difference, again, is between the Westphalian concept of sovereignty and the competing idea of universal individual rights. Genocide is perhaps the most telling example. Had Kant shared the collective experiences of the twentieth century, he would probably have seen it differently. The genocide in Rwanda – involving the mass-killing of more than 600,000 Tutsis – happened in the context of a civil war. Few would seriously argue, with the benefit of hindsight, against a case for military intervention in Rwanda in 1994 in order to stop the genocide. Up until World War II, however, genocide was not considered a violation of international law.[16]

Kant did not, and could not, foresee the development and consequences of nuclear weapons, nor the development of international law and institutions as framed in the international system of today. Nor did he have any possibility to envision how vastly more interdependent the states of the world are today than in his own day. Kant's perspective was to avoid military conflict, but he could not see far beyond the Westphalian Paradigm of his own time. The global challenges of today necessitate far more extensive international co-operation than merely to avoid military conflict. This includes, for example, climate change, the rules of international trade, and the role of transnational corporations. Furthermore, the issue of dealing with non-compliance in the international system today entails far more than issues of military conflict and wars of aggression. An example is the challenge of tax paradises, which allow money to be concentrated on the hands

---

[14] Kant, 1795, p. 8, see *supra* note 22 in Chapter 1 (Preliminary Article 5) (http://www.legal-tools.org/doc/dc079a/).

[15] *Ibid.*, p. 8.

[16] D'Amato, 2010, p.1, see *supra* note 60 in Chapter 3.

of the few and well-off, in violation of rules that apply within a domestic legal context.

What the future holds remains elusive even to the best and brightest. That being said, reasoning about the future is both natural and useful, as long it simulates debate rather than dictates direction.

INDEX

A

African (Banjul) Charter on Human and
Peoples' Rights, 108, 109, 116
Agreement Establishing the World Trade
Organisation, 75, 77
Anti-Personnel Mine Ban Convention, 50
Association of South-East Asian Nations,
vii, 110, 111, 121, 124, 125
ASEAN Human Rights Declaration,
110

B

balance of power, 7, 8, 9, 10, 15, 22, 23,
32, 35, 40, 41, 42, 47, 49, 55, 56, 88,
90, 107, 137, 138, 188, 189

C

Cassese, Antonio, 4, 5, 11, 12, 34, 46, 56,
62, 63, 64, 66, 68, 69, 119, 148, 149,
150, 153, 163, 179, 186
Children and Armed Conflict, 47, 145
China, 18, 19, 29, 33, 34, 35, 41, 44, 52,
59, 61, 74, 78, 81, 86, 97, 100, 101,
104, 105, 111, 114, 117, 118, 122, 127,
130, 135, 136, 137, 139, 141, 142, 145,
152, 160, 164, 165, 175, 176, 180, 181,
182, 183, 184
Chinese Taipei (Taiwan), 18, 44, 81, 104,
111, 175
Concert of Vienna, 8
constructivism, 2, 3, 171
Convention on Cluster Munitions, 50,
169, 178, 179
Convention on Rights of the Child, vii,
51, 101, 103, 121, 123
Convention on the Elimination of all
Forms of Discrimination Against
Women, vii, 100, 103, 123

Convention prohibiting Certain
Conventional Weapons, 179

D

Dahl, Robert, 57
Darfur, 18, 19, 49, 165, 166
derogable (human rights), 96, 118
Draft International Convention on the
Condition and Protection of Civilians
of enemy nationality who are on
territory belonging to or occupied by a
belligerent (Tokyo Draft), 151, 154

E

European Court of Human Rights, 18, 21,
63, 64, 87, 117, 125
European Union, 18, 20, 21, 49, 52, 57,
58, 73, 74, 78, 79, 82, 86, 137, 139,
180, 181, 184, 185, 186, 187

F

France, 4, 7, 8, 9, 10, 11, 13, 14, 27, 28,
29, 30, 33, 34, 35, 45, 65, 71, 104, 148,
152, 165, 175, 186, 187
Frederick the Great, 8
future paradigm, 188, 189

G

Gaza, 28, 153, 162
General Agreement on Tariffs and Trade,
vii, 71, 72, 73, 74, 76, 79, 93
Geneva Conventions, 147, 148, 150, 151,
152, 153, 154, 155, 156, 157, 158, 159,
160, 163, 168

H

Hague Convention (IV) on War on Land
and its Annexed Regulations, 1907, 29,
151
Havana Charter for an International Trade
Organization (The Havana Charter), 81
Hobbes, Thomas, 6

I

Independent National Human Rights
Institutions, vii, 136, 137
India, 19, 33, 43, 50, 52, 58, 61, 101, 104,
112, 152, 160, 164, 165, 166, 175, 180,
181, 184, 185
International Committee of the Red Cross,
vii, 48, 67, 68, 147, 151, 152, 155,
157, 158, 159, 161
International Court of Justice, vii, 20, 25,
26, 39, 41, 42, 47, 53, 55, 60, 61, 62,
63, 64, 65, 66, 67, 68, 69, 70, 75, 85,
87, 88, 119, 124, 125, 138, 155, 167,
172, 174, 176
International Covenant on Civil and
Political Rights, vii, 100, 107, 109,
112, 113, 114, 115, 118, 121, 122, 123,
124, 142
International Covenant on Economic,
Social and Cultural Rights, vii, 100
International Criminal Court, vii, 2, 18,
19, 20, 28, 39, 49, 51, 69, 145, 149,
155, 162, 163, 164, 165, 166, 167, 168,
169, 170, 171, 172, 175, 178
International Criminal Tribunal for
Rwanda, vii, 162, 166
International Criminal Tribunal for the
Former Yugoslavia, vii, 162, 166, 169
International Law Commission, 163
International Military Tribunal, 150

J

Japan, 16, 29, 30, 32, 33, 43, 61, 62, 73,
78, 112, 150, 152, 176, 180, 183, 184,
185
jus cogens, 64, 118, 119, 124, 160

K

Kant, Immanuel, 15, 188, 190

L

League of Nations, 11, 12, 16, 23, 30, 31,
32, 44, 50
Covenant of the League of Nations, 14,
15, 16
liberalism, 2, 3, 171
Locke, John, 6

N

National Human Rights Institutions, vii,
134, 136, 137
national interests, 22, 28, 32, 36, 37, 38,
39, 40, 42, 53, 61, 80, 135, 136, 172
Non-governmental Organisation, vii, 19,
36, 48, 51, 52, 53, 54, 57, 60, 67, 76,
77, 78, 80, 82, 83, 84, 89, 90, 91, 92,
102, 111, 129, 130, 131, 132, 133, 134,
136, 139, 143, 156, 157, 163, 164, 165,
168, 174, 178
Non-state actors, 19
North Atlantic Treaty Organisation, vii,
46, 97, 181, 182, 184, 185

O

Office of the High Commissioner for
Human Rights, 100, 101, 124, 128,
132, 134, 137
Organisation of Islamic Conference, viii,
110
outer boundaries, 1, 21, 60, 131, 139, 140,
141

P

paradigm, 1, 2, 3, 7, 8, 9, 10, 11, 14, 15,
16, 17, 18, 19, 21, 23, 25, 26, 27, 30,
40, 42, 43, 44, 45, 47, 48, 49, 52, 55,
56, 57, 59, 60, 66, 68, 72, 77, 80, 83,
85, 89, 90, 93, 96, 97, 100, 114, 124,
134, 137, 138, 139, 140, 141, 150, 166,
169, 171, 172, 174, 179, 185, 186, 188,
189, 190

paradigm shift, 1, 9, 21, 27, 44, 138, 179, 185, 186
Permanent Court of Arbitration, 61, 65, 155
Permanent five of the UNSC, viii, 30, 31, 32, 33, 34, 35, 36, 40, 42, 46, 49, 61, 65, 66, 67, 70, 164, 174, 175, 176
Popular Sovereign Paradigm, 11, 12, 15, 16, 17, 19, 23, 24, 25, 26, 27, 28, 30, 34, 42, 47, 48, 51, 59, 64, 67, 80, 82, 90, 95, 96, 123, 124, 140, 145, 151, 153, 162, 171, 172, 179, 185, 186, 189
Protocols Additional to the Geneva Conventions, vii, viii, 151, 155, 157, 158, 160

R

realism, 2, 171, 172
realist, 4, 172, 188
representativity, 31, 58, 60, 104, 105, 107, 116, 132, 175
responsibility to protect, 45, 46, 48, 175
Rome Statute of the International Criminal Court, 162, 163, 164, 165, 167, 168, 169, 170
Rousseau, Jean-Jaques, 6
Russia, 7, 8, 10, 11, 13, 16, 18, 29, 30, 32, 33, 34, 35, 40, 41, 61, 74, 81, 97, 99, 101, 103, 104, 124, 130, 136, 145, 152, 158, 160, 164, 166, 176, 180, 181, 182, 183, 184, 186
Rwandan crisis, 37, 126, 172, 175

S

self-determination, 11, 13, 14, 53, 82, 97, 98
Sharia law, 113, 120, 121, 123
sovereign, 1, 3, 4, 5, 6, 7, 9, 10, 11, 12, 15, 16, 17, 18, 19, 20, 21, 23, 24, 25, 26, 27, 28, 30, 34, 35, 40, 42, 43, 47, 48, 51, 52, 53, 54, 56, 57, 59, 63, 64, 65, 66, 67, 68, 69, 72, 76, 77, 80, 81, 82, 83, 85, 88, 89, 90, 91, 95, 96, 97, 99, 111, 117, 122, 123, 124, 134, 135, 137, 138, 140, 142, 145, 147, 150, 151, 153, 155, 158, 161, 162, 168, 170, 171, 172, 174, 179, 185, 186, 187, 188, 189

sovereign rights, 5, 16, 17, 18, 19, 20, 21, 24, 34, 35, 42, 43, 47, 53, 54, 57, 65, 66, 67, 68, 69, 77, 81, 82, 85, 89, 97, 111, 122, 124, 134, 135, 137, 138, 142, 161, 168, 170, 187, 189
sovereign state, 1, 3, 5, 6, 10, 11, 12, 17, 18, 19, 40, 51, 52, 56, 63, 64, 65, 67, 72, 76, 81, 83, 85, 88, 97, 99, 117, 124, 140, 147, 155, 158, 162, 168, 172, 174, 179, 187, 188
supranational independence, 22, 78
supranational powers, 18, 21, 22, 29, 31, 34, 35, 40, 61, 79, 83, 137, 168, 169, 178
Swebel, Stephen, 62
system integrity, 40, 49, 63, 66, 93
System Integrity, 40, 55, 66, 88, 137

T

The Vienna System, 9
The World Trade Organisation, vii, viii, 19, 71, 72, 73, 74, 75, 76, 77, 78, 79, 80, 81, 83, 84, 85, 86, 87, 88, 89, 90, 91, 92, 93, 136, 140, 172, 174, 177, 178, 181, 183, 185
   Disputes Settlement Body, 76, 83
   Disputes Settlement Mechanism, vii, 74, 76, 77, 79, 83, 84, 85, 86, 87, 90, 93, 178
   International Trade Organisation, vii, 72, 81, 82
The World Trade Orgnisation
   Dispute Settlement Body, 76, 83
   Dispute Settlement Mechanism, vii, 74, 76, 77, 79, 83, 84, 85, 86, 87, 90, 93, 178
Treaty of Versailles, 13, 14
Treaty of Westphalia, 4, 5, 11

U

UNGA Resolution 377 (Uniting for Peace resolution), 41, 47, 88
United Kingdom, viii, 8, 11, 13, 14, 15, 20, 27, 28, 29, 30, 33, 34, 35, 39, 44, 61, 65, 71, 81, 101, 103, 104, 106, 107, 114, 152, 165, 175, 176, 186

United Nations, vii, viii, 2, 3, 12, 16, 18, 19, 21, 23, 24, 25, 26, 27, 29, 30, 31, 32, 33, 34, 35, 36, 37, 38, 40, 41, 43, 45, 46, 47, 48, 49, 50, 52, 53, 54, 55, 56, 60, 61, 63, 66, 68, 70, 71, 80, 81, 88, 97, 98, 99, 100, 102, 103, 104, 105, 106, 107, 108, 111, 112,113, 118, 119, 120, 121, 122, 124, 125, 126, 127, 128, 129, 130, 131, 132, 134, 135, 136, 137, 138, 139, 142, 143, 144, 145, 152, 159, 164, 168, 171, 172, 173, 175, 176, 177, 183, 184
Trusteeship Council, 25, 26, 27, 28, 29
United Nations Charter, 16, 21, 23, 24, 26, 29, 32, 33, 41, 43, 46, 47, 66, 68, 97, 125, 126, 128, 168
United Nations General Assembly, viii, 24, 25, 26, 30, 31, 41, 42, 47, 50, 51, 52, 53, 54, 55, 56, 57, 58, 59, 60, 61, 65, 66, 67, 70, 76, 80, 88, 98, 99, 104, 106, 111, 112, 113, 115, 118, 123, 125, 126, 127, 131, 132, 133, 134, 135, 136, 137, 138, 140, 142, 143, 156, 163, 172, 174, 176, 177, 184
United Nations Office of the High Commissioner for Human Rights, viii, 100, 101, 124, 128, 132, 134, 137
United Nations Security Council, viii, 3, 18, 19, 24, 25, 26, 29, 30, 31, 32, 33, 34, 35, 36, 37, 38, 39, 40, 41, 42, 43, 44, 45, 46, 47, 48, 49, 50, 51, 53, 55, 56, 61, 62, 63, 65, 66, 68, 70, 79, 80, 88, 97, 115, 124, 125, 132, 134, 135, 136, 139, 145, 163, 164, 165, 166, 171, 172, 175, 176, 177, 178, 180, 181, 182, 183, 184, 185
United Nations Economic and Social Council, vii, 25, 51, 71, 103, 104, 126, 128, 132
United Nations Human Rights Council, vii, 44, 54, 98, 111, 125, 126, 127, 128, 129, 130, 131, 132, 133, 134, 135, 136, 137, 138, 139, 140, 141, 142, 143, 144, 145, 174, 178, 182, 183, 184
United States of America, viii, 5, 9, 10, 11, 13, 15, 16, 18, 19, 29, 30, 32, 33, 34, 39, 41, 55, 61, 62, 65, 71, 73, 78, 79, 81, 82, 83, 86, 97, 99, 100, 101, 103, 104, 111, 116, 119, 120, 126, 141, 142, 145, 150, 152, 159, 160, 161, 164, 166, 167, 175, 176, 180, 181, 182, 184, 185, 186
Universal Declaration of Human Rights, viii, 99, 100, 102, 103, 104, 105, 106, 107, 108, 109, 110, 111, 112, 116, 120, 121, 123, 124, 128, 142
Universal Periodic Review, viii, 98, 128, 129, 130, 132, 133, 136, 137, 138, 140, 141, 143, 144, 178

V

veto (of the Permanent five at UNSC), 18, 29, 31, 32, 33, 34, 35, 44, 62, 66, 82, 166, 172, 175

W

Westphalian system, 4, 6, 7, 8, 10, 11, 72, 78, 96, 185

TOAEP TEAM

OTHER VOLUMES IN THE PUBLICATION SERIES

Morten Bergsmo, Mads Harlem and Nobuo Hayashi (editors):
Importing Core International Crimes into National Law
Torkel Opsahl Academic EPublisher
Oslo, 2010
FICHL Publication Series No. 1 (Second Edition, 2010)
ISBN: 978-82-93081-00-5

Nobuo Hayashi (editor):
National Military Manuals on the Law of Armed Conflict
Torkel Opsahl Academic EPublisher
Oslo, 2010
FICHL Publication Series No. 2 (Second Edition, 2010)
ISBN: 978-82-93081-02-9

Morten Bergsmo, Kjetil Helvig, Ilia Utmelidze and Gorana Žagovec:
The Backlog of Core International Crimes Case Files in Bosnia and Herzegovina
Torkel Opsahl Academic EPublisher
Oslo, 2010
FICHL Publication Series No. 3 (Second Edition, 2010)
ISBN: 978-82-93081-04-3

Morten Bergsmo (editor):
Criteria for Prioritizing and Selecting Core International Crimes Cases
Torkel Opsahl Academic EPublisher
Oslo, 2010
FICHL Publication Series No. 4 (Second Edition, 2010)
ISBN: 978-82-93081-06-7

Morten Bergsmo and Pablo Kalmanovitz (editors):
Law in Peace Negotiations
Torkel Opsahl Academic EPublisher
Oslo, 2010
FICHL Publication Series No. 5 (Second Edition, 2010)
ISBN: 978-82-93081-08-1

Morten Bergsmo, César Rodríguez Garavito, Pablo Kalmanovitz and Maria Paula Saffon (editors):
Distributive Justice in Transitions
Torkel Opsahl Academic EPublisher
Oslo, 2010
FICHL Publication Series No. 6 (2010)
ISBN: 978-82-93081-12-8

Morten Bergsmo, César Rodriguez-Garavito, Pablo Kalmanovitz and Maria Paula Saffon (editors):
Justicia Distributiva en Sociedades en Transición
Torkel Opsahl Academic EPublisher
Oslo, 2012
FICHL Publication Series No. 6 (2012)
ISBN: 978-82-93081-10-4

Morten Bergsmo (editor):
Complementarity and the Exercise of Universal Jurisdiction for Core International Crimes
Torkel Opsahl Academic EPublisher
Oslo, 2010
FICHL Publication Series No. 7 (2010)
ISBN: 978-82-93081-14-2

Morten Bergsmo (editor):
Active Complementarity: Legal Information Transfer
Torkel Opsahl Academic EPublisher
Oslo, 2011
FICHL Publication Series No. 8 (2011)
ISBN print: 978-82-93081-56-2
ISBN e-book: 978-82-93081-55-5

Morten Bergsmo (editor):
Abbreviated Criminal Procedures for Core International Crimes
Torkel Opsahl Academic EPublisher
Brussels, 2017
FICHL Publication Series No. 9 (2018)
ISBN print: 978-82-93081-20-3
ISBN e-book: 978-82-8348-104-4

Sam Muller, Stavros Zouridis, Morly Frishman and Laura Kistemaker (editors):
The Law of the Future and the Future of Law
Torkel Opsahl Academic EPublisher
Oslo, 2010
FICHL Publication Series No. 11 (2011)
ISBN: 978-82-93081-27-2

Morten Bergsmo, Alf Butenschøn Skre and Elisabeth J. Wood (editors):
Understanding and Proving International Sex Crimes
Torkel Opsahl Academic EPublisher
Beijing, 2012
FICHL Publication Series No. 12 (2012)
ISBN: 978-82-93081-29-6

Morten Bergsmo (editor):
Thematic Prosecution of International Sex Crimes
Torkel Opsahl Academic EPublisher
Beijing, 2012
FICHL Publication Series No. 13 (2012)
ISBN: 978-82-93081-31-9

Terje Einarsen:
The Concept of Universal Crimes in International Law
Torkel Opsahl Academic EPublisher
Oslo, 2012
FICHL Publication Series No. 14 (2012)
ISBN: 978-82-93081-33-3

莫滕・伯格斯默 凌岩（主编）：
国家主权与国际刑法
Torkel Opsahl Academic EPublisher
Beijing, 2012
FICHL Publication Series No. 15 (2012)
ISBN: 978-82-93081-58-6

Morten Bergsmo and LING Yan (editors):
State Sovereignty and International Criminal Law
Torkel Opsahl Academic EPublisher
Beijing, 2012
FICHL Publication Series No. 15 (2012)
ISBN: 978-82-93081-35-7

Morten Bergsmo and CHEAH Wui Ling (editors):
Old Evidence and Core International Crimes
Torkel Opsahl Academic EPublisher
Beijing, 2012
FICHL Publication Series No. 16 (2012)
ISBN: 978-82-93081-60-9

YI Ping:
戦争と平和の間――発足期日本国際法学における「正しい戦争」の観念とその帰結
Torkel Opsahl Academic EPublisher
Beijing, 2013
FICHL Publication Series No. 17 (2013)
ISBN: 978-82-93081-66-1

Morten Bergsmo and SONG Tianying (editors):
On the Proposed Crimes Against Humanity Convention
Torkel Opsahl Academic EPublisher
Brussels, 2014
FICHL Publication Series No. 18 (2014)
ISBN: 978-82-93081-96-8

Morten Bergsmo (editor):
Quality Control in Fact-Finding
Torkel Opsahl Academic EPublisher
Florence, 2013
FICHL Publication Series No. 19 (2013)
ISBN: 978-82-93081-78-4

Morten Bergsmo, CHEAH Wui Ling and YI Ping (editors):
Historical Origins of International Criminal Law: Volume 1
Torkel Opsahl Academic EPublisher
Brussels, 2014
FICHL Publication Series No. 20 (2014)
ISBN: 978-82-93081-11-1

Morten Bergsmo, CHEAH Wui Ling and YI Ping (editors):
Historical Origins of International Criminal Law: Volume 2
Torkel Opsahl Academic EPublisher
Brussels, 2014
FICHL Publication Series No. 21 (2014)
ISBN: 978-82-93081-13-5

Morten Bergsmo, CHEAH Wui Ling, SONG Tianying and YI Ping (editors):
Historical Origins of International Criminal Law: Volume 3
Torkel Opsahl Academic EPublisher
Brussels, 2015
FICHL Publication Series No. 22 (2015)
ISBN print: 978-82-8348-015-3
ISBN e-book: 978-82-8348-014-6

Morten Bergsmo, CHEAH Wui Ling, SONG Tianying and YI Ping (editors):
Historical Origins of International Criminal Law: Volume 4
Torkel Opsahl Academic EPublisher
Brussels, 2015
FICHL Publication Series No. 23 (2015)
ISBN print: 978-82-8348-017-7
ISBN e-book: 978-82-8348-016-0

Morten Bergsmo, Klaus Rackwitz and SONG Tianying (editors):
Historical Origins of International Criminal Law: Volume 5
Torkel Opsahl Academic EPublisher
Brussels, 2017
FICHL Publication Series No. 24 (2017)
ISBN print: 978-82-8348-106-8
ISBN e-book: 978-82-8348-107-5

Morten Bergsmo and SONG Tianying (editors):
Military Self-Interest in Accountability for Core International Crimes
Torkel Opsahl Academic EPublisher
Brussels, 2015
FICHL Publication Series No. 25 (2015)
ISBN print: 978-82-93081-61-6
ISBN e-book: 978-82-93081-81-4

Wolfgang Kaleck:
Double Standards: International Criminal Law and the West
Torkel Opsahl Academic EPublisher
Brussels, 2015
FICHL Publication Series No. 26 (2015)
ISBN print: 978-82-93081-67-8
ISBN e-book: 978-82-93081-83-8

LIU Daqun and ZHANG Binxin (editors):
Historical War Crimes Trials in Asia
Torkel Opsahl Academic EPublisher
Brussels, 2016
FICHL Publication Series No. 27 (2015)
ISBN print: 978-82-8348-055-9
ISBN e-book: 978-82-8348-056-6

Mark Klamberg (editor):
Commentary on the Law of the International Criminal Court
Torkel Opsahl Academic EPublisher
Brussels, 2017
FICHL Publication Series No. 29 (2017)
ISBN print: 978-82-8348-100-6
ISBN e-book: 978-82-8348-101-3

All volumes are freely available online at http://www.toaep.org/ps/. For printed copies, see http://toaep.org/about/distribution/. For reviews of earlier books in this Series in academic journals and yearbooks, see http://toaep.org/reviews/.